MAKING WAVES

MAKING

The 50 Greatest Women in Radio and Television

WAVES

As Selected by American Women in Radio and Television, Inc.

Edited by Jacci Duncan

Contributing Writers:

Jane Lawrence

Louisa Peat O'Neil

Judith Marlane

Tom Dunkel

Rebecca Reisner

Lynn Page Whittaker

**Andrews McMeel
Publishing**

Kansas City

01 02 03 04 05 QUF 10 9 8 7 6 5 4 3 2 1

Library of Congress Card Cataloging-in-Publication Data

Making waves : the 50 greatest women in radio and television / American Women in Radio and Television.
    p. cm.
  ISBN 0-7407-1401-5
    1. Women broadcasters—United States—Biography. I. American Women in Radio and Television Inc.

PN1991.4.A2 M35 2001
791.44'028'0820973—dc21
[B]

00-067674

Book design and composition by Holly Camerlinck

──────── Attention: Schools and Businesses ────────

Andrews McMeel books are available at quantity discounts with bulk purchase
for educational, business, or sales promotional use. For information, please write to: Special Sales Department,
Andrews McMeel Publishing, 4520 Main Street, Kansas City, Missouri 64111.

Contents

CONTENTS

CONTENTS

viii

CONTENTS

Introduction

Nearly every woman, at some point in her life, has been told "Don't make waves." Don't try something you've never done before; don't try to change things; above all, don't call attention to yourself—just go along to get along. Fortunately for all of us, the women in this book did not heed that advice and, as a result, went on to change the face of radio and television, and influence the impact broadcasting has had on our society and the world. As super-successful television producer Marcy Carsey says elsewhere in these pages, "This country was built on wave making; I believe in wave making."

So do all the women included here, and this book is designed to salute them and their accomplishments. They not only broke down doors in a profession initially closed to women, but once in, they used their intelligence, creativity, hard work, and dedication to expand the definition of what television and radio can do.

While many women have made significant contributions to the industry, these fifty were chosen as worthy of particular note by American Women in Radio and Television, Inc., the world's oldest and most respected organization in support of women in broadcasting, as part of our fiftieth anniversary celebration. With the assistance of the Library of American Broadcasting at the University of Maryland, the AWRT membership selected each of the honorees based on four criteria: her positive impact and influence within the broadcast and cable industry; her positive impact and influence on viewers and listeners; her positive impact and influence on the advancement of women in the industry; and her vision and the resulting impact she will have on future generations. We are thrilled to pay tribute to these women who have made a difference.

Honoring these pioneering women is, however, only part of the reason for this book. The other part is creating an opportunity for us, their collective audience, to be inspired by their example. Many of the fifty are well-known celebrities whose faces and voices have come into America's homes on a regular basis. Others are women behind the scenes, whose names and faces may be less familiar but who wield tremendous power in their areas of media. Still, for all their successes, none of them found their journey easy, and in their profiles and first-person essays, you will share their stories and learn what they had to overcome and what helped them most to get to the top. Sometimes the resistance they faced was from the outside: executives who resisted giving them jobs, bankers who didn't want to lend them money, bosses who were reluctant to let them even try something new. At other times, the challenge was getting beyond what they feared were their own limitations: having the wrong kind of accent, considering themselves not pretty, overcoming a previous image of being too glamorous or too feminine or too smart.

As you read about these women, you will therefore see that, in many ways, they are like the rest of us, trying to make a place for ourselves in the world, wherever it may be. We hope you will also be inspired to do a little wave making of your own in the process.

Gracie
Allen

■ AFTER A MUTUAL FRIEND INTRODUCED THEM in the early 1920s, vaudeville performers Gracie Allen and George Burns decided to try out a comedy act together. At first, Allen served as the "straight man," handing her partner lines he could hit home with a joke. But the audience didn't laugh at Burns. It was Allen's seeming guilelessness and comic timing that delighted them. So the two switched roles—and became an instant hit, prompting a Chicago reviewer to write, "Miss Allen, who is just about the best characterization of 'Dumb Dora' seen on vaudeville boards in many a day, is thoroughly at home in her role; Mr. Burns is a good feeder for Miss Allen and that's about it for him."

Vaudeville loved Gracie Allen. The gently chiming, squeaky voice that producers once had said would hinder her success turned out to be her greatest asset. The skillful way in which she used that voice and fine-tuned her delivery enabled her to become one of the few performers who made a successful transition from vaudeville to radio to television. During much of her long career, Allen was so popular she could not step out of her house without attracting a crowd of autograph hounds.

But as much as the public adored her, they never knew how much her comic persona differed from her true self, for she stayed in character for interviews and

public appearances. One thing, however, is certain: Gracie Allen was not dumb. "She was about as scatterbrained as Albert Einstein," says Dick Moore, spokesperson for the American Federation of Television and Radio Artists.

While Allen's comedic abilities, business savvy, and dedication to her craft ensured her own extraordinary career, her pioneering role in the entertainment industry also opened doors for future generations of female comedians. In recognition of that significance, her name appears on the broadcast industry's preeminent awards honoring women in the industry: the Gracie Allen Awards, presented each year by the Foundation of American Women in Radio and Television.

Grace Ethel Cecile Rosalie Allen acquired her show business smarts early in life. She grew up in San Francisco in an Irish Catholic family and sometimes toured with her father, a vaudeville song-and-dance man. She and her three older sisters developed an Irish dancing and harmony act they performed all over the country starting when Gracie was just five.

After the sister act disbanded, Gracie got a $22-a-week gig with Larry Reilly, an Irish dramatist with a traveling show. When Reilly dropped the "& Co." part of the act's billing, Allen quit. She met George Burns when he was part of the song-and-dance act Burns and Lorraine. They hit it off immediately, and the act soon became Burns and Allen.

"She sounded like a bird who had been thrown out of the nest for singing off-

Allen and George Burns

key," Burns wrote years later. "It turned out to be a perfect act because it had no lows, so it projected beautifully in a theater."

On stage, Allen would talk to her partner about her many mythical relatives, such as Cousin Audubon Allen, who taught hummingbirds to sing lyrics and an owl to say "whom." Audiences loved it. In 1925, the pair got a five-year contract for $450 to $600 a week to play at New York City's Jefferson Theatre. The show did consistently well, but by the 1930s they could see that radio would mean the death of vaudeville. They tried out a radio act in England but then got their big U.S. break when Eddie Cantor invited Allen to be on his radio show—without George. Fortunately Burns had no objections, and her solo appearance was a hit. But the two continued to perform together in radio spots.

Then the couple received an offer to star in their own radio series for $2,000 a week. *The Adventures of Gracie* used a sitcom format to showcase Allen's comedic talent. First biweekly and then weekly, the series featured Allen's loony but lovable travails—such as the time she decided to become an actress at the Upstairs Greek Art Theater (over the Acropolis Greek restaurant) and implored guest star Brian Donlevy to work with her in *The Sins of Madeline Fudnick*.

As the medium grew, so did the number of competing radio shows, prompting Allen to embark on a series of publicity stunts to retain her popularity. In 1933, she launched a search for her "lost brother" (she did indeed have a real brother, but she knew where he was). She would wander onto other radio shows, pleading on air for information about her brother, noting that he worked as a marketer of umbrellas with holes "so you could see when it stopped raining." The gag captivated the country, and Burns and Allen received 350,000 letters. When surrealist art came into vogue in the 1930s, she mounted her own farcical exhibit with paintings such as *Man with Mike Fright Moons over Manicurist*. She also took her "One Finger Concerto" to Carnegie Hall and the Hollywood Bowl; she played the scales with her index finger, hitting the wrong note at the end. Her 1940 campaign for president—on the "Surprise Party" ticket—attracted national attention and garnered thousands of write-in votes.

Gracie Allen's popularity was holding fast, but radio was losing out to TV, so the couple ended *The Adventures of Gracie* and started their television sitcom, *The George Burns and Gracie Allen Show,* in 1950. The visual aspect only added to Allen's comic genius as she executed sight gags such as plugging in an electric clock to find out what time it was. "She could be dumb without looking stupid," says *Houston Chronicle* TV critic Ann Hodges. "A lot of times if someone looks stupid, you feel sorry for that person instead of laughing. She could say a dumb thing that made you feel comfortable with laughing at it. It was part of her charm."

By 1958, Allen was ready to retire from show business, despite the huge audiences the TV show was still drawing. The announcement of her retirement was met with great disappointment; one newspaper even ran an editorial begging her to reconsider. But her health problems, including a bad heart and migraine headaches—which

she hid from the public—were worsening. She also longed to spend more time with the couple's daughter and son, Sandy and Ronnie, and her grandchildren. After the show went off the air, Burns, with his wife's blessing, tried a sitcom on his own but couldn't make a go of it.

Allen died in 1964 at age fifty-nine—although at least one biographer has suggested that, like many performers, she falsified her age and was actually sixty-nine. Burns claimed he never asked her how old she was. And in his 1988 book *Gracie: A Love Story,* he provides only a modicum of insight into the woman behind the character, noting, however, that she was strict with the kids, prudent with money, and meticulous about any details that could improve their routines. Gracie Allen died an entertainment legend, a woman loved by millions but known by few. ∎

Allen and Helen Sioussat at the Democratic National Convention in Chicago, 1944

On her presidential campaign:

I will make no fireside chats from the White House between April 15 and October 15. It is asking too much and I don't know how President Roosevelt stands it. Washington is awfully hot in summer.

On her "missing" brother:

GRACIE: He was going to go into the restaurant business, but he didn't have enough money. So he went into the banking business.

JACK BENNY: Your brother didn't have enough money so he went into the banking business?

GRACIE: Yes. He broke into the banking business at two o'clock in the morning and was kidnapped by two men dressed as policemen.

On buying a ranch:

George: You don't know anything about ranching.

Gracie: What's to know about ranching? White cows give white milk; brown cows give chocolate milk.

Maybe we could get animals that used to be in vaudeville that sleep as late as we do.

I don't want a ranch where you can hear the cattle rustling every time the wind blows.

On why she's searching the Sears, Roebuck catalog:

I'm looking for sweaters for cows. They must be very scarce. Fred told me that he has forty Holstein cows and only twenty-two jerseys.

On her Uncle Harvey:

Remember when my Uncle Harvey went to the doctor's to find out why walking uphill made him shortwinded? The doctor said he wasn't walking uphill. He just needed new heels.

GEORGE: This check for $65. It's marked "The bare necessities for Uncle Harvey." What does that mean?

GRACIE: Oh, yeah, that's how much he asked for in his letter. He said that the cost of life is going up so that the bare necessities of life cost $65 a case now.

On her neighbor Blanche Morton's husband:

BLANCHE: Casey pushes Harry around all day and then Harry comes home and pushes me around.

GRACIE: Blanche, wouldn't it save a lot of time if Casey came right to your house and pushed you around?

On budgeting:

GEORGE: I wish now that you'd lived within your income.

GRACIE: Within it? Oh, that's easy. I was afraid you were going to ask me to live without it.

What Gracie wrote on the back of a $67 check to Dr. Howard's Dog and Cat Hospital (though she has no pets):

Dear Doctor Howard, Please run across the street and give this check to the May Company. I bought a dress, and I don't want my husband to find out.

To George:

You know what gives me a thrill? The hair on your chest. It's such a cute little curly one.

On George:

George is money mad. I noticed it the very first night we were married. He only rented one hotel room for the two of us. It wasn't the one room I minded but I don't think George should have sublet the divan to a hosiery salesman. And that wasn't the worst of it. George wouldn't let me buy anything from him.

I don't want a husband with money or good looks and personality. I'd rather have George. And I'm not the only one who feels that way about him. Plenty of women have told me how relieved they are that he's with me.

To actor Brian Donlevy:

We'd be magnificent together. Can't you just see us doing *Macbeth?* You could be Mac, and I could be Beth.

On herself:

In the winter I seem much taller because the days are shorter.

I'm as old as my little finger and a little older than my teeth.

I was so surprised at being born that I didn't speak for a year and a half.

GEORGE: Did the maid ever drop you on your head when you were a baby?

GRACIE: Don't be silly, George. We couldn't afford a maid. My mother had to do it herself.

—GRACIE ALLEN

Christiane
Amanpour

■ THIS IS WHAT "ROOM SERVICE" CAN MEAN when you're a war correspondent. Christiane Amanpour, CNN's roving international correspondent, getting some sleep at a Sarajevo hotel when a howitzer shell came a-knockin' two doors down the hallway.

"I heard the whistle of incoming artillery," she said afterward. "I thought, 'Well, this is it. Good-bye.'"

Actually, it was just hello. The shell failed to detonate, sparing the lives of all those lucky souls sleeping on that floor of the hotel. It was a terrifyingly close call—close enough that many journalists would've immediately left town and requested transfer to a safer beat. Not Amanpour. She held her ground in Sarajevo, just as she had a few years earlier in Bosnia, when her camera had been shot by a Serb sniper. "It's like being a doctor," she has coolly said of reporting under fire. "You know, if you're going to scream every time you see blood, you're not going to be able to do your job."

Amanpour is no stranger to wartime bloodshed: in Yugoslavia, Bosnia-Hercegovina, Afghanistan, Haiti, Somalia, Rwanda, and the Persian Gulf War, among other hot spots. Amanpour is, in the estimation of decorated broadcast veteran Mike Wallace, "the best-known foreign correspondent in the world." Foreign cor-

respondents have been around since Herodotus chronicled ancient Greeks clashing with ancient Persians. But never before in history have they had the impact and influence they enjoy in today's satellite-enhanced, instant-information age. As the *Washington Post* observes, "Amanpour figures in the worst nightmares of generals and diplomats alike."

She is here, there, and everywhere, memorialized by a bumper-sticker-type slogan that has worked its way into the journalism vernacular: "Where there's war, there's Amanpour." Pentagon officials once gave Amanpour a world map decorated with push pins representing her various reporting campaigns. They called it the "Amanpour Tracking Chart." Globe

MAKING WAVES

Reporting from Sarajevo, Yugoslavia, early 1990s

hopping has rewarded her handsomely with an obscene number of frequent-flyer miles and a trophy case full of journalism honors. Her reporting from Bosnia alone won a News and Documentary Emmy and a George Foster Peabody Award. The Peabody committee proclaimed, "She reminds us of all that is good and great in television journalism."

But Amanpour's stature can perhaps best be measured by the fact that she is the first person to drive in two lanes on the journalism superhighway. In 1996, she signed a unique contract worth a reported $2 million a year that lets her continue to report for CNN while simultaneously contributing occasional pieces to CBS's *60 Minutes*. There is only one reason somebody gets to cut that kind of deal: she is one of the best in the business.

She brings to the table firsthand experience with political and social chaos. Amanpour was born in London in 1958, the oldest of four daughters. Her father, Mohamed, was an Iranian Muslim airline executive; her mother, Patricia, a British Catholic housewife. The family moved to

Teheran when Christiane was eight months old. The Amanpours were affluent and well connected. Young Christiane got to race Arabian horses and go on vacations to Switzerland. Those good times abruptly ended when the shah was deposed in 1979. An uncle of Amanpour's, who was the director of the military police hospital, was arrested and subsequently died in jail. Her immediate family fled the fundamentalist revolution and resettled in London. "My father lost everything," Christiane later told *People* magazine.

She was educated in British Catholic schools, where the nuns hit her with rulers more than she hit the books. After graduation, Amanpour went to work in a department store and stumbled into what would become her chosen profession. One of her sisters had enrolled in a London journalism school and then changed her mind about going. When the school wouldn't refund the tuition money, Amanpour asked if she could attend in her sister's place. She had found her calling. The Amanpours had friends in Rhode Island and, at twenty-two, she came to the United States and entered the University of Rhode Island, graduating summa cum laude in 1983 with a degree in journalism.

Amanpour had worked part-time at a local TV station, and after she graduated, a professor put her in touch with then-fledgling CNN. Amanpour got hired over the phone and moved to Atlanta in September 1983. Despite being self-conscious about her heavily accented English, she was not shy about telling superiors she intended to "be a star." She earnestly built her own launching pad by coming in on weekends to practice scriptwriting and paying her own way to the 1984 Democratic National Convention to help with coverage. In 1986, she was promoted to producer-correspondent in the New York bureau.

Four years later, a slot opened up in the network's Frankfurt bureau that several reporters turned down. Amanpour jumped at the opportunity. It proved to be a serendipitous move: Shortly after she moved to Germany, the Ceausescu regime was toppled in Romania, and Amanpour witnessed her first revolution. Her field reporting and Farsi language skills next won her a supporting role with CNN's Persian Gulf War team. Then it was on to Bosnia. CNN was in the thick of the ethnic cleansing early on, for which Amanpour readily takes some credit: "I believe I forced CNN to cover Bosnia on a regular basis because I was willing and eager and hungry to stay there."

For years Amanpour was all reporting work and no play. That changed when she met James Rubin, at the time chief spokesman for the U.S. State Department. The couple had a breakthrough date at a dive bar in battered Bosnia in June 1997. Two years later, they married, and they now reside in London with their infant son, Darius-John.

Amanpour conducting an interview with President Khatami of Iran, December 1997

Amanpour reporting from Bosnia-Hercegovina during the Balkan War, early 1990s

Love has been a blessing but not exactly a life-altering experience. Christiane has no intention of retiring from the field, of turning her back on informing the world about international crises. Where there's war, there will still be Amanpour. "I'm really uncomfortable with people assuming I'm going to give up my life's work because I'm going to become a mother," she said during her pregnancy. "There's no doubt it's going to be a challenge, and I'm going to have to figure out the challenge. But I want—deeply want—to continue doing what I do. I can't imagine not doing it. It's my passion. It's my mission." ∎

I've often said that I'm an accidental journalist because I really didn't decide on journalism as a career until my early twenties. I was the product of a massive upheaval in my home country, Iran. We had a revolution in 1979, and it was only after that happened that I realized that I could not carry on living the nice, privileged, laid-back life that I was leading then. I needed to make my living in the world, and I needed to go out and fight for myself. I was so fascinated by the events of the Iranian revolution that I thought perhaps one way of staying involved in this kind of world event, crisis, upheaval, was to become a journalist.

I am satisfied that I have been able to keep the idea of a foreign correspondent alive in an era, regrettably, in the United States, where foreign news is almost invisible these days. U.S. news organizations, for whatever crazy reason, are in retreat from the kind of news coverage that I do. Of course, foreign news coverage used to be the crown jewel of any news organization. I grew up hearing about Edward R. Murrow and Eric Sevareid, all of these great foreign correspondents, the legends of our business. Today it's celebrity journalism, trivial journalism, stock market–mad journalism. So I think I'm satisfied I have been able to keep foreign news in the spotlight.

I'm also satisfied that I have been able to give a human face to crises and disasters, whether a famine or an earthquake or a war. I think that I've been able to get beyond the bang-bang, get beyond the heavy weaponry, get beyond the sort of technospeak of war, and relate in a human way to what's going on wherever I happen to be.

I connect with people because my instinct is to be a human being. I think that I tell the stories, or at least I try to tell the stories that I do, in a way that everybody can connect with. For instance, a war like Bosnia wasn't the traditional army against army on a battlefield. It was a war of ethnic cleansing, of racism, of one army against civilians. I was able to tell the story of the women who were affected, the children who were affected, the old men who were affected. People who could have been your brother and sister, my parents. It was that basic, and I try to tell every story in that manner.

I really believe passionately in the kind of work that I do and that many foreign correspondents do because I think it is important. We have to be there; we have to go to these crazy parts of the world and explain what's going on. We live in a globalized society. We can't sit back and say that what happens out there doesn't affect us, because it does. This is obviously the age of information, and information is the power broker of our time. I enjoy being able to disseminate information.

I would like to be able to encourage a new generation of foreign correspondents. Two of my colleagues were recently killed on assignment in Sierra Leone. They were two highly talented, highly experienced people. It makes me very angry that the kind of work we do and risk our lives for day after day, month after month, year after year, is now all but ignored. I want to get the journalism establishment, the news estate, to reconsider and to realize that what we do is vital. You can't have an informed citizenry or a thriving democracy if people don't know what's going on.

I once facetiously told an interviewer, when I was still young and at the start of my career, that I didn't want to get married or have children because being a wife or being a parent imposed upon you a responsibility to stay alive. I was doing the kind of work where anything could happen, and I was responsible only for myself.

These days it's a little bit different. I have a responsibility to my husband and my child, and so it makes my life much more complicated. It makes doing this kind of work much more difficult, and I guess I will have to think many times about the dangers and the risks I take. But I'm also committed to this kind of work; I'm not about to give it up. I want to figure out how to do both in the best possible way, and it's difficult. I think women are much more troubled by this kind of decision than men. It's a real burden for women because we have to balance personal and professional roles that men still do not have to.

It's going to be extremely tough for me, but I'm going to figure out how to do it and I'm going to do it. This is not just a job for me; it is more of a mission because I feel passionately that foreign news stories have to be told. That will keep me motivated to continue. It is a real gift to have a job you adore, a husband you love passionately, and a child who is the center of your life. All of that is truly more than most people dare to hope for.

—CHRISTIANE AMANPOUR

Lucille
Ball

■ IN THE FALL OF 1951, A NEW TV SHOW changed the habits of an entire nation. From 9:00 to 9:30 P.M. on Monday nights, traffic disappeared from city streets. Stores cut back their evening hours, and television-owning households were besieged by neighbors vying for seats in their living rooms. All were gathering to watch *I Love Lucy*.

What Lucille Ball had envisioned as a "pleasant little sitcom" turned into the hottest entertainment vehicle around. As cocreator, -producer, and -star, she put all her talents to work, delivering physical comedy no other TV performer had—or has to this day—matched. Her flair for transforming any situation into an occasion for Chaplinesque antics captivated the American public and spawned an entertainment empire rivaling the Hollywood studios. When she bought Desilu Studios, she became the first woman to head a major movie studio.

As a child growing up in Celoron, New York, Lucy exhibited a determined yet clownish spirit that survived despite the loss of her father to typhoid fever when she was four years old. Life improved briefly when the family moved in with Lucy's beloved maternal grandfather, only to collapse after he lost everything in a lawsuit. As a result, the family relocated to a tiny apartment in Jamestown, New York.

When a teenage Lucy began to misbehave—first with pranks such as roller skating across the school's freshly varnished floor, then by running away from home—a principal suggested she channel her energies into school plays. She took to the stage immediately, and her mother worked late into the night sewing costumes and even let Lucy's theater group borrow family furniture for props.

In 1932, Lucy moved to New York City to attend the John Murray Anderson–Robert Milton theater school. A petite classmate named Bette Davis received encouragement there, but all Lucy got was a letter saying she lacked talent and her mother should stop wasting her money. Reluctant to return to Jamestown a failure, she sought modeling work. Her lovely features and tall, slender figure gained her many assignments, including an appearance in a slinky evening gown on a Chesterfield cigarettes billboard towering over Times Square.

But Hollywood needed hundreds of pretty faces for movie extravaganzas, and Lucy soon headed west with a $50-a-week contract. The studios used her primarily in secondary roles, but Ball soon gained popularity with both the public and colleagues. "I took the slapstick parts the other starlets spurned, and never whined about the siphon water and pies in the face," she wrote years later. "I considered myself lucky to be paid while learning a business I adored."

One day in 1939, Lucy heard some friends raving about a sexy young Latino musician causing a sensation in Broadway's *Too Many Girls*. She attended the show to see what all the fuss was about. When twenty-eight-year-old Lucy met twenty-two-year-old Desi Arnaz, the attraction was instant, and their marriage in 1940 led to a twenty-year partnership that changed television forever.

The couple shared a drive to succeed and to compensate for the wrongs done to their families. Arnaz had lived like a prince in his native Cuba until a rebel political group had seized his parents' assets and rendered the family exiles. In America, young Desi started out working in restaurants, then used his talents as a singer and bongo-drum player to work his way up in the entertainment business.

During their courtship and the early years of their marriage, the couple

One of the many tricky situations Lucy found herself in on *I Love Lucy*

endured many weeks of separation while Lucy worked on movies and Desi toured as a bandleader. They sought movie projects they could work on together, but Hollywood had few roles for an actor with a heavy Spanish accent.

When Ball decided to advance her career via the growing medium of radio, she requested Arnaz for her costar in the comedy *My Favorite Husband*. Producers said that audiences would not accept him as a "typical American husband." Nonetheless, she did the show, with Richard Denning in the spouse's role, and found that radio made an excellent proving ground for getting laughs out of a studio audience.

In 1951, Ball and Arnaz gave up their high-paying separate careers to star in a CBS situation comedy they developed themselves. Ball insisted they shoot

I Love Lucy in front of a live audience—she wanted to see viewers' reactions instantly. Arnaz, whose idea it was to record the shows (other series at that time were broadcast live and untaped), constructed a complicated diagram for maneuvering the three cameras so they wouldn't interfere with the audience's view. When the network balked at the production costs, the couple agreed to pay the extra money themselves in return for ownership of the show.

The series revolved around housewife Lucy Ricardo, whose quest for self-

Lucy's classic look

actualization inevitably leads to inventive wackiness, especially when circumventing the control of her practical-minded but hot-tempered husband, Ricky. Audiences delighted in seeing Lucy come up with zany solutions to wrapping candy on a fast-moving conveyor belt, drinking an entire bottle of the alcoholic elixir Vitameatavegamin, or appearing in a fashion show despite a sunburn so bad she could barely walk. As her straight man, Desi Arnaz was superb, but it was Lucy who caused a sensation. "God, was she made for TV," says John Cannon, president of the Academy of Television Arts & Sciences. "She was totally prepared to take her dignity and throw it away in the course of creating that character," says American Comedy Institute director Stephen Rosenfield. "In comedy you have to slip and fall."

Ball was also an astute businesswoman. *I Love Lucy* proved so popular that the sponsor, Philip Morris, renewed the couple's contract for $9 million. Ball and Arnaz received an additional $5 million when CBS bought back the rights to all 179 episodes. And in 1959, when the stars tired of producing a weekly show, they secured a $12 million contract to make monthly hour-long specials. These were unheard-of sums at the time, and Ball and Arnaz made millions more from licensing agreements for dolls, tea towels, and other products.

But all the professional success couldn't heal the emotional wounds between the couple, and they divorced in 1960. Ball went on to do a series based on the book *Life Without George,* about two women raising their children alone. The *Lucy Show*—also starring *I Love Lucy* veteran Vivian Vance—premiered in 1962 and was a hit with audiences and critics.

After that show ended its run in 1968, Ball scored another hit with *Here's Lucy,* featuring her real-life children, Lucie and Desi Jr., as well as guest appearances by dozens of showbiz friends. By that time, Ball had bought out her ex-husband's stake in Desilu Studios, which had grown to include the old RKO movie studio lot, a staff of a thousand, and shows such as *Star Trek* and *Bewitched.*

After she temporarily retired from television in 1974, Ball starred in the remake of the movie musical *Mame* with Beatrice Arthur. Her final TV series, ABC's *Life with Lucy,* made when the star was in her late seventies, lasted for only a handful of episodes before she passed away in 1989.

In the years since her death, Ball's legacy has only grown. Many experts say that Lucy Ricardo is the most popular TV character ever created; *I Love Lucy* ranks as the most successful sitcom (playing three times a day in some markets); and Lucille Ball reigns supreme—still the one, the only queen of comedy. ■

When I was going into my fourth month of pregnancy, CBS suddenly gave Desi the green light: they would finance a pilot for a domestic television show featuring the two of us as a married couple. A show that might go on the air that fall.

"What show?" I asked our agent, Don Sharpe. "We don't have a television show."

"You've got a month to put one together," he answered. "They want the pilot by February 15th."

For ten years, Desi and I had been trying to become parents and co-stars. Now our dearest goals were being realized much too fast. We suddenly felt unprepared for either and began to have second thoughts.

It would mean each of us would have to give up our respective radio programs and Desi would have to cancel all his band engagements. It was a tremendous gamble; it had to be an all-or-nothing commitment. But this was the real chance Desi and I would have to work together, something we'd both been longing for for years.

We continued to wrestle with the decision, trying to look at things from every angle. Then one night Carole Lombard [a film star and dear friend] appeared to me in a dream. She was wearing one of those slinky bias-cut gowns of the '30s, waving a long black cigarette holder in her hand. "Go on, kid," she advised me airily. "Give it a whirl."

The next day I told Don Sharpe, "We'll do it. Desi and I want to work together more than anything else in the world.". . .

Desi and I were so excited and happy, planning our first big venture together. I thought that *I Love Lucy* was a pleasant little situation comedy that might survive its first season. But my main thoughts centered on the baby. The nursery wing was now complete, and I planned to have a natural delivery late in June. . . .

The weeks passed and still no baby. Finally my obstetrician decided on a cesarean delivery. Lucie Desirée Arnaz was lying sideways with her head just under my rib cage: when they performed the cesarean, the surgical knife missed her face by a hairsbreadth. But miss her it did; she was complete, healthy, and beautiful. . . .

I had to go right back to work after Lucie was born, so I missed hours and hours and hours of her earliest life. . . . During the early days of the *I Love Lucy* show, I only had Sundays free. So I spent this time entirely with my new baby, marveling at her. . . .

We rehearsed the first show 12 hours a day. Then on Friday evening, August 15, 1951, the bleachers filled up by eight o'clock and Desi explained to the audience that they would be seeing a brand-new kind of television show. He stepped behind the curtain and we all took our places.

Sitting in the bleachers that night were a lot of anxious rooters: [my mother] DeDe and Desi's mother, Delores; our writers; Andrew Hickox; and a raft of Philip Morris [our sponsor] representatives and CBS officials. To launch the series, the network had paid out $300,000. They hoped it would last long enough to pay back that advance.

We were lucky all the way. The first four shows put us among the top ten on television. Arthur Godfrey, one of the giants, preceded us and urged his watchers to stay tuned to *I Love Lucy*. Our 20th show made us number one on the air and there we stayed for three wild, incredible years. . . .

In May 1952, Desi and I both walked into [writer] Jess Oppenheimer's office, elated.

"Well, amigo," Desi told Jess, "we've just heard from the doctor. Lucy's having another baby in January. So we'll have to cancel everything. That's the end of the show."

My feelings were mixed. I felt bad for the cast, the crew, and the writers. I regretted that our dream of working together was again busted. But my predominant feeling was still one of elation. Another baby! And I was almost 41!

Jess sat looking at us silently. Then he remarked casually, "I wouldn't suggest this to any other actress in the world—but why don't we continue the show and have a baby on TV?"

Desi's face lit up. "Do you think we could? Would it be in good taste?" No actress had ever appeared in a stage or television play before when she was obviously pregnant.

"We'll call the CBS censor and see," said Jess. That wonderful guy said, "I don't see why not," and with his active encouragement, Philip Morris and the network went along with it. We had just finished 40 Lucy shows, 10 months of backbreaking work with hardly a letup, but now we made feverish plans to get back into production for the next season as fast as possible.

The baby would be delivered by cesarean section, so we had a definite date to plan around. . . . All through the hot, steaming Hollywood summer we worked, 10 and 12 hours a day, six days a week.

In the early fall, when I was beginning to look pretty big, we did seven shows concerning my pregnancy. These films were screened by a priest, a minister, and a rabbi for any possible violation of good taste. It was the CBS network that objected to using the word "pregnant." They made us say "expecting." The three-man religious committee protested, "What's wrong with 'pregnant'?" They were heartily in favor of what we were doing: showing motherhood as a happy, wholesome, normal family event.

[In one of those shows, we did a scene in which] Lucy tells Ricky she is having a baby. She sends an anonymous note to him at his nightclub, requesting that he sing "Rock-a-Bye Baby." Ricky complies, going from table to table singing the old nursery rhyme. In front of Lucy's table, he looks into her eyes and suddenly realizes that *he* is the father.

When we did this scene before an audience, Desi was suddenly struck by all the emotion he'd felt back when we discovered, after childless years of marriage, that we were finally going to have Lucie. His eyes filled up and he couldn't finish the song; I started to cry, too. Vivian started to sniffle; even the hardened stagehands wiped their eyes with the backs of their hands.

—LUCILLE BALL

Candice
Bergen

■ CANDICE BERGEN WAS BORN AT THE TOP, literally and figuratively. Born May 10, 1946, the first child of popular ventriloquist Edgar Bergen and former model Frances Westerman, she spent her youth at Bella Vista, a Beverly Hills estate overlooking a canyon and resplendent with flower gardens, a citrus orchard, and a waterfall cascading into a swimming pool. Little Candice's friends included Liza Minnelli and oil-fortune heir Timothy Getty. Birthday parties featured rented carousels and maypoles, a governess in tow for each guest. Family friend Walt Disney sent Candice a Christmas gift each year.

With little effort, the teenage Candice found work as a model and actress. But before she could realize the most satisfying and longest-sustained success of her career—playing the hard-hitting reporter on TV's *Murphy Brown*—she had to contend with a challenge or two. The first one also resided at Bella Vista, in a bedroom of his very own: Charlie McCarthy, a forty-pound wooden dummy with red hair. The public considered the wisecracking half of Bergen and McCarthy to be Edgar Bergen's "son." "I wished that I could be Charlie, always up there with my father," Candice said of her semianimate brother. "I wished I could take his place in the sun."

Not that Bergen herself ever failed to attract attention. Tall for her age, by thirteen she had begun to catch the eye of adult men, some of them the movie star friends of her parents. She learned how to handle that attention and by sixteen had her first real boyfriend, Doris Day's son, Terry Melcher. Soon, at the University of Pennsylvania, classmates voted her freshman homecoming queen. But after failing two classes during her sophomore year, she found herself booted out of school and in need of a job.

Photojournalism had always fascinated her. In fact, she used the money she earned from a Revlon lipstick advertisement to buy a Nikon camera and thought of following in the footsteps of her idols, Brenda Starr and Margaret Bourke-White. Before she had a chance, director Sidney Lumet offered her a role in the film adaptation of Mary McCarthy's best-selling book *The Group*. Critics' reviews of her performance ranged from lukewarm to scalding, but directors continued to seek her out. She appeared in a string of movies in the mid-1960s, including *The Sand Pebbles, The Magus, The Adventurers,* and *Getting Straight*.

The roles she wanted most, however, went to acclaimed dramatic actors such as Jane Fonda and Faye Dunaway. Even after she wrote an essay for *Esquire* about her experiences making *The Group,* some readers refused to believe that Bergen could have penned such a well-written story herself.

A turning point came when critics praised her performance in Mike Nichols's 1971 film *Carnal Knowledge,* in which she played a college student torn between affection and forbidden-fruit intrigue. Deciding to work more diligently at her film career—and defeat her other major worry, that she would never rise above her image as an elegant mannequin—Bergen enrolled in acting classes. There she learned the meaning of terms such as "character arc" and "sense memories" that her more experienced colleagues tossed about.

Over the next couple of decades, Bergen continued her acting and freelance photojournalism work, once even combining the two when she played the role of her idol Margaret Bourke-White in Richard Attenborough's *Gandhi*. And she

always seemed to wind up where the action was: at Joan Collins's "hippie party," at prochoice events and Black Panther meetings, with Jane Goodall and her chimpanzees in Tanzania.

In 1975, Bergen started her TV career with a stint as a *Today* show correspondent. About that same time, producer Lorne Michaels invited her to serve as the first female host of his new show, *Saturday Night Live.* "He showed me tapes of the first two shows, and I said 'I'll do whatever you ask,'" she says. "It was the best experience. The cast members were unbelievably talented and amazingly energetic. It was as though the inmates had taken over the asylum." Bergen appeared in the popular *Jaws*-parody sketch "Land Shark" and, in a sequence with Gilda Radner, tried to answer a question oft posed to her: "What is it like to be so beautiful?" Her performance was so impressive that she was invited back to host several more shows.

The comic bent suited her, and in 1979, she appeared in the comedy film *Starting Over,* portraying a self-involved aspiring singer who callously tosses aside her husband, played by Burt Reynolds.

That persona, of a humorous, strong career woman, foreshadowed the character she would play in TV's *Murphy Brown.* The Murphy Brown role also represented the artistic convergence of several of Bergen's life themes: journalism, feminism, politics, and comedy. *Murphy Brown* debuted in 1988 and lasted ten seasons. "The show was a windfall for all of us who took part in it," she says. "We liked one another so much, and the writing was so good. All of us knew we would never have professional kismet like that again."

When *Murphy Brown* creator Diane English suggested a storyline that would involve Murphy having breast cancer, Bergen immediately threw her support behind the idea. "Doctors and hospitals told us that the incidence of mammograms went up thirty-three percent as a result of the show," she says.

Of course, it would have been hard to top the massive dose of publicity the show received in 1992, when Vice President Dan Quayle made a speech criticizing

Real-life newswomen give Murphy a surprise baby shower on an episode of *Murphy Brown*. Standing left to right are: Faith Ford, Faith Daniels, Joan Lunden, and Katie Couric. Seated are Mary Alice Williams (left) and Paula Zahn.

Single mom Murphy Brown enters motherhood and breaks ground on national television.

Murphy Brown for bearing a child out of wedlock. Overlooking deadbeat parents, domestic violence, drugs and alcohol, and the paucity of affordable day care, Quayle blamed the deterioration of the American family on Bergen, for portraying a modern career woman "mocking the importance of fathers" by choosing single parenthood. Scriptwriters wove the controversy into the show's storyline, pretending that Quayle had criticized the "real-life" Murphy.

Sadly, Bergen had to play the role of a single parent in real life when her husband, French film director Louis Malle, died of cancer in 1995, leaving her with daughter Chloe, born to the couple in 1985. Bergen and Malle had been introduced by a mutual friend, photographer Mary Ellen Mark, and discovered they were soul mates on their first date; they wed in 1980.

Murphy Brown ended its run in 1998. Three years later, Bergen took her interest in journalism a step further. As host of the Oxygen TV cable show *Exhale,* she conducts nightly one-on-one interviews with celebrities, politicians, and other newsmakers. She married philanthropist Marshall Rose in 2000 and lives in Beverly Hills near both her mother and her brother Mark (born when Candice was fifteen; Edgar Bergen died in 1983). *Architectural Digest* featured photos of the Spanish-style hilltop villa she had custom-designed so that her daughter would have an agreeable place to entertain friends. As she entered the new millennium, Bergen found herself still on top, but this time on her own terms. ▪

My sixth Christmas I made my radio debut as a guest on the *Edgar Bergen Show,* appearing in a skit with my father and Charlie in 1952. My father rehearsed the lines with me in his study and again in his car as we headed down Sunset to the studio for the read-through, where I proudly took my seat at the long table in the rehearsal room with my father and the writers and the other guests. "Now remember, Candy," my father warned me sternly, "wait till it's quiet to say your lines. *Don't step on the laughs.*"

The night of the show, my hair brushed and burnished, taffeta ribbons tied crisply and tight, I hovered backstage, faint, heart fluttering. It was my first time to be up there with the two of them, to make my mark, and as the program began, I waited for Charlie to give me my cue.

"And now, here are Edgar Bergen and Charlie McCarthy. . . . Our guests tonight are Mimi Benzell and *Candy Bergen.* . . ." (Applause)

EDGAR: Ah, Charlie, my dear, sweet little Charlie, this is going to be the happiest Christmas of my life.

CHARLIE: Oh? You mean you're not giving out any presents?

EDGAR: No, Charlie, this is an occasion for which I've waited six years, ever since my little daughter, Candy, was born.

CHARLIE: You mean you're sending her to work?

EDGAR: No, Charlie, tonight Candy's going to be on this show and that's why I'm so happy. You know, she's the apple of my eye.

CHARLIE: Yes, of course, but don't forget, I'm the cabbage of your bankbook.

EDGAR: Charlie, I hope you're not jealous of Candy.

CHARLIE: Oh no, Bergen, I welcome a little competition. Ha, what have I got to worry about? Let the kid have her chance.

There it was, and someone squeezed my shoulder, crumpling my puffed sleeve, and I walked out on stage to my first burst of applause, stepping up to my little low microphone alongside my father and Charlie. Reeling at the rows of faces smiling up from the darkness that spread out below us—pleased, expectant, friendly—I recited my well-learned lines with considerable poise and polish—a perfect little ham, a windup doll—a dummy. A daughter determined to make good.

CANDY: Hello, Daddy, hi, Charlie. (Applause)

CHARLIE: That's enough folks. That's enough. Let's not let things get out of hand. Goodbye, little girl, get outta here, goodbye.

EDGAR: Now, now, please, Charlie. Candy, my own little Candy, tonight is the happiest night of my life. Tonight, my little girl steps out into the footlights of life.

CANDY: Down, Daddy, down.

CHARLIE: Hey, this kid's getting laughs. Watch it, kid. Remember—there's only one star on this show.

CANDY: Yes, Mortimer [Edgar's other dummy] is clever.

CHARLIE: Well that does it. This kid has gotta go.

CANDY: But I want to be on the show. I want to be just like Daddy.

CHARLIE: Just like Daddy, huh? No ambition, eh?

CANDY: Now, Charlie, you don't mind my being on the show, do you?

CHARLIE: No, Candy, not at all. After all, you're growing up and it's about time you helped me support your old man.

CANDY: You shouldn't have said that, Charlie. Daddy resents the idea that you support him.

CHARLIE: Does he deny it?

CANDY: No, but he resents it.

CHARLIE: How do you like that? A trial-sized Lucille Ball.

My father had trained me well. Not only was I letter-perfect, I also waited for and got the laughs, commenting casually to him later, "Gee, Daddy, I had to wait a long time."

— CANDICE BERGEN

Dr. Joyce Brothers

■ AT THE TURN OF THE TWENTY-FIRST CENtury, when people willingly air the most intimate details of their lives on radio and television, it's almost hard to believe that there was once a time when such personal topics were believed to be inappropriate for public consumption. In the late 1950s, one concerned psychologist who also happened to love the media changed the relationship between broadcasting and people's lives—opening the airwaves not only for herself, but for all the on-air advice givers who would follow. That trailblazer, known as the "mother of media psychology," is Dr. Joyce Brothers.

For more than four decades, through both broadcast and print media, Dr. Brothers has been dispensing advice and encouragement to help women and men lead happier, emotionally healthier lives. Her soothing voice, warm yet authoritative manner, and ability to cite relevant research have reassured troubled callers and helped millions of individuals. Though this process, Dr. Brothers transformed radio and television into a place where people go for advice.

"In the 1950s, there was a lot of information on psychology in libraries and textbooks," she says, "but it was not readily available to the general public. It seemed to me that if I wanted to communicate it, I should go where the people are—so I went into the media."

The connection between psychology and broadcasting seemed natural for Dr. Brothers, but it was a white-knuckle experiment for her first television bosses. She recalls, early on, responding to a letter from a viewer seeking advice—a technique that became a hallmark of her show—but this question was about premature ejaculation. As she discussed this previously taboo subject on the air, she remembers looking up to see a ring of terrified TV executives, all male, "with white faces drained of blood, and they were waiting for phone calls." When the calls came, they were all positive—men saying, " 'This is something I've had all of my life, and you've helped me,' " she says.

Brothers and cartoonist Charles Schulz, 1984

"Not one negative call. So the [executives] left me alone and I went my own way, and I was on my own way."

The confidence to go her own way grew from Joyce's early years with her high-achieving, supportive parents, Morris and Estelle Bauer. Born October 20, 1927, young Joyce Diane Bauer grew up in the New York City suburbs. Her parents, both of whom were attorneys and the children of eastern European Jewish immigrants, instilled in Joyce and her younger sister, Elaine, a high regard for

hard work and academic achievement.

Even as an adolescent, Joyce was known for her inquisitive mind, her superb memory, and the level-headed advice she gave to family and friends. After skipping two grades and still graduating from high school with honors, Joyce attended Cornell University. Although she was on a scholarship requiring her to major in home economics, she became fascinated with a course in psychology and made it her second major. After earning a B.S. with honors in 1947, she

Brothers is congratulated by Colonel Eddie Eagen, president of the New York State Boxing Commission, on the set of *The $64,000 Question.*

enrolled in Columbia University, earning an M.A. in 1949 and a Ph.D. in 1953. Her professors told her they were making her graduate work especially difficult to try to get her to leave and create space for a male student, but she relished the challenge and met it. Her marriage in 1949 to a medical student, Dr. Milton Brothers—along with her doctorate in psychology—gave her the name for which she'd become famous, pronounced almost as one word, "Doctorjoycebrothers."

Then, in 1955, after Dr. Brothers had left her teaching position at Hunter College to care for daughter Lisa, she decided to try to make some money for the young family by becoming a contestant on the most popular TV game show of that era, *The $64,000 Question.* After

teaching herself all about her selected topic, boxing, she became only the second person and the only woman ever to win the top prize. She went on to win the follow-up show, *The $64,000 Challenge,* which pitted her against boxers in answering questions about the sport. In both competitions, TV executives asked the most obscure, hardest possible questions because they thought a woman with a Ph.D. would be unappealing to viewers and were hoping to get her off the air.

But audiences loved her, and Dr. Brothers beat her opponents every time. She walked away with not only the money but national celebrity, which gave her the opening to the television career she'd wanted. She appeared on *Sports Showcase* and on talk and late-night shows, where her charm, intelligence, and dignity reinforced her favorable image.

Soon after, she decided not to return to university teaching but, as she says, become "a teacher in a different sense." She approached NBC executives with her idea for a local afternoon television show. They reluctantly agreed, and in September 1958 she began a four-week trial giving counseling on marriage, child rearing, and even sex. To the surprise of the producers, who had offered the program as a publicity stunt, she became an immediate hit with viewers, generating thousands of letters each week. Soon the show was broadcast nationally, and within a year a late-night program was added. The ratings soared. A new type of television had begun.

In various television formats and on radio as well, her programs stayed on the air for the next three decades. Throughout that time and up to today, she has also often appeared on television talk shows and game shows, and she has frequently played herself in guest spots on series when a little counseling is needed. In this guise, she has advised characters ranging from Cybill Shepherd's on *Moonlighting* to Fran Drescher's on *The Nanny.*

In addition, her articles have appeared in magazines from *Parade* to *Good Housekeeping* to *Reader's Digest.* She has also written nine books, from *The Successful Woman,* which advised women how to balance family and career, to *Widow,* which provided comfort and encouragement to women who'd lost their husbands, written after her own died in 1989.

Throughout her career, Dr. Brothers has received hundreds of awards and been named among the most influential and admired women in America and the world in numerous polls and surveys. The public acknowledgment, however, reflects the personal gratitude millions of women and men feel for her. Over a tumultuous period of American social history, when women began facing bewildering choices about their personal and professional lives, when women and men entered new realms of relationships and sexuality, Dr. Joyce Brothers made it okay to ask for help. By linking broadcasting and psychology, she expanded the possibilities of both. ■

I did not grow up wanting to be a psychologist. My secret wish was to be in show business. But those were the days of the glamour stars: Rita Hayworth and Paulette Goddard, Ginger Rogers and Claudette Colbert. I was attractive enough, with the scrubbed look of the nice girl next door, but I was not glamorous. I was afraid I didn't have a chance.

So, being practical, I decided to become a psychologist. This was something that interested me very much. I had very definite goals. I wanted to be a professor of psychology at a major university, and I also wanted to be a good wife and mother. At Cornell, I took a double major, home economics and psychology, so I could be as well prepared for domestic life as for professional life.

But every time I went to the movies, I could see myself up there on the screen, a star. After Milt and I were married, I auditioned for several television shows. I thought that if I did get a role, I could still continue working for my doctorate in psychology at Columbia.

All I got was turndowns. The final one was the most devastating. My mother-in-law had a good friend who was head of an advertising agency and had considerable clout in the television world. As a favor to her, he agreed to see me. I asked him if he could advise me on how to break into show business.

"Joyce, go home," he said. "Be a good wife and have nice kids. You have no chance in a million years. Forget it."

And that was that. Right from the shoulder. I stopped auditioning for television roles. But I will tell you right now that it was the last time I took no for an answer without challenging it.

Then *The $64,000 Question* came along. For those of you who were not watching television in 1955, it was a quiz show—not just *a* quiz show, but the hottest show on television. On Tuesday nights, everyone watched *The $64,000 Question,* following the efforts of contestants to win the $64,000, which was a fortune at that time. The more I watched it, the more I thought, "I could do that."

I did not think of it in terms of show business. What I was thinking about was money. I had stopped teaching and doing research when Lisa was born. As a psychologist, I was convinced of the importance of full-time mothering for the first three years. Now I was ready to get back to work.

Not only had I had enough of staying home (I was climbing the walls with boredom), but we were broke. We were living on Milt's salary as a hospital resident: $50 a month. It went a lot further in those days, but not far enough.

I did not even dream of winning the $64,000. My goal was a smaller prize: the Cadillac. If I could win the Cadillac, Milt and I could drive around in it all summer. Show off to our friends. Go to the beach. Visit my folks in the country. And when winter came, we would sell it and have a nice little nest egg.

I analyzed the show. All the contestants were similar in one respect. There was a shoemaker who knew all about opera, for instance, and there was a burly Marine who was a gourmet cook. Every contestant had a built-in incongruity.

I was short and blond and pretty, a psychologist and the mother of an almost-three-year-old. There was nothing paradoxical about me, nothing that would catch the attention of the powers that be that cast the quiz show. After some thought, I decided to become an expert on either plumbing or boxing. Either would be sufficiently incongruous with my image. Milt advised me to go with boxing. "No one wants to hear about stopped-up toilets," he said. So I went to work to turn myself into a boxing expert. I ate, drank, and slept boxing: its history, its statistics, its personalities.

When I felt I was ready, I applied for the show and was accepted. I went on and won. I kept on winning. I was on every week. I loved being in front of the television cameras. And one night, I won big. I won the $64,000!

It changed my life. I was on television and radio. I was making personal appearances. I was in show business! My two interests, show business and psychology, dovetailed as if I had been planning this kind of career ever since I was a freshman in college. But I had not.

It was not until after I won *The $64,000 Question* that I even dreamed of a career as a psychological journalist, working in front of television cameras and translating the results of psychological research into terms that people could use in their everyday lives. At the time, there was no such job description. Once I glimpsed the possibility of what I could be, however, there was no stopping me. It was what I wanted more than anything else in the world. I shiver sometimes when I think about how I almost missed out because I believed that man who told me to "go home and be a good wife."

When I look back, I realize that unless I had really loved the idea of appearing on television in front of an audience of hundreds of thousands, I would never have considered trying out for *The $64,000 Question*. So while it was the Cadillac that I wanted, there was an unconscious inner force pushing me on, saying, "I want to be in show business. This might be my chance."

The moral of this little story is that you cannot let other people's opinions stop you from trying to do what you want.

—DR. JOYCE BROTHERS

Dorothy
Stimson Bullitt

■ WHEN DOROTHY STIMSON BULLITT CHOSE the name "Mike" to adorn her prized boat, it wasn't to honor her father, her husband, or a treasured friend; rather, it was short for "microphone," and she wanted it to symbolize the industry she grew to love. Although Bullitt entered the industry by chance, her pioneering role as a founding mother of broadcast ownership proved anything but chancy as she turned a single radio station into a broadcasting empire and blazed a trail for other women to follow.

As founder of King Broadcasting Company, the Pacific Northwest's premier broadcasting company, Dorothy Stimson Bullitt was acclaimed nationally for her innovative, award-winning programming and influential management style. King Broadcasting (later purchased by Belo Corporation) was recognized throughout the country as one of the best broadcasting companies. During its peak years, the King empire included a string of radio and television stations that extended through the Pacific Northwest, south to San Francisco, and west to Hawaii.

Bullitt may have been a relative newcomer to the competitive arena of broadcasting when she bought the financially strapped Seattle radio station KEVR in 1946, but she quickly proved her business savvy by acquiring and changing the call letters to KING to represent King County, where the station was located. A feisty businesswoman who secured a loan for nearly $200,000—a huge sum in those days—she consistently did her homework, conferred with colleagues, and picked strong employees.

Radio first captured Bullitt's interest when her cousin Fred Stimson suggested that owning a radio station might be a fun way to earn a living. She had been managing family-owned commercial real estate up to that time, but the idea intrigued her. Realizing that she was a novice in the field, however, she proceeded only after conducting thorough research and forming a brain trust of broadcasting experts to advise her.

The King facility in Seattle in the early years

Bullitt's career in broadcasting began in 1946 with the purchase of her first radio station in Seattle; she soon expanded into television and other regional markets. Throughout the company's growth, she was widely recognized as the reason King Broadcasting succeeded. Her tenacious management style, enhanced by her long-standing political and business contacts, certainly boosted her success. But it was Bullitt's strength of character, leadership, and vision that enabled King Broadcasting to sustain its role as a voice for the Pacific Northwest and her role as a leader in the broadcast industry.

Bullitt also had timing and luck on her side. Soon after she entered television broadcasting, the Federal Communications Commission (FCC) ordered a freeze on broadcast licenses, which allowed KING to temporarily secure a local monopoly for network affiliations. One of Bullitt's favorite sayings was

"Long-range planning is great, but dumb luck is better."

Only two years after purchasing KEVR Radio, Bullitt wasted no time getting in on the hot new craze of television. At the time, few in Seattle had TV sets, so people would congregate outside a hardware store to watch the flickering black-and-white images on the sets for sale inside. Bullitt could see that the new medium had promise, so in 1948 she purchased KRSC-TV,

Bullitt at KGW-TV, 1958

Bullitt with John F. Kennedy in 1962

the first television station sold in the United States. This purchase secured her place in this vibrant new medium, giving her Seattle's only TV station.

Bullitt herself traveled to Washington, D.C., to apply for station licenses once the FCC resumed issuing them in 1952. Her testimony before congressional hearings earned her the respect of FCC officials and legislators, impressing them with her presentation of complex broadcast information.

King Broadcasting was a family-run company, and Bullitt remained in charge of the finances, watching the books like a hawk, including her own travel expenses; she was notorious, for instance, for insisting on flying coach. Yet she was also known for her great loyalty to and respect for her friends and employees. When World War II broke out in the Pacific and American citizens of Japanese descent were interned in camps, Bullitt secured a house and job in Connecticut for a long-

time Japanese employee and got him out of Seattle before he was taken away.

Early in her broadcast career, Bullitt recognized the power of aligning with other women in the broadcasting business, even though there were very few at the time. When friend Georgia Davidson, who owned KTVB in Boise, Idaho, decided to sell her station, her first call was to Bullitt. Out of both friendship and recognition of the opportunity, Bullitt snatched it up, adding it to her company's growing conglomerate of regional broadcasting properties.

Dorothy Stimson was born on February 5, 1892, into a prominent Seattle family. Her mother was a music lover originally from New York, and her father's family had made a fortune from timber harvesting around the Great Lakes and moved to the Pacific Northwest to expand operations. Though Dorothy didn't attend high school or college, her training at Mrs. Dow's Finishing School in Briarcliff Manor, New York, was typical for a girl of her social class at that time. She was an avid reader who loved sports and travel. In 1918, Dorothy married Scott Bullitt, a member of a family of Kentucky bluebloods, and the couple had three children.

Bullitt's father had a significant influence on her success and management style. Father and daughter shared a strong interest in business strategies and negotiating techniques, and he taught her skills that she utilized first in real estate and then in broadcasting. Whenever Bullitt came to an impasse in a deal or confronted a thorny management

Bullitt with her prized boat, the *Mike*

problem, she would consider what her dad would do.

In 1961, after fifteen years presiding over her broadcast entities, Bullitt retired and turned the management of King Broadcasting over to her son. Bullitt then turned to her other passion: boats.

Aboard her prized yacht, the *Mike*, she traveled frequently, but she continued to visit the King offices almost daily until her death in 1989 at the age of ninety-seven. Her boat may have provided many fond memories, but her heart belonged to the industry. ∎

After World War II, a lot of new avenues opened up. Broadcasting was a road I'd never taken and it included a pretty risky investment in a business I knew nothing about. So I gathered a handful of people [to form a brain trust] and we started out with only an idea to see what would happen. [Radio broadcaster] Gloria Chandler was on the staff of the NBC station in Chicago and she knew the mechanics of programming, about which I knew nothing. A program for me was just something that came on the air.

A tenant in a building we owned happened to own a radio station, KEVR. We knew each other pretty well, but I didn't know much about his station except that it wasn't very good. He came up to the office and said, "Don't apply for another radio station here in Seattle. I have one and it doesn't have an audience. If you bring another in, it will just dilute the audience further. Why don't you buy mine?" I began to dicker with the owner (Arch Talbot) on his price, while [my business associates] were in the next room with the door closed playing gin rummy. Finally we made a deal and while it was being written up, I slipped a piece of paper under the door saying "We got it!" so we were in business.

The price was $190,000 and I didn't have the money to spare, so I borrowed it from banks. The bankers were very nice—but then those were the days when I knew the bankers personally. They were Father's friends and they knew me a little and knew what the securities were. It was a great gamble, but we didn't know how great. We were just happy to be in business.

We had been told that the station didn't have an audience, but I didn't realize that it had literally no audience, until Henry sat down at the manager's desk and opened the mail. A check fell out and we yelled, "Hooray, we got some money." The letter was from Mr. Hooper of the audience measurement surveys, who said, "We're returning your check because there was no one listening to your station." No One. He also enclosed a chart of station performance and ours had zero, zero, zero, all the way down. I said, "Well, we can't do worse than that—it shouldn't take much to do better."

The format was the worst I have ever heard. The air was full of paid religion—fundamentalists who advertised figures of Christ to hang in your car for 25 cents. I hated that coming in! It was a terrible format that featured religious hucksters begging the listeners to "put their hands on the radio and be saved" and "send in a dollar or God will punish you." That was the station's only source of revenue—they paid to get on the air so they could ask for contributions.

So the decision had to be made about how shall we taper this down—get rid of the paid religion a little at a time, or just cut it all out and put on our own records or whatever we can find, which I thought we might just as well do. We also made a policy decision to support and give free time to the three basic faiths—Catholic, Protestant, and Jewish—whose programs would talk about God and not just talk to raise money. . . . Bit by bit we took steps. We improved the personnel, got a better station manager, and bought some programs.

We produced a symphony evening, the way an orchestra would, by having one conductor for the entire evening. And we programmed the way a symphony concert was programmed—one piece to start with and then an entire symphony with all three or four movements under the same conductor. So, when we had Toscanini, it was a Toscanini evening. I did the timing and produced it every Wednesday evening or so. It really was a lot of work and I did it for almost a year until one of the salesmen came in and said, "I have a program sold for that time unless you want to continue with your symphony." I said, "Heavens no! If it's paid for, we take it." And that was the end of the symphony, except that letters came in by the heap.

We needed to change the call letters. I wanted the letters K-I-N-G for obvious reasons—it signified the tops and we were in King County. So, I wrote KING, KING, KING for all three choices on the application form. It wasn't long before Andy Haley called to ask if I was crazy. He said, "You don't imagine you're the first person to want those call letters, do you? They're the best call letters there are." I said, "I'm sure they are; that's why I want them. Find out who has them because we want them." A few days later he called to say he'd traced the call letters through various departments to a tramp steamer called the *Watertown,* a big old ship going round delivering packages here and there in the world. I said, "For a ship called the *Watertown,* all they need is dots and dashes—they don't have to advertise to promote a tramp steamer, they don't even have to say it. We need those letters."

I don't know how Andy did it, whether he went through the Maritime Commission or the Catholic Church or where, and I don't know what it cost him, maybe a case of scotch or champagne. I never knew what he did to get those letters; he never billed me for them, but he got them. More people have asked me how much it cost to get those call letters. It's one of the best things that ever happened to us. That's how King Broadcasting was born.

—DOROTHY STIMSON BULLITT

Carol
Burnett

■ THE YEAR WAS 1945, AND YOUNG CAROL Burnett had a plan. A junior high school student, Carol was helping out with her grandmother's secret job as a cleaning lady at the Warner Bros. office on Hollywood Boulevard. The job was kept secret because it would have prevented her family from receiving relief payments. One night, Carol, who loved to draw cartoon figures, left an original creation on a desk in the art department. "I would surprise Nanny with a job offer from the Warner Bros. art department the next day," Burnett remembers. "We'd be rich and famous, and the Relief Lady could just go to hell." The following night, she sprinted to the anointed desk, only to find a note asking that she clean the office "period" and stop messing with the pencils.

Few stars start out big, but Burnett—who became the top female television entertainer of the 1970s—lays claim to a particularly hardscrabble legacy she keeps close to her heart (as evidenced by the animated Carol-Burnett-as-a-cleaning-lady featured in the credits of *The Carol Burnett Show*). Little Carol's family suffered from a combination of divorce, alcoholism, tuberculosis, underemployment, and unemployment.

After moving the family from San Antonio (where Carol had been born on April 26, 1933) to a poor section of Hollywood, Carol's mother gave birth to another daughter. Carol considered herself plain-looking in contrast to her adorable baby sister and fetching mother. Yet she won friends among her well-to-do schoolmates at Hollywood High with her fun-loving personality. Though Carol still wanted to become an artist, she was also impressed by two teachers with a flair for dramatic storytelling. "I started thinking that wasn't a bad way to get noticed," she says.

When graduation time came, Carol longed to attend UCLA, but the family could scrape up only enough money for a local secretarial school. Fortunately, an anonymous do-gooder left Carol an envelope with $50—enough to register as a freshman at UCLA—and she was off. There, blessed with a loud voice and double-jointed hips conducive to physical comedy, she gravitated to the theater department and within months attained success as a comic actor in school productions. "She gave off a magical feeling," recalls Jim Klain, then UCLA campus activities director. "When she auditioned, people just perked up."

As a result, Burnett was invited to join a UCLA summer ensemble group in San Francisco. She made costumes, built scenery, set up lighting, and performed—loving all of it. There, Burnett decided that "the only thing that was reliable in the whole wide world was the stage, and it would be my life." During her sophomore year she appeared in three shows, while taking classes and working five mornings a week.

Before long Carol left school and headed straight to Broadway. While living at the Rehearsal Club, the legendary New York boardinghouse for young women aspiring to the stage, Burnett convinced her housemates they could break out of the no-work-without-an-agent/no-agent-without-work cycle by mounting their own show. When Burnett's slapstick rendition of the Eartha Kitt song "Monotonous" was lauded, she received numerous offers from talent agencies. A cabaret act in which she sang "I Made a Fool of Myself over John Foster Dulles" won her guest spots on *The Jack Paar Show* and *The Ed Sullivan Show* and, eventually, a permanent gig on *The Garry Moore Show*. At the same time, she was

Guest star Roddy McDowall and Burnett take part in a movie spoof in an episode of *The Carol Burnett Show.*

making a name for herself in the lead role of the hit play *Once upon a Mattress,* directed by her idol, George Abbott.

In 1967, Burnett found the vehicle that would transport her to the pinnacle of television success and, incidentally, breathe life into the variety-show genre. *The Carol Burnett Show,* a musical comedy variety hour, enabled Burnett to use her talents as a singer, physical comedian, and comic actor while working with stars she admired, such as Dinah Shore, Julie Andrews, and Jim Nabors.

A key part of the show's originality was the roles Burnett created and performed herself. In perhaps the most memorable of many hilarious movie parodies, Burnett played Scarlett O'Hara wearing the famous green dress made from a curtain—but Burnett wore it with the rod still attached. Later in the series' run, a recurring sketch introduced viewers to Eunice, Ed, and Mama, a wacky, dysfunctional southern family. These vignettes spawned the spin-off *Mama's Family.*

During its twelve successful seasons, *The Carol Burnett Show* received twenty-five Emmy awards, owing to excellent writing, the compatibility among long-time cast members Vicki Lawrence, Harvey Korman, and Tim Conway, and Burnett's strong anchoring of the show. "Carol Burnett defied the rule that the variety show was dead," says Syracuse University TV historian Robert Thompson. "That genre had exploded in popularity in 1950s, but when rock 'n' roll came along in the early 1960s it became hard for a TV show to appeal to everyone. Ed Sullivan hung on for a couple of years by having the Beatles and Doors on, but the genre was dying. Carol Burnett had the only network variety show with broad enough appeal to survive in prime time."

In 1979, with the show's ratings still respectable, Burnett decided to end its run. "I always like to leave the party before the host looks at his watch," she says. She went on to appear in big-screen films such as *The Four Seasons* and *Pete 'n Tillie,* as well as numerous TV specials and movies, including her highly praised dramatic portrayal of a mother who dis-

Burnett with guest Betty White on *Carol & Company*

covered her son had been killed in the Vietnam War by friendly fire. In 1996, she won her fifth Emmy, for portraying Helen Hunt's mother in the TV series *Mad About You.*

Burnett has three daughters from her marriage to producer and director Joe Hamilton (they divorced in 1984). Although she never did receive that job offer from the movie studio's art department, in 2000 she paid homage to such bittersweet memories by collaborating with one of her daughters to write the play *Hollywood Arms,* based on her memoir of her early years. ■

Growing up, I didn't feel pretty. I was gangly and skinny. All bones and no meat. I also had the famous "Burnett lower lip," which meant I had no chin. Andy Gump. Gopher Girl. Ugly. I showed some promise in other areas. I had artistic talent and liked reporting for the school newspaper. My mother would say things like, "Listen, kid, no matter what you look like, you can always draw or write." She meant well but, to me, her words translated into, "Good God, I'm really quite unattractive."

It didn't help to share a household with two man-magnets. My maternal grandmother, Nanny, had been pretty enough to snare six husbands in her day. My mother looked like Joan Crawford.

I loved to watch Mama getting ready for a date. She'd put setting lotion on her fingers and fashion a wave in the hair on one side of her face, setting it with two bobby pins. She'd apply her red, red lipstick right from the tube and then smooth it out with her little finger. Then came the black mascara that accentuated her big blue eyes. She'd spit into the mascara and squish the brush around and sweep it up under the top eyelashes, which were pretty long to begin with. When her hair was dry, she'd take out the bobby pins and fluff the wave with her hands. She'd look at her face in the mirror and smile and rub her teeth with her little finger to get off any lipstick that showed. She looked really good. She wasn't tall, and she was round everywhere. Her legs were slim with little ankles. She'd put on her high heels and back away from the mirror and look this way and that and pose a lot. She sure got a kick out of looking at herself.

And Christine, my baby sister, was striking from the day she was born. She was my half-sister. Her father was Italian. She was the kind of baby who made people stop and turn around. They'd say, "Why, look at those big, brown, beautiful eyes! Where did those come from?" She had feather-duster eyelashes, too. Mama said Chrissy was the most beautiful baby she had ever seen. I loved having a little sister, although I looked—and felt—more like her mother. But I was never jealous of Mama or Chrissy—I was proud of them. I just wished I could get in on a little of the boy action, like my cousin Janice did. She was a raving beauty with blond hair. When we played Tarzan and Jane together, you can probably guess which role went to whom. She's the reason I learned the Tarzan yell. By our teenage years, Janice looked like a baby Lana Turner. At dances boys would be lined up to wait for even a 10-second round with her.

I also had started growing up—straight up. At first I liked getting taller. But soon it was a royal pain, because the boys only came up to my neck. And they liked the short girls. I was a fast runner and, since I wasn't so hot in the looks department, I figured I could attract some of the cuter guys with my athletic ability. There was a new boy in school, a ninth grader, Joey. He was Italian, and he made the girls drool. The guys liked him, too, because he was a sensational athlete.

I developed a crush on Joey. My friend Norma was nuts about him, too. He started to pay attention to Norma, and I became desperate, so I challenged him to a footrace. That would make him look at me all right. Then we would run through life together, Joey and me, hand in hand. I nagged and nagged him and he finally agreed, reluctantly, to the race. "Come on, let's get this thing over with. I gotta get home," he said.

"Ready."

There we were side by side—Joey and me—bent over, touching shoulders.

"Get set . . ."

I pictured a perfect photo finish with him hugging me and saying that I was really something.

"Go!"

He tore up the alley like Superman, and it was over. I was left way behind, eating dust. He never even came back. A couple of weeks later he asked Norma out.

After high school, when I enrolled at UCLA, I was supposed to take journalism classes. Still, I found myself leafing through the Theater Arts section of the course offerings. I registered as an English major, but what I couldn't tell anyone was that deep down I wanted to be an actress. Am I crazy? They'd laugh me right off the face of this Earth. Actresses are supposed to be gorgeous.

Later that year, there was a festival of "all-student-acted-written-directed One-Acts." I tried out for nearly every one. I finally got a role as a hillbilly woman named Effie. Opening night I was pretty nervous, but I got lots of laughs during the first scene, using a kind of down-home Texas/Arkansas accent. When I exited to the wings, I had the funniest feeling that the audience had come offstage with me, that they hadn't wanted me to leave, and I wasn't nervous anymore, just excited and feeling . . . wanted. When I re-entered the stage, the audience started screaming, laughing, and stomping its feet. At first I thought something had happened behind me, like maybe the scenery had fallen down, but I turned around and looked and everything was the way it was supposed to be. Then it dawned on me . . . they were reacting to Effie, to me.

It began in my stomach: a feeling, a good feeling, a warm something. Whatever it was, there were no words to describe the sensation. It quickly spread its way up to my heart and down to all ten toes, to my arms, to my fingers, my head. . . . I was a helium balloon, floating above the tiny stage. I was . . . happy. At the end of the show, some total strangers stopped me in the hall and said they didn't remember the last time they'd had such a good belly laugh.

Nobody cared if I wasn't pretty. It didn't matter. *It didn't matter.*

—CAROL BURNETT

Diahann
Carroll

■ AT THE AGE OF SIXTEEN, CAROL DIANN Johnson and her friend Elissa Oppenheim auditioned to appear on the TV show *Arthur Godfrey's Talent Scouts.* Under their selected stage names, Diahann Carroll and Lisa Collins, Diahann sang "Tenderly" while Lisa accompanied her with a fancy piano arrangement.

"All right, kids, here's the story," the producer announced after the tryout. "We'd like to use the singer but not the piano player."

That scenario of being singled out early on became a theme in Carroll's life and has continued throughout her career. Sometimes it was a bad thing. Junior high schoolmates bullied little Diahann for wearing her fussy hairdos and the pristine clothing her mother outfitted her in every morning. It didn't help matters that Carroll's parents—her father was a subway conductor who rented out apartments—were wealthier than most of their neighbors and dropped her off at school every morning in a brand-new Chevy.

Fortunately, most people who singled Carroll out had good intentions. *Ebony* magazine fashion editor Freda DeKnight picked out an unsolicited snapshot and letter from fifteen-year-old Diahann and hired her as a model. Under DeKnight's tutelage, the teenage Diahann learned a sense of fashion—which dresses

call for short white gloves and which are right for long black gloves—that would, years later, lead to her being selected for the international best-dressed list, along with Jacqueline Kennedy Onassis. At Stitt Junior High School in Washington Heights, New York, a guidance counselor took note of Diahann's vocal talent (born in 1935, she had been singing publicly since her choir debut at age six at the Abyssinian Baptist Church) and suggested she enroll in Manhattan's High School of Music and Art. After graduating, Diahann won a talent contest on TV's *Chance of a Lifetime,* receiving $4,000 and a singing engagement at the Latin Quarter. The nightclub's owner, Lou Walters, sought out Diahann as a client for his management agency and pledged himself to groom her for stardom as a cabaret singer and Broadway player.

No one could deny the talent, sophistication, and sense of style that set Diahann apart. Sometimes, however, she was denied a chance. Even after her 1974 Academy Award nomination, top Hollywood talent agent Sue Mengers declined to represent her, saying it would have taken too much work to find quality film projects for a black female actor.

Fortunately, by that time, Carroll was skilled at zeroing in on, and fighting for, the occasional prime opportunities that did come along, and creating her own when they didn't.

But before she could change TV history, she had to hone the actor's craft. The journey started after Carroll attained prominence as a nightclub singer in the late 1950s. Her work came to the attention of playwright Truman Capote, who cast her as the innocent Ottilie in *House of Flowers,* choreographed by George Balanchine and Herbert Ross and directed by Peter Brook. "That play was like four years of college," Carroll says. "I learned that it is quite a complicated process to pull a character apart and put it back together."

The effort paid off, and Carroll won a Tony Award for her next major stage role, as a fashion model in *No Strings,* a 1962 musical that Richard Rodgers wrote with her in mind.

Carroll's charm and grace made an impression on others as well, namely her four husbands (club owner Monte Kay, with whom she had a daughter, Suzanne;

businessman Freddie Glusman; entrepreneur Robert DeLeon; and singer Vic Damone), on-again-off-again love Sidney Poitier, and onetime fiancé David Frost. At times, her glamorous, jet-setting personal life mirrored that of Dominique Deveraux, the character she would play in the glitzy television drama *Dynasty.*

However, it was her ability to adapt to the role of a middle-class character that enabled Carroll to pull off her greatest career coup: the title role in the 1960s TV sitcom *Julia,* about a widowed nurse raising a young son. Producer Hal Kanter had set out to prove that the American public would take an interest in a series—the first in TV history—featuring an African-American woman in the central role. *Julia* debuted at the number one spot in the Nielsen ratings and stayed

Carroll with costar Billy Dee Williams on the set of ABC's *Dynasty*

near the top for three seasons. At first Carroll was ecstatic about the show. Then controversy descended as critics charged that the series, with its middle-class setting, failed to confront the harsh realities faced by the majority of black Americans. And as the lead actor, Carroll took the brunt of the attacks.

After the third season of *Julia*, Carroll declined to renew her contract. Had she re-signed, she would have stood to make a fortune from syndication, but she had had enough annoyance and decided instead to concentrate on her singing career.

In 1974, Carroll came into possession of the script for the movie *Claudine* and loved it immediately. Still known for the haute couture wardrobe she wore for her singing engagements, Carroll again took the initiative to take on a role that overturned viewers' expectations of her. This time she persuaded director John Berry that she could convincingly play an impoverished single mother with six children. She received an Academy Award nomination for her work as the title character.

The next big splash came in 1984, when TV producer Aaron Spelling greenlighted an idea Carroll had proposed herself: to play television's "first black bitch," as she called it, on *Dynasty*. "My comment to the producers was 'Please write for this character as though you are writing for a white male who is interested in succeeding and has greed,'" Carroll recalls. Dominique Deveraux delighted *Dynasty* fans, who lapped up every second of the fights between her and series star Joan Collins.

Subsequent TV appearances included an Emmy-nominated turn as Jasmine Guy's image-conscious mother on *A Different World* and a starring role as 103-year-old Sadie Delany, the first black home economics teacher in New York, in the 1999 movie *Having Our Say*. In between acting gigs, Carroll still indulges in her first love, singing in nightclubs. "There's a wonderful song by James Taylor called 'Isn't It a Lovely, Lovely Ride?'" she says. "I feel quite privileged to have had the professional and personal life that I've led." ■

It was the mid-1960s, and every now and then, I heard a rumor that NBC was toying with the idea of a TV series starring a black actress, but it didn't really matter to me. I was doing what I loved. I was perfectly content. . . .

Then my agent called one day. "There is a man named Hal Kanter," he told me, "a very successful television writer-producer, who is putting together a project for NBC and Twentieth Century–Fox. It's a TV series, a sitcom about a black woman, and I'd like you to meet with him for five minutes."

I heard a certain reticence in his voice that piqued my curiosity.

"Oh," I answered. "Tell me more."

"Well, the truth of the matter is, Hal Kanter doesn't really want to see you. But he's talking to every black actress he can find. I think I can set up a quick meeting with you."

That's all I had to hear. Tell me I'm not right for a part, tell me you *don't* want me, and I'm yours. I'll do pratfalls, I'll do handstands, I'll do anything—but please tell me you love me. Suddenly I was very interested in Mr. Kanter and his project. It wasn't so much that I wanted the part; I wanted to be wanted for it.

"Why isn't he eager for me to have the role?" I asked.

"He thinks you're too sophisticated, Diahann. You represent glamour and elegant nightclubs and couture clothes, and that's not the image he wants to project. He's going for a different audience."

"But I am an actress," I answered. "I hope my range is a little broader than that. Can you send me a script? I'll read it immediately."

The script was about a young, very middle-class Vietnam War widow named Julia who goes to work as a nurse in the aerospace industry. The only really special aspect of the plot was that Julia and her five-year-old son were black. . . .

What captured my attention was Julia herself. From the very first scene I understood her completely. She was a situation comedy version of many ladies I had known my entire life, most certainly part of the product Mrs. Mabel Johnson had brought up to be Carol Diann Johnson a.k.a. Diahann Carroll. Behind the stylized cuteness of the dialogue, Julia's conversations with her son reflected many of the same middle-class attitudes toward parenting I experienced in my own childhood. I could relate to that very easily, just as I could relate to Julia's desire to make a place for herself in the world. She wanted a good job. She wanted a nice apartment. She wanted to give her child a decent education.

By the time I finished the script, I had gone beyond understanding Julia's character—I saw her actual physical presence. I knew exactly how she should look.

I asked my agent to set up a meeting with Hal Kanter the next day . . . and began forming myself into this lady. My hair stylist brought his scissors and hair dryer to my suite at the Beverly Hills Hotel; a blunt bob haircut was our final decision. I hunted through my closet and found exactly the right dress: black wool with a short skirt, simple and understated. . . . And I wore subtle makeup and no jewelry.

By the time I entered the polo lounge, I was positive I was just what Hal Kanter wanted to bring into the homes of America.

I spotted him sitting with my agent the second I stepped through the doorway. To make sure he had a good look at me before we got down to business, I pretended I didn't see him and stopped to ask the maître d' for his table. When Hal swiveled around in his chair to watch me walk across the room, I knew I had his attention and headed for his table like a nice middle-class housewife meeting her husband for dinner. From the smile on his face, he seemed to like what he saw. I hoped what he saw was Julia. . . .

Kanter, a tall, pleasant-faced man with a black mustache, seemed a bit cold and aloof at first as he explained why he hadn't wanted to see me. (I later learned that, like me, Hal is a bit shy!)

"This is a very simple middle-class woman. I want her attractive but not glamorous. The television audience has to be able to relate to her."

I assured him I understood. Over the years, the long fingernails and coiffed hair and designer clothes had become something of a personal trademark. But clearly such attire and attitude were not appropriate for Julia.

Once we realized we had no disagreement, we both relaxed, and Hal began telling me about how he got the inspiration for the show. He had heard Roy Wilkins, then head of the NAACP, speak at a luncheon and was so moved that he wanted to do something to forward the cause of mutual understanding and goodwill. *Julia* was to be his contribution, using the most powerful communications medium of our time to help counteract the hateful effects of racial bigotry.

"You must remember some indignities that happened to you in the past?" he asked.

I had heard that one before. It is often assumed that once a black person achieves a little success, all the problems that come with the color of your skin automatically disappear.

"What do you mean in the past?" I answered. "The day before I left New York I waited on Fifth Avenue for an hour before a cab would stop for me."

"Oh, well, that's just New York for you. It happens to me all the time," he smiled.

"Really, Hal? Do they slow down for you, stick their heads out of the window and shout, 'I ain't goin' uptown, baby!'?"

We both laughed—out of discomfort—but the point was made.

Hal went on to say he thought a series starring a black woman was timely and could attract a large audience. A number of black actors were already appearing regularly on popular TV series. There was Bill Cosby on *I Spy* (I adored that show), Greg Morris on *Mission Impossible,* and supporting performers on *Ironside* and *Star Trek.* We were ready for the next step forward, for a show that had a black actor as the lead, not just the sidekick to the star or part of the supporting cast.

Despite a few bumpy spots, the meeting went well. As it came to an end, I noticed Hal was no longer talking quite so much, but I knew his silences did not mean a rejection. Believe me, I recognize rejection when I see it! He smiled as he stood up to shake hands and said, "Well, Julia, it's nice to have met you."

"My pleasure," I answered, thrilled that the part was mine.

—DIAHANN CARROLL

Marcy
Carsey

■ IN THE EARLY 1980s, TELEVISION PRODUCER Marcy Carsey pitched a rather tame-sounding idea for a new sitcom to NBC executives. But the show about marriage and family life seemed too simple to the executives and they dismissed it. Carsey forged ahead anyway, contacting Bill Cosby—whose comic monologues had inspired her proposal—to gauge his interest in such a series. Also zero.

Carsey's determination, however, was still 100 percent. Having recently left a successful career as an ABC programming executive to form the independent production company Carsey-Werner with longtime associate Tom Werner, she knew her idea could pay off.

Things happened even faster than she had imagined. Carsey arranged for Werner and herself to have dinner at the Cosby house, then used her renowned powers of persuasion to talk the star into doing the show.

That dinner was in February 1984. Later that year, the first episode of *The Cosby Show* debuted at number one in the Nielsen ratings. The show stayed there for five years, becoming the first of a string of successes that have cemented Carsey's reputation as a programming genius.

Not only was *Cosby* popular; it had an important social impact—another characteristic of Carsey's work. "That

show changed the perception of African-American people," she says. "It was nice to have a show about a black family neither hurting for money nor surprised that they had it."

The success of *Cosby* also validated Carsey's decision, viewed skeptically by many, to leave the security of a high-salaried network job to join the dwindling, maligned league of independent production companies. "Billions of dollars later, she has proved them wrong," says Peter Ross, president of Warner Bros. Television and one of Carsey's protégés.

Carsey's drive to create began with a love of television that goes back to her childhood in Weymouth, Massachusetts. Born in 1944 to a homemaker and a shipyard draftsman, little Marcy liked to watch shows such as *Father Knows Best* and *Maverick*. "I was always interested in TV," she says, "but I didn't yet understand the breadth of jobs there were." As New England offered little entree into the world of entertainment, Carsey moved to California and worked as an NBC Studios tour guide after graduating from college in 1966. She then segued into the quintessential job for newcomers: production assistant for *The Tonight Show*, starring Johnny Carson. "I was basically a schlepper," Carsey recalls. "But I learned the mechanics of television, like how talent gets booked. I had contact with agents."

Her next position, as a program supervisor at William Esty Advertising, taught her how to schmooze for fun and profit as she was responsible for ferreting out information about new TV shows for advertising clients.

By 1974, Carsey had worked her way up to being a general programming

Carsey with her business partners, Tom Werner and Caryn Mandabach, 2000

executive at ABC-TV, then was promoted to vice president of prime-time comedy and variety programs and senior vice president of prime-time series. She won the respect of superiors and associates with her intuition, sense of humor, and impeccable taste—qualities that enabled her to recognize a potential hit show before anyone else. Among the shows she shepherded into production were the hits of the 1970s: *Laverne & Shirley, Taxi, Barney Miller, Soap,* and *Mork & Mindy.*

"She was a revelation to work with," says Caryn Mandabach, who met Carsey when they were among the few female executives at the network. "Her style was antithetical to the corporate guys'. She was fun-loving but extremely common-

Carsey, 2000

sensical, full of good ideas, and always ready to help at any stage of the process."

At ABC, Carsey also demonstrated her knack for recognizing nascent talent and matching the right actor to the right role. In 1977, she talked Billy Crystal, then known only as a stand-up comic, into playing one of television's first sympathetic gay roles, in *Soap,* the nighttime send-up of daytime dramas. After seeing Robin Williams perform at a comedy club and guest-star on *Happy Days,* Carsey and her associates realized they would need to act fast to corral him into their corner. "We were so excited about Robin, we put together *Mork & Mindy* over the weekend," said Carsey.

Carsey credits then–ABC network boss Michael Eisner (who hired Carsey despite her being three months pregnant, an unusual move in 1974) with giving her the opportunity to grow professionally and setting an example for how to foster confidence and decision-making ability in junior colleagues. "Michael Eisner believed that in order to go out and try new things and succeed, you must have the freedom to fail sometimes. And Marcy gave me that freedom too," says Ross, who worked under Carsey as a young executive at ABC.

She took that attitude with her when she formed Carsey-Werner in 1981 after management changes at ABC left her feeling restless. "I encourage employees to go home early. If you're not leading a rich and fulfilling life, what are you bringing to work?" she says.

Cosby called for frequent travel to New York City, where the show was shot, so Carsey dedicated weekends entirely to her husband, writer John Carsey, and two children in Los Angeles. She maintained her attentiveness at home even as Carsey-Werner burned up the airwaves by adding *A Different World* and *Roseanne* to the company's stable. Together with *Cosby,* this trio made up the roster of Nielsen's first-, second-, and third-ranked television shows for the 1988–89 season.

The company also broke ground by showing people and situations seldom seen on network TV. *Roseanne* was the first series to address problems faced by working-class women who put in eight hours a day at an hourly wage, then return home to care for a home and children. *A Different World* was the first series set in a primarily black college, and the student roles were predominantly female.

Another Carsey-Werner sitcom, *Third Rock from the Sun,* became a hit for NBC in the mid-1990s and again proved Carsey's talent for picking the right actors. When executives eager for a hit wanted to rush the show into production, she insisted they hold out for John Lithgow, who she knew was the one and only choice for the lead.

With a company that has made her the first name in independent production, what's left for Carsey? Well, there's that $400 million project called Oxygen Media, a twenty-four-hour cable channel for women, whose investors include America Online and ABC. Carsey will apply her production skills to make the venture a success.

The TV and on-line industries are carefully watching Oxygen as an indicator of whether interactive shows can draw dynamic, upwardly mobile female viewers and sell them products. Leave it to Marcy Carsey to turn TV viewing into an exercise of career fulfillment for women all over the country. ■

Working-class upbringing. Hard work. Good grades. First generation to graduate college. "Oh, Marcy, we're so proud! When do you get your teaching credential?"

"No, Mom, I'm getting a job in television."

Silence. "Repairing them, dear?"

A decade or two passes. Hard work. Motherhood. Balancing acts that rival the Flying Wallendas'. Quick rise through network corporate structure, ending in a near-fatal blow to the head from a heretofore invisible ceiling. Pause to regroup and get anger in check.

"Fine. I'll start my own company."

Hard work. Balancing act. This time with the dexterity of Cirque du Soleil. Another decade or two passes. Lots of failures. Enough successes. More hard work. (Question: If this is show business, why is it that the closest I ever got to a glamorous life was occasionally not eating over the sink?) Children almost grown now, marriage still intact, wolf no longer at door. In fact, wolf would need security code to get in.

Besides recounting the journey that brought me here, I'm also asked sometimes to give advice. This is ironic, because I never took advice. I don't believe in advice. Information, yes. Insight, yes. But advice implies that what worked for someone else is going to work for you. See, we know different. We're entrepreneurs. By definition, we throw out the old ways of doing things and find new ways. So, just for fun, I'm going to share with you the top ten bits of bad advice I've been given over the years, all of which I've thrown out:

1. "Don't watch so much TV. That'll never get you anywhere."

2. "That which you do, do with all your might. That half done is never done right." There must be mental institutions chock full of people who thought they had to do everything perfectly. There are lots of things that ought to be only half done, and only a very few things in any given day, or in any given lifetime, that need to be done with all your might. The most important thing you can ever do is to figure out the difference.

3. This from my college boyfriend: "Just leave it to me, I've got it all worked out. After we graduate, I'll go to med school, and you'll work and put me through. Then I'll be a doctor and everything will be great."

4. This one came from a variety of sources, most of them corporate: "Don't make waves." Usually followed by "honey." Well, I come from a long line of wave makers. My great-grandfather was a minister who got thrown out of the church because he refused to preach hellfire and damnation. My mother at seventeen almost lost her job as a bank secretary during the Depression—a job she desperately needed to support her mother and sister—because she had

everyone sign a petition protesting the long hours of overtime without pay. This country was built on wave making, I believe in wave making.

5. "Just do those Lamaze breathing exercises, and you'll barely feel it." No comment.

6. "Don't worry, mothering comes naturally, just follow your instincts." Uh-uh. Sorry. I believe every school in America should be teaching parenting skills from fourth grade on, alongside history, math, and English. Or are they instinctual too?

7. This one was from my boss at ABC, upon my decision to leave and form my own production company, rather than keep banging my head on that pesky glass ceiling: "Don't try for a hit show . . . just try for a nice, middle-of-the-road show." This is the same guy who explained that glass ceiling by saying he assumed I had no interest in upper management because "Well, you know, because you're a mother." I replied that since he was a father he'd apparently made a big mistake in his own career and had better request a demotion and go home. This guy was later fired, shortly after we pitched him *The Cosby Show* and he passed on it because he said a black family show would be "demographically limiting."

8. "Be assertive, not aggressive." You say tomato, I say tomahto. You can be perfectly assertive, just the right amount of assertive, not an ugly trace of aggressive, and they still won't let you run the *Fortune* 500. This is a first cousin to some other bits of wisdom: Dress for success, let your boss think that really good idea of yours is his, etc. Call me crazy, but it all sounds like a corporate version of that song "Hey little girl, better wear something pretty." I always say my version of dressing for success was Gerber rice cereal tastefully thrown all over my nice silk blouse.

9. and 10. Because this one's a killer: "A woman can't have it all, something has to suffer." I remember one year I was commuting every week from Los Angeles to Brooklyn to do *The Cosby Show,* and I was so concerned about being away from my kids so much that every day I was in Los Angeles, I was home every minute. The net effect was that I was always more available than the mothers who didn't work—to carpool, drive to soccer games, help at the school fair, solve homework problems, whatever. Until my daughter finally said to me, "Mom, can we spend a little less time together?"

Of course you can have it all, if you want it. And it won't be perfect, but it won't be perfect anyway, so you might as well do what you want.

I say to my daughter, "You know, someday you'll be forty. Your daughter will tell you to go to hell in a handbasket. No matter what. You might as well also have a career."

She told me to mind my own business. "Yes, dear, that's my point. I will."

— MARCY CARSEY

Peggy
Charren

■ PEGGY CHARREN KICKED OFF THE MEET-
ING at her home in Newtonville,
Massachusetts, with a simple question:
"What can we do for children's television
without saying 'Take it off the air'?" She
had invited friends and neighbors she'd
never even met to talk about starting an
organization to improve the quality of
children's programming. Speaking out
on behalf of children seemed a logical
path for this concerned suburban mother
at the time. She couldn't have known
then that her informal meeting was just
the beginning of a grassroots odyssey
that would span more than three decades
of her life and launch her career as one of
the most effective advocates in the
industry.

As founder of Action for Children's
Television (ACT), Charren has championed
the cause of quality kids' programming
and changed how television advertising is
presented to children. Her persistence,
knowledge, and commitment to the cause
found focus through ACT, the 10,000-
member national child advocacy organization she founded in 1968. What she
calls her "bare-bones nonprofit" lobbied
Congress for two and a half decades,
finally achieving success when the
Children's Television Act of 1990 was
passed and thus changed the nature of
television broadcasting aimed at children.

Charren's bent for advocacy was
nurtured in her childhood, when she
learned the lore of labor unions and the
bohemian Left from her activist, artisti-
cally oriented parents. She was born
March 9, 1928, in New York City to a
businessman father, who was a serious
amateur photographer, and a pianist
mother whose music, Chopin especially,
filled the household. Since Walzer was
the family surname and *Walzer* (German
for "waltz") appeared so often on her
mother's sheet music, as a child Peggy
thought her mother had composed the
music. At Robinson Crusoe camp in
Sturbridge, Massachusetts, Peggy also
learned the lyrics to union anthems and
civil rights songs.

After graduating from Hunter College High School and earning a B.A. from Connecticut College, Peggy got a job as director of the film department at WPIX-TV in New York City. This position, which she held from 1949 to 1951, gave her the opportunity to observe the business of television from the inside. Later, she switched to educational work and became director of the Creative Arts Council in Newton, developing artistic programs for schoolkids. As a young mother, Charren next created "Quality Book Fairs," which presented children's books in public and private schools. Part of her motivation for starting her own business was the ability to schedule her work around the responsibilities of caring for her young children.

Even so, she found it difficult to balance her work and family life. When she couldn't arrange day care to meet her book

Charren testifies on Capitol Hill in the 1970s.

fair obligations, she disbanded the business, planning to reopen it when her children started school. In the meantime, she refocused her energies on another at least potentially educational medium: television. When she began to consider how to make children's television more like a library in presenting educational opportunities to kids, the seeds of ACT were sown.

After the initial meeting in her living room, it took Charren twenty-six years to marshal support for national guidelines that mandated that television stations air educational programming. The culmination of her effort to improve the quality of the images, stories, songs, commercials, characters, and cartoons aimed at children was the Children's Television Act of 1990. In April 1991, in response to the act, the FCC issued regulations requiring stations to broadcast programs to meet the educational and informational needs of children age sixteen and younger. Rules that limited advertising abuses aimed at young audiences were also part of those requirements.

In acknowledgment of her work, Charren was awarded an Emmy in 1988 and a George Foster Peabody Award in 1992. She has received numerous awards and honors, including the Presidential Medal of Freedom, the Annenberg Public Policy Center Award from the University of Pennsylvania for Lifetime Contribution to Excellence in Children's Television, and a "Women That Made a Difference" Award from the International Women's Forum. In June 2000, KIDSNET, a clearinghouse for information about children's radio and television, honored her with

Charren and Jay Leno at Action for Children's Television's twentieth birthday party in New York City, 1988

the First Annual Lamb Chop Award Honoring Excellence in Children's Programming. Charren is the author or coauthor of four books about television for children; she and her husband, Stanley Charren, an engineer and entrepreneur, have two children and four grandchildren.

Even though the objectives of ACT have mostly been addressed, Peggy Charren continues to work for improving what she calls "delicious choices in children's television programming" and continues to be a role model and beacon for community activists. ∎

When I think back to how I got to be who I am, I am reminded of something John Kennedy said when asked how he became a hero. He replied, "It was involuntary! They sank my boat!"

My career as a child advocate was also largely involuntary. Particular events can refocus your options, and your responses can change the direction of your life. I started Action for Children's Television because I couldn't get day care organized when my second daughter was born. I decided to close a small business I had started running children's book fairs until after my children started school.

ACT began as a volunteer effort in my living room, and it grew and grew . . . and now it's thirty years later, and my grandchildren have started school and I'm still talking about children's television.

By the late 1960s, parents, teachers, and Congress were calling for an end to TV sex and violence. ACT's goal, however, was not to get rid of what was ghastly but to create a market for what was missing from service to children in an industry licensed to serve the public.

The model for a diverse, delicious TV service to children exists in every community in America. My response to television executives who bemoan the lack of specifics on what constitutes serving the interests of children is "Get thee to a library—a children's library! You will discover an astonishing variety of stories and subjects to turn into terrific TV for kids."

The role of television is not to replace families and teachers as the chief influence on children, but TV can encourage kids to discuss, wonder about, and even read about new things. It can empower young people to get involved in efforts to improve the neighborhood, the town, and the planet. It can help children understand the rights and responsibilities of citizenship in a democracy. Above all, it can lead them to ask questions.

As an advocate for better children's TV, I needed to be able to articulate a particular set of values, to encourage others to adopt those values, and to take action based on them.

So where did my values come from? First, from my mom and dad. The most important gift I received from my parents was a sense that you can go out there and fix how the world works. They were Roosevelt Democrats, and they talked to me about the power of the ballot box, about prejudice and discrimination, and about the rights of people of color before civil rights became a movement. They sent me to camp, where I didn't do too well at soccer but managed to learn just about every labor song. To this day, I can recite the words to Pete Seeger's "Talking Union." I don't remember a time when I wasn't worried about the rights of others. It started young for me, and it stuck.

In school, I learned to love books for information and education, for delight and discovery. I learned about constitutional values and rights, particularly the importance of free speech in a democracy. This turned out to be the bedrock principle of my efforts to get more TV choices for children and to fight censorship as a solution to children's TV problems.

To lead, you also need support, and I am lucky to have the enthusiastic support of a husband who understood that women were people too, even before Gloria Steinem. And I had the somewhat less than enthusiastic support of my two children, who often wished that I would spend more time cooking and less time turning off the TV set.

When I speak to parents about the problems and pleasures of children's television, they often ask about how to control TV viewing in the home: How much is too much? When to say no? How to decide what's good and what's bad?

Although answers to these and other TV questions differ depending on family circumstances, I thought up a variety of strategies designed to help hassled parents. And I tried them out first on my own children!

This homegrown research almost got me in trouble when my younger daughter rebelled.

"No other mother dreams up so many TV rules," she complained when she was about nine years old. "I'm going to picket ACT," she said.

"Good grief!" I thought. "Wait until the press hears about this!" I had visions of headlines like "ACT President's Child Marches Against Mother!"

But then I figured, "So what?" At least she has come up with a reasonable political response to a problem. Like mother, like child.

She never carried out her threat. But when I remember her indignation, I still feel a surge of pride.

Another time that I felt particularly full of pride was during what was perhaps the most unusual event in the thirty-year history of ACT: an invitation to participate in a weeklong meeting on "Media and Society" in Tokyo, sponsored by NHK's Bunka Hoso Foundation. Featured speakers included two representatives from each of seven countries: thirteen males who were in charge of their governments or a major communications system—and me, the president of Action for Children's Television. I was invited to represent not only the United States, but also the audience.

There were almost no women at the conference until the morning of my presentation. At that point, the room filled with women who had come from all over Japan. They had arranged a press conference, and my remarks and photo landed on the front page of Japan's major national newspapers the next day. With that, I felt that ACT had truly arrived on the international scene.

— PEGGY CHARREN

Sylvia
Chase

■ WHEN SYLVIA CHASE BROKE INTO NET-work television in the early 1970s, her long blond hair attracted her CBS bosses' attention: they asked her to restyle it so it didn't look, in their words, like an "unmade bed." Viewers, however, noticed that something quite different made Chase stand out even among the handful of women on national television in those days. That was her forthright focus on controversial social issues. Throughout her broadcasting career, Chase has used her tenacious intelligence and her commanding voice to expose an impressive range of social ills, consumer frauds, and gender inequalities.

Because Chase began her career at a time when there were few role models,

she established her own—as a serious investigative journalist. Her career progress mirrored the rise of the women's movement, from demands for control over their own bodies to organizing for equal pay for equal work. And after she had helped direct public attention to women's issues, Chase broke ground by covering other tough issues: drug abuse, police brutality, prison reform, and insurance fraud by hospitals.

Born February 23, 1938, in Northfield, Minnesota, the youngest of three children, Sylvia spent her earliest years with her family in a small house on White Bear Lake. Though her mother and father came from comfortable backgrounds, the cramped summer cottage was all they could afford at the time. After her parents divorced, Sylvia was moved from relative to relative, spending only brief amounts of time with her mother, who experienced both emotional and financial difficulties.

Feisty and a fast learner, Sylvia was often bored in school until an English teacher sparked an interest in writing and reading. In high school, she was active in theatrical productions and edited the school paper. But this early start toward a journalism career was neither straight nor smooth.

Her college years began with tragedy. Turning down a scholarship to Wellesley

College in Massachusetts, she had acceded to her father's urging to join him and her sister, Ruth, in Los Angeles and attend UCLA, where Ruth was already a student. But five days before school started, their father died. Despite their grief, the sisters decided to stay on in Los Angeles, with Sylvia attending college and Ruth stepping into the management of their father's business.

A few years into college, Sylvia married a student in UCLA's graduate school of journalism and moved to Wisconsin with him. When the couple separated two years later, she returned to Los Angeles and finished a B.A. in English through part-time extension courses at UCLA, all the time working to support herself.

For most of the 1960s, Chase held a variety of jobs, from modeling at I. Magnin on Saturdays to temporary secretarial work to a significant stretch in politics, working in the California state legislature and managing election campaigns. A short-lived position as a receptionist at a newspaper was as close as she came to journalism.

But these varied experiences served Chase well when she finally landed a broadcasting job in 1969 as a reporter and producer at KNX Radio News in Los Angeles. For the next two years, she

Chase with colleagues on the ABC News set, 1978

worked as an advocate for her listeners—reporting, investigating, and resolving consumer problems and complaints against government agencies. This radio work began to establish her reputation as the voice of people in need.

Then, in 1971, Chase moved to New York City to accept a job in television. As a general-assignment reporter for CBS Television when social issues were exploding onto the public scene, Chase found herself in the right place at the right time. While she's done her share of celebrity interviews, her stories on issues of concern enabled her to build on her consumer advocacy experience while taking advantage of her combination of empathy and rigorous investigative skills. Off camera, she joined rank and file women at CBS in demanding better job opportunities, acknowledgment of their contributions, and serious television coverage of women's issues such as abortion rights, child care, and workplace equity.

At CBS, as Chase worked her way up, she anchored *CBS Newsbreak,* hosted a

Chase interviewing Diana Ross, 1983

monthly daytime newsmagazine for women, and made "vacation relief" appearances on *60 Minutes.* After moving to ABC News in 1977, she coanchored *The ABC News Weekend Report* and did general-assignment reporting before becoming a charter member of the correspondent team of *20/20.*

After seven years with *20/20,* Chase moved to San Francisco for a five-year stint anchoring the local news for KRON-TV. She later returned to the national scene to rejoin ABC News, alternating time as a correspondent for *PrimeTime Live* and *20/20.*

While her hard-hitting reports on social issues cemented her reputation as a champion of the voiceless and downtrodden at home, her work has also extended worldwide at times. Frequently on assignment where news was breaking, Chase spent a month in Teheran just before the fall of the shah, covered the war zones in Yugoslavia, and was the first television journalist to reach the remote mountains of southeast Turkey during the Persian Gulf War to report on Iraqi Kurds fleeing Saddam Hussein.

Chase's reporting and documentaries have won numerous awards, including one of journalism's most prestigious: the George Foster Peabody Award, which she received in San Francisco in 1989 for a documentary about homeless children in the Bay area. In addition, she has received five Emmy awards—three for local news broadcasting and two for national investigative reports on car safety. She also received the National Headliner Award in 1979, 1983, and 1994.

Chase interviews Hedda Nussbaum, 1995

Sylvia Chase continues to serve the viewing public with incisive reporting on social issues of the day. Yet her equally important legacy may be giving young reporters in the twenty-first century something Chase never had: an enduring role model for using the spotlight of broadcast journalism to create an awareness of problems and the investigation of solutions. ■

I was anchoring the weekend news at ABC, and Victor Neufeld (later, a longtime executive producer of *20/20*) was an associate producer on the weekend news. He dug up this story about a woman in Michigan on trial for murdering her husband. Her case had been taken up by women's liberation groups there. She was a battered wife who went back to college, something that made her husband, she said, even more abusive. He beat her severely one night after she'd served the family TV dinners. He got drunk then and passed out, and she ringed their bed with gasoline and set it on fire.

I'd always wanted to do a story on battered wives. I just couldn't figure out how to approach that subject from a new angle. The woman was Francine Hughes and the story became the movie *The Burning Bed.* . . .

There were some remarkable things about the story. I couldn't interview Francine Hughes. I don't think they would allow me to interview her at the jail where she was being held, but I did interview her children. Of course the cameramen and Victor kind of snickered about the fact that I conducted this interview in which the kids were teary. I think they never expected the depths of a child's emotions, the searing memory of a mother who tells them to go to the basement and lock the door when dad is on the rampage. Francine's daughter, perhaps nine or ten at the time, was able to express her fear of her father and love for her mother. The years of beatings were unthinkable, yet the woman had committed a murder. So the story that we put on was very moving, and I think maybe we took five, six minutes to tell it. . . .

It's my job to get intimacy in [any] interview. And that's a challenge when you are trying to have an intimate conversation with two cameras grinding away and recording equipment strewn all over the room. The subject will adjust to the lights after a time, but then the perspiring begins. It's one thing if you have an actor or politician in the chair; they know what to expect. But, because of the kinds of stories I do, the subject is likely to have never been in front of a camera. The person in that chair is likely to be someone who has something perfectly awful to talk about—some painful, life-changing event. A child who became gravely ill following a routine vaccination. A surgery that has caused permanent, life-altering damage. A rape. A loved one murdered.

It's amazing to me that people agree to be interviewed at all under these circumstances, but it is also perfectly understandable. Something so awful, so senseless, so unfair has walked into your happy life or your struggle with life or your perfect health, marriage, parenthood. And once the shock wears off, you're boiling to warn people it could happen to them too.

Helping people to do that is part of my job. Calming them down. Reassuring them. Some correspondents are not good at that at all. Producers complain and so do cameramen that their job is made really, really hard by some correspondents who are incapable of making small talk. They just sit there and they wait in silence and fume if the camera's not ready. Well, you can't do that. You want everything to look good, for one thing. . . . And you want that person in the chair opposite to feel safe and secure.

So, I would say that I am unusual in that I'm very keenly attuned to what's going on in the room with everybody, and I really think that has a lot to do with what happened to me as a child. I grew up this way, with craziness and insecurity all around. A child who's always under some kind of threat is going to learn how to sniff the wind, so I think I'm pretty much aware if the cameraman's in a snit, if he's having a quarrel with the producer or can't get the light right. I can sense when the cameraman is ready to run out the window and jump into the swimming pool. And at the same time, I carry on a conversation with the person who is about to be interviewed about how this awful thing has happened to them. I do think that my having a childhood full of all kinds of fright and terror does get your antennae going in any situation. You can't shut it off just because you're grown up and you don't feel threatened anymore.

I like to think that people in trouble can sense that I'll make it okay for them to be honest and that they'll be portrayed with respect and sympathy.

— S Y L V I A   C H A S E

Julia Child

■ IT WAS THE OMELETTE THAT LAUNCHED THE career of the most prominent chef in television history. While promoting her first cookbook on the Boston public broadcasting show *I've Been Reading* in 1961, Julia Child became an instant hit by demonstrating her technique of beating egg whites in a copper bowl with a balloon whip. Child's humor and culinary style appealed to audiences and left them wanting more—which is exactly what they got. That single appearance led to her own cooking series, launching her lengthy career in front of the camera as the "French Chef." She has been on the air regularly since the day she began.

It's no surprise that Child has been such a television success. Her voice is unmistakable, its timbre as commanding as her jolly spirit is contagious. Her speech is authoritative with culinary expertise perfected during years of living and studying in France. Equally important, Child seemed from her first appearances to enjoy French cuisine so much that she demystified it for American audiences, who then accepted it as a desirable part of life. Whether viewers decided to tackle the recipes themselves or not, all have enjoyed watching Julia deftly assemble a tart or laugh at herself as the whole chicken she is preparing to roast slips out of her hands.

Child's televised cooking demonstrations also had an impact on the broadcasting industry. Because her programs appeared on the Public Broadcasting Service (PBS), her show's popularity helped build support for public broadcasting in its developing years. Subsequently, her shows and her personal appeals have successfully convinced viewers to make pledges during those all-important fund-raising drives.

Child was born Julia McWilliams in Pasadena, California, on August 15, 1912. After graduating from Smith College in 1934, she did what few women did at the time: she got a job. She first found work as a copywriter in New York, but once World War II broke out she felt compelled to find a way to help support the

Allied effort. She moved to Washington, D.C., where she worked as a clerk with the Office of Strategic Services (OSS), precursor of the CIA. But she longed to serve her country abroad and finally got her chance after seeking and receiving an assignment in the Far East. This experience would change her life.

While stationed in Ceylon, she met her future husband, Paul Child, who was also serving in the OSS. The war ended when the two were on their next assignment, in China; from there, they returned to the United States and were married.

In 1948, Paul joined the United States Information Agency and, after two years in Washington, was assigned to the American Embassy in Paris. Although Child had been teaching herself to cook while the couple lived in Washington, the move to Paris thrust her into the

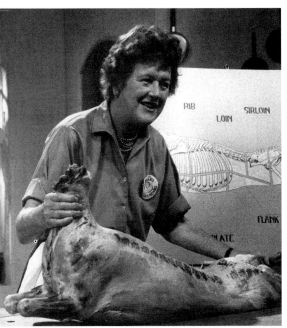

The French chef explains cuts of beef with visual aids, 1965.

gourmet world. French cooking captivated her, literally from the first bite. As soon as she and her husband were settled in Paris, she enrolled in the renowned cooking school Cordon Bleu, where she attended classes for about six months. She also studied cooking techniques privately with chefs Max Bugnard, Claude Thilmond, and Pierre Mangelatte.

Soon Child was invited to join the French women's gastronomical society Le Cercle des Gourmettes. Her friendship forged there with two other women eventually led to their opening a cooking school in Paris, L'École des Trois Gourmands—that is, "the school of the three hearty eaters."

Together, the trio put their expertise into print. In 1961, they coauthored *Mastering the Art of French Cooking,* published by Alfred A. Knopf. Following publication, the Childs and one of Julia's coauthors, Simone Beck, embarked on a two-month book tour of the United States, doing cooking demonstrations at some stops. It was on that tour that Child was discovered during her appearance on Boston's WGBH-TV. By then her husband had retired, and the couple decided to settle in nearby Cambridge, Massachusetts.

In the summer of 1962, WGBH asked Child to prepare three pilot shows for a possible cooking series. It was a risky experiment, for there were no cooking shows on television at the time, but Child seized the opportunity, adopted the name "The French Chef," and went on the air February 11, 1963.

The public loved her immediately. Her audience quickly grew as the series

Julia Child, 1999

Dinner at Julia's, a thirteen-part series first aired in 1984, featured salmon fishing in Puget Sound, artichoke and date farming, a chocolate factory, and appearances by celebrity chefs. Child has also hosted such PBS series as *Cooking with Master Chefs, Julia Child and Company, Baking with Julia,* and *Julia and Jacques Cooking at Home,* in collaboration with Jacques Pépin. Her televised cooking "concerts" with Pépin in auditoriums full of fans have also been extremely popular. Her latest special, aired in December 2000, was *Julia's Kitchen Wisdom.*

Child's television programs have often been accompanied by cookbooks. She has also written stand-alone cookbooks and columns for *McCall's* and *Parade* magazines. In addition to her numerous awards from culinary societies, Child is the recipient of a George Foster Peabody Award for distinguished achievement in television. In 1981, she was among the founders and honorary chairmen of the American Institute of Wine and Food, a nonprofit international scholarly and education organization.

After nearly forty years on the air, Julia Child still has the magic touch for promoting good cooking and eating through the medium of television. She's taught viewers everywhere to say *"Bon appétit!"* ∎

was publicized with her appearances on talk shows with hosts such as Johnny Carson and Dick Cavett, all of whom appreciated her colorful and funny stories. In the late 1960s, *The French Chef* began to be televised in color, including episodes filmed in France. During this time, Child also developed cooking specials on public television.

Child continues to win accolades from the television and food industry while sustaining her vast audience and capturing the affection of new viewers.

I grew up in the teens and '20s in a comfortable middle-class family in Pasadena, California, and like most families of that class and income in that era, we had a cook. My mother knew how to eat, but she didn't cook—anything, that is, but her two-dish repertoire, a cheese thing and baking powder biscuits. We always ate well in a very conventional middle-class way. For Sunday breakfasts we often had codfish balls with egg sauce, and for the big Sunday lunch, to which she always invited all the relatives for miles around, we'd have roast chicken, roast beef, or a leg of lamb, well done, with gravy and mint sauce. I was always hungry, and I ate everything with enthusiasm. However, I never learned to cook until I married Paul Child.

Paul had been brought up by a mother who was a fine cook, and they moved to Paris when he was a young man. Thus he had developed a sophisticated palate and he loved both food and wine. I realized, after we married and settled down into our nice little house in the Georgetown section of Washington, D.C., that I'd better get busy in the kitchen. So I started in quite elaborately with *Gourmet* magazine for great ideas and *The Joy of Cooking* for down-to-earth instruction. I was enjoying the challenge, and Paul and our friends were encouraging, but I rarely managed to get dinner on the table before 9:30 or 10 p.m.

Then, because Paul spoke beautiful French, we were sent to France, arriving by boat at Le Havre with our old blue Buick near the end of 1948. I'll never forget our ecstatic drive on that first day. Paul was thrilled to return after many years away, and I couldn't get over my first view of that country I had so longed to visit. We marveled at the ancient buildings in the towns we passed through, and Paul decided we should lunch in Rouen. We had picked up a *Guide Michelin* on our last visit to New York, and the obvious restaurant was La Couronne on the place where Joan of Arc met her fiery finish. What a lunch we had—my first meal in France—oysters and white wine, roast duck, a great fresh salad, beautiful cheeses, delicious little petits fours with our fresh fruit dessert. The service was charmingly attentive, and the whole atmosphere of friendly concern made for a happy, deeply felt first impression. In fact it took me several years to get over my euphoria for just being in France.

After we got settled in our apartment in Paris, and Paul felt at home in his job at the American Embassy, I decided I should really learn how to cook. I couldn't get over how absolutely delicious French food was, and I decided that it was for me. When I enrolled at the Cordon Bleu, the usual housewifey courses didn't interest me, but at that time, shortly after World War II, the school was also giving courses to former GIs studying on the GI Bill of Rights. To my great delight, the wonderful chef teacher, Max Bugnard, allowed me to join them.

We started in at 7:30 in the morning, cooked nonstop until noon, and then I would rush home to get lunch for Paul. In those days the embassy people followed the French system of a two-hour lunch—a happy custom, and I wonder if they still follow it. With Chef Bugnard we did everything from green beans and mashed potatoes to how to cut up a chicken or push a ham mousse through a drum sieve to elaborate chaud-froids, aspics, veal Orloff, ris de veau, and quenelles Nantua. He was an infinitely kind and gentle man, and he was tireless in his explanations and examples. He drilled us in his careful standards of doing everything "the right way," and insisted on thorough analyses of "how does it taste?"

We had not only practical cooking with Chef Bugnard in the mornings, but in the afternoons, we had two hours of demonstration by other professional chef teachers. Two of them I remember with particular pleasure and gratitude. Pierre Mangelatte, chef in the fine small Restaurant des Artistes on la Rue Lépic on the way to Montmartre, gave wonderfully stylish and intense classes on cuisine—beef en daube, sole meunière, pâté en croute, trout in aspic, ratatouille, quiches, and so forth. He was particularly explicit and easily understandable in his explanations, and taking copious notes as I did, I found it easy to follow his recipes when I tried them out later in my own kitchen.

Claude Thilmond, former pastry chef at the Café de Paris, demonstrated with great authority and kindness desserts like Charlotte Malakoff, puff pastries, pie doughs, brioches, croissants, tarts, and layer cakes. Incidentally, he had worked with the author herself on that seminal volume for the French home cook *La Cuisine de Mme Sainte-Ange.*

It was my supreme good fortune to have had such remarkably able and devoted teachers. It was through them that I received my introduction to French cuisine, and through them that I know why good French food makes such sublimely good eating. Nothing is too much trouble if it turns out the way it should.

—JULIA CHILD

Connie
Chung

■ POISED AND POLISHED, CONNIE CHUNG delivers the news with a hint of a smile at the corner of her lips. She is a woman who is not afraid of showing her humor and humanity on the air. We know her confident personality instantly because she's appeared on television since 1970, making her the most recognizable Asian-American woman in TV news. She was the first woman to coanchor the *CBS Evening News,* has had several news programs bearing her name, and has worked at all three major commercial networks: NBC, CBS, and, since 1997, ABC. Chung has thrived in the national spotlight of the sometimes vitriolic world of television news, proving that she is not only a top-notch journalist but also a survivor who has endured bruises to her career and still come out on top.

Underneath her celebrity recognition among television viewers beats the heart of a serious journalist. As the first Asian-American woman to be assigned as a national network news anchor and to have a national signature news program, Chung had to sharpen her survival skills early in her career to compete and succeed.

Constance Yu-Hwa Chung was born in Washington, D.C., on August 20, 1946, the youngest of ten children, five of whom had died as infants before her parents emigrated from China. Her father,

William Ling Chung, a financial manager who had served as an intelligence officer under General Chiang Kai-shek, and her mother, Margaret Ma Chung, moved their family to Washington in 1945. Though it couldn't have been easy for a young first-generation Chinese American, Chung grew up in a city that was multicultural even in the 1950s and attended a public high school known for academic rigor. Early on, she was determined to excel, to bring the family honor. Chung graduated from the University of Maryland in 1969 with a B.S. degree in journalism and a commitment to make her mark in her chosen profession.

Right after graduation, she joined WTTG-TV (now Fox) in Washington,

Chung interviews Rep. Barbara Jordan during the Watergate hearings, 1973–74.

D.C., where she fielded phones, conducted research, and ran copy until she got a handle on how a newsroom operates. She then progressed to writing and reporting the news. After only two years of newsroom experience, she joined CBS News in 1971 as a general-assignment reporter based in Washington. She covered the 1972 George McGovern presidential campaign, the Democratic National Convention, Watergate, and other political stories. She also traveled overseas to report on the Nixon/Brezhnev SALT I talks and President Richard Nixon's final trip to the Middle East.

In 1976, Chung moved to Los Angeles, where she spent seven years as an anchor at KNXT-TV (now KCBS), with occasional stints as substitute

anchor for the *CBS Morning News.* In 1983, she joined NBC News as a correspondent and anchor for such programs as the Saturday edition of the *NBC Nightly News, NBC News at Sunrise, NBC News Digests,* prime-time specials, and a newsmagazine. She also stepped in as substitute anchor for *NBC Nightly News.* Chung's work as a political reporter and analyst continued as well, and she was an NBC correspondent at the 1984 and 1988 national conventions.

She rejoined CBS News in 1989 as anchor and correspondent on *Saturday Night with Connie Chung* and anchored the Saturday edition of the *CBS Evening News.* The following year, she hosted another signature program that aired during the week, the Emmy Award–

winning *Face to Face with Connie Chung.* Her interviews included an exclusive with Captain Joseph Hazelwood of the Exxon *Valdez,* which had caused a devastating oil spill off the coast of Alaska, and the first interview with basketball star Magic Johnson after his announcement that he was HIV-positive.

Though Chung headlined a news series, she remained involved with her roots in political reporting. During the 1992 national political conventions, she reported from the floor for CBS News and provided analysis during election-night coverage in 1990, 1992, and 1994.

Then, in 1993, Chung made history by taking a seat as coanchor of *CBS Evening News* alongside Dan Rather. During that period, she covered such historic events as the Israel/PLO signing ceremony at the White House and the Israel/Jordan signing ceremony in the Middle East. She also arranged an exclusive interview with Chinese leader Li Peng five years after the massacre at Tiananmen Square. The on-air partnership, however, fizzled after two years, when the program's ratings failed to meet the network's expectations, and her program *Eye to Eye with Connie Chung,* begun in conjunction with her coanchoring duties, was also ended. Lasting such a short time on the coanchor assignment was a temporary low point in her career

Election night, 1992

and might have discouraged others, but it only served to spur her onward.

Since then, Chung has been a fellow at the Joan Shorenstein Center on the Press, Politics, and Public Policy at Harvard's John F. Kennedy School of Government, and she joined ABC News in 1997, appearing on *20/20* as a correspondent and later coanchor.

Throughout her career, Chung has made her mark on news with her ability to follow a story, get essential interviews, and, in the process, effect change. One of her most significant recent reports, "Justice Delayed," came from her investigation into the 1966 murder of Ben Chester White, an elderly black farmhand in Mississippi. As a result of new information uncovered by her investigation, the U.S. Justice Department reopened the case after more than three decades and brought a federal indictment against Ernest Avants, who had been acquitted on state murder charges in 1967. Chung won the 1999 National Association of Black Journalists Salute to Excellence Award for this investigation.

Chung also received awards for her *20/20* report "Roy Smith's America," which aired during the 1998–99 season, about a black man tormented in brutal racist attacks by his Colorado neighbors. She was awarded the Amnesty International Human Rights Award for her 1999 report revealing that young women in Bangladesh were being burned with acid for turning down men's advances.

Her many broadcasting honors include three Emmy Awards, two of which were for Best Interview/Interviewer, and a George Foster Peabody Award. Chung married television journalist Maury Povich in 1984, and they have a son, Matthew. She also has two stepdaughters, Susan Povich and Amy Povich Agus, and three grandchildren.

After three decades in broadcast journalism, Connie Chung continues on as a consummate professional—informing the viewing public, uncovering stories that change people's lives, and providing inspiration and leadership to women beginning careers in news broadcasting. ■

My foundation in journalism was solidly laid at CBS News in Washington, D.C., in the early 1970s. I had begun my television news career in 1969 at a Metromedia station (now Fox), WTTG-TV. There, I advanced from copy person to writer to on-air reporter.

But when I was hired as a CBS News reporter in 1971 by William Small, the Washington Bureau Chief, I began a learning process that would ultimately provide me with the standards of journalism that I live by to this day.

The CBS News Washington Bureau was arguably the best bureau in television news. William Small created an aggressive group of reporters and correspondents who would compete against not only other news organizations but each other as well. There was no better training ground for me, a twenty-five-year-old cub reporter. Covering the nation's capital meant covering the White House, Capitol Hill, the State Department, the Pentagon, the Justice Department, government agencies, presidential campaigns, political conventions, and elections.

One of my first major assignments was to cover the 1972 presidential campaign of Senator George McGovern. In those days, the big three broadcast networks—ABC News, NBC News, CBS News—would send at least two correspondents to follow the presidential candidate day in and day out, as he crisscrossed the country in search of votes.

The first-string CBS News correspondent reported on the McGovern news of the day on Walter Cronkite's *CBS Evening News*. I was the second-string correspondent who reported primarily for CBS radio and, at times, the *CBS Morning News*. I thought I was doing my job well. I knew what McGovern's positions were on all the issues. I practically knew his speeches by heart. Each night, I'd scurry to my hotel room, order room service, and dutifully write and record my last radio spot to be fed to CBS Radio.

I knew the other reporters were having dinner together or were downstairs in the bar, drinking late into the night, but I had no time for that. I was much too dedicated a journalist to engage in such decadence.

Even Timothy Crouse, who wrote *The Boys on the Bus: Riding with the Campaign Press Corps,* noticed: "Connie Chung . . . occupied the room next to mine at the Hyatt House and was always back by midnight, reciting a final 60-second radio spot into her Sony or absorbing one last press release before getting a good night's sleep. So here she was this morning, bright and alert, sticking a mike into McGovern's face and asking something about black ministers. The print reporters stood around and watched, just in case McGovern should say something interesting."

Some mornings, though, I'd wake up, get a copy of the *New York Times* or get information on the latest news in the *Washington Post* or *Boston Globe* and discover that another reporter covering McGovern had broken a story. How could that have happened? I hadn't been out all night. How could I have missed the story? It was not I who was bleary-eyed in the mornings. They were.

In fact, it didn't take me long to wake up. Those reporters weren't having "fun" at the bar at night. They were working their sources—the candidate's aides. They may have been drinking, but they were gathering information at the same time. I obviously had not learned the art of working a source. That revelation turned a very green reporter into the beginning of a reporter who would later be prepared to cover the biggest story of the decade: Watergate.

Those of us who covered Watergate knew the gravity with which we were dealing. A presidency was at stake. Accuracy had always been paramount, but now there was a higher degree of oversight. The rule in the CBS News Washington Bureau was clear: triple-check information. The honing of my reporter skills at CBS News paid off. I had some Watergate-era successes in breaking stories, such as information on Nixon's Enemies List.

By the time I covered Vice President Nelson Rockefeller, starting with his confirmation hearings, I had come of age as a reporter. I remember Lou Cannon, the veteran *Washington Post* correspondent, telling me that I was the reporter to go to if anyone had a question about Rockefeller. He made me feel as if I were the dean of correspondents covering the Rocky beat.

The ensuing years brought on the era of the feeding frenzy and the world of "gets"—newsroom parlance for the cutthroat competition for the big interview, the hot celebrity, the tell-all tattler *du jour*. It's where the supermarket tabloids, the morning wake-up shows, and even the network news broadcasts collide in a mad scramble for an exclusive that will sell papers and draw viewers. It's a symbiotic world where it's hard to tell who is manipulating whom: the media or the newsmakers. I was mired in that morass until I found my way clear.

While the flavor of the week was still the hot property of the day, the 1999–2000 season brought a new day for me. With ABC News *20/20* producer Harry Phillips, I broadcast a story that returned us to our hard-news roots in journalism. Harry and I investigated four unsolved murder cases that occurred in the 1960s civil rights period.

One of the cases involved the 1966 murder of Ben Chester White, an elderly black farmhand in Mississippi. The alleged killers were all suspected members of the Ku Klux Klan. Today, two of the alleged killers are dead. The remaining suspect, Ernest Avants, was tried in 1967 on state murder charges. Despite his confession to the FBI, Avants was acquitted.

During our investigation, we discovered that the murder of Ben Chester White might have been planned to lure Dr. Martin Luther King to the area and make an attempt on his life. We also discovered a fact that had gone unnoticed for more than thirty years: that the White murder had occurred on federal park land. That meant federal charges could be brought against Ernest Avants for the murder of Ben Chester White. After we broadcast that report, the FBI reopened the White case, and the Justice Department indicted and arrested Ernest Avants on federal murder charges. Our cameras were there in Bogue Chitto, Mississippi, when Avants was arrested.

Our story represents the essence of journalism: solid investigative reporting, using sources to uncover information that had been buried with time, and creating change to right wrongs of the past.

—CONNIE CHUNG

Joan
Ganz Cooney

■ JOAN GANZ COONEY DIDN'T SET OUT TO make a seven-foot bird, a cookie-eating monster, and a lovable grouch known throughout the world. But three decades later, the famous residents of *Sesame Street* are still accomplishing what Cooney did set out to prove: that TV can both teach and entertain children.

Cooney has dedicated herself to making a difference in the lives of children—and what a difference she has made. She changed the way millions of children around the world learn by laying the groundwork for innovative children's programming, including the amazingly successful preschool series *Sesame Street* with its unforgettable characters such as Big Bird, Cookie Monster, Oscar the

Grouch, and all the other Muppets. With her passion for education, broadcasting experience, and dedication to social causes, Cooney has had the right combination of skills and contacts to use television as a way to instruct children, wherever they may be. Children's educational programming is, as she puts it, "the job I was born to do."

But creating *Sesame Street* wasn't what she originally set out to do. In 1966, Cooney was an award-winning public affairs producer for New York's educational channel, now WNET/13. One evening she hosted what turned out to be a serendipitous dinner party that brought together several individuals who were, like herself, interested in both education and television. Afterward, Lloyd Morrisett, one of Cooney's guests and an official at the Carnegie Corporation, proposed launching a Carnegie-funded study on using television to educate children. Cooney surprised herself by agreeing with Morrisett's suggestion that she head up the study, seeing it as an opportunity to have a meaningful impact in an area of great social concern.

The report Cooney presented from that study concluded that because television could reach millions of children in families of various economic levels, it should be used to teach children about

Cooney in the Muppets' early days with Bert and Ernie and Frank Oz

the "three Rs" (reading, 'riting, and 'rithmetic) and, probably even more important, about life. While those conclusions now seem obvious, in 1966 they were startlingly new.

Then it was time to bring the study to life. Within a year, Cooney, along with Morrisett, founded the Children's Television Workshop (CTW), dedicated to producing quality educational programming for children. *Sesame Street* was the flagship program, and Cooney became president and CEO (she held those positions until 1990 and now serves as chairman of the executive committee of the company under its new name, Sesame Workshop).

Cooney has led CTW with conviction and creativity, whether rounding up financial support or beating the drum for programming that both teaches and entertains. With her knack for merging education and broadcasting, she enlisted expertise from all relevant areas—bringing together researchers, child development experts, and educators to work side by side with television writers and producers.

The result shows kids that learning is fun, whether they're practicing numbers with a charming, numeral-loving, Dracula-like "Count" or mastering word combinations with best friends Bert and Ernie. In addition, *Sesame Street* has an important impact on the way children socialize in the world's multicultural environment. The program shows Muppets and humans of various racial and ethnic origins cooperating, sharing, and learning together. The program thus prepares children for school and life by demonstrating how to get along and respect one another. On *Sesame Street,* the Muppet characters interact with affection and respect; they make mistakes, and they recover. The puppets are effective stand-ins for kids who are just learning to communicate feelings and develop self-respect.

Cooney herself learned to value education early. She was born on November 30, 1929, into a middle-class family in Phoenix who counted among its forebears one of the founders of the Arizona territory. Her mother, an Irish Catholic from Michigan, sent Joan and her older brother and sister to parochial schools, where the spirit of community service ran strong. A

Cooney with Jim Henson, 1975

Catholic priest, James Keller, who advocated the application of Christian principles to the media and communications, especially influenced her.

After receiving a B.A. in education from the University of Arizona, Joan began her career as a reporter at the *Arizona Republic,* her hometown paper. Soon, however, she was on her way to New York City, where from 1954 to 1962 she worked as a publicist for NBC and for *The U.S. Steel Hour,* a highly acclaimed CBS drama series. These career-advancing jobs put her in touch with Manhattan's literary circles and grounded her in the broadcast industry she would come to affect so significantly.

Under Cooney's direction, *Sesame Street,* which began as an experiment, has been a resounding success. Broadcast daily since 1969 on more than three hundred stations of the Public Broadcasting Service in the United States, the program is also seen in more than 140 foreign countries. Indigenous coproductions reflecting local languages, customs, and educational needs have been produced for kids across Europe, the Middle East, Latin America, and Asia and in Russia and South Africa.

Following the successful launch of *Sesame Street,* Cooney and her colleagues have created other award-winning children's series on network and public TV. *The Electric Company, 3-2-1 Contact, Square One TV, Ghostwriter, CRO, Big Bag,* and *Dragon Tales* present science, mathematics, reading, and new experiences for young audiences. These programs have been awarded more than seventy Emmys and have received scores of other honors

in the United States and around the world. The newest development is Noggin, Sesame Workshop's twenty-four-hour, commercial-free cable channel and on-line service for children ages two to twelve. Sesame Workshop's other activities include publishing, on-line services, CD-ROMs, extensive product licensing, and community outreach programs.

Married to businessman Peter G. Peterson, former U.S. secretary of commerce, Cooney has five stepchildren and six grandchildren. Over the years, she has received numerous awards, including a Daytime Emmy for Lifetime Achievement in 1989. In 1990, she was inducted into the Television Academy Hall of Fame and received the Founders Award from the International Council of the National Academy of Television Arts and Sciences.

In 1995, Cooney was awarded the Presidential Medal of Freedom, the nation's highest civilian honor, and in 1998, she was inducted into the National Women's Hall of Fame—fitting tributes to a woman who has made television a place of learning and wonder for children everywhere. ■

How did I get to Sesame Street? I followed my heart, spoke my mind, and, with the help of great partners and real visionaries, was lucky enough to be the right person in the right place at the right time.

The year was 1966, and I was working as a documentary producer at WNDT (now WNET), the local educational television channel in New York City. I had just finished *A Chance at the Beginning,* a program about Martin Deutsch's work with young children in Harlem that was a precursor to Head Start. At the time, I was intellectually and spiritually involved in the civil rights movement and with the educational deficit that poverty created. I was also passionately committed to the idea of television as an educational medium, although not as yet focused on young children.

The idea for *Sesame Street* was actually first raised in a dinner-party conversation. There were six of us that night in March: Mary and Lloyd Morrisett (then a vice president at the Carnegie Corporation of New York); my former husband, Tim Cooney; my assistant and associate producer at Channel 13, Ann Bement; and my then-boss, Lewis Freedman, director of programming and a stunning, dramatic, and brilliant man.

Lewis began talking about the great untapped potential of television as an educator. He was so persuasive and so interesting that he triggered something that night in Lloyd, who had long been interested in cognitive development in young children and who, as the father of two young children, had been astounded to find them watching test patterns on television one morning while waiting for cartoons. Lloyd was so interested, in fact, that several days later he invited Lewis and me to come to the foundation and meet with him and several others to discuss the possibility of Carnegie financing a small study on the subject.

I'll never forget what happened next. Lloyd very clearly asked Lewis if I would be interested. Lewis very clearly replied, "No, Joan wouldn't be interested; she's a public affairs producer"—to which I remember saying, "Oh yes, I would!"

I didn't know it until that moment. I just suddenly saw that I could do little documentaries on Channel 13 for the rest of my life and have no impact on the lives of those in need, or I could use television to help children, particularly disadvantaged children, learn. I saw it so clearly that it really was a kind of Saint Paul on the highway.

But translating that vision didn't come quite so easily. Lewis was determined to keep me as a public affairs producer, and it wasn't until several days later, when, as fate would have it, my then-husband was scheduled to have lunch with Lloyd on an unrelated matter. He knew my feelings, of course, and so asked if he should bring them up again at lunch. I said yes.

Lloyd then simply called Lewis and said, "I've decided we want Joan to do the investigation." Carnegie granted $15,000 to Channel 13 to cover my expenses and salary for three months, and I traveled around the country asking experts in a variety of disciplines about the potential of television to educate children.

Even after Lloyd put his faith in me, there was still quite a bit of resistance to having a woman at the helm. Loud voices clamored that a woman would diminish the project's credibility, that this particular woman didn't have enough experience to head such a project. One of those funders even asked me if I had given any thought to how this responsibility would affect my marriage and whether I could "handle" it. Funny to think of that now. I knew then as I know today that this was the job I was born to do; I knew it totally and with complete conviction.

And so we presented the study to Carnegie in October 1966, held a press conference about eight months later to announce the formation of Children's Television Workshop, and put *Sesame Street* on the air in November 1969. The rest, as they say, is history.

With one postscript: while we knew *Sesame Street* was a hit, none of us had any idea that it and the Children's Television Workshop would grow into the international institutions they are today, or that *Sesame Street,* winner of more Emmys than any other single show, would also become the longest street in the world, benefiting more children in more countries than any other programming in history.

None of us had any idea that the characters we were creating—Muppets to teach children letters, numbers, and concepts—would become so much a part of our culture, or that we were creating a television family for every child watching. We only knew that we wanted to make a difference in the lives of children and families.

Thirty-one years later, we continue in this spirit. Today, as I write this, we've changed the name of our organization from Children's Television Workshop to Sesame Workshop. Why? Because the world in which our children live, in which we all live, is influenced by other media as well as television: CD-ROMs, the Internet, books, videotapes, radio, and so on. The challenge and the responsibility—as true today as it was three decades ago—are to channel children's natural attraction to media in positive and constructive ways, to use all media to help educate children, and to help them achieve their highest potential.

—JOAN GANZ COONEY

Katie
Couric

■ MILLIONS OF AMERICANS TUNE IN TO Katie Couric on the *Today* show to hear hard-hitting interviews with world leaders and other newsmakers. They also watch to see her bright smile and likable personality and get their morning under way. That's why it's so hard to imagine that Couric was banned from the air early on in her career at CNN by the network's president for her high-pitched, squeaky voice. True story. So how did Couric go from a career low to coanchor of the *Today* show? Persistence, hard work, a strong ability to overcome adversity, and simply being herself, all traits that have defined her career.

Couric's authoritative yet down-to-earth style makes her interviews with people from all walks of life look effortless. In describing her interview style, Couric says, "People get a sense that I really enjoy talking to whom I'm talking to, that I don't see it as a duty, that I see it as a pleasure. I think I have the ability to laugh at myself, which perhaps people find appealing." Continually described as perky, Couric presents an attractive, rather than glamorous, persona; and viewers love it.

But behind that easy manner are years of hard work invested in becoming a serious journalist—not just sessions with a voice coach to learn how to deepen and project her voice but years of working in the trenches. Some of her accomplishments include reporting on immigration, crime, and drug issues from Miami's WTVJ, as well as winning an Emmy and an Associated Press award while at Washington's WRC-TV for a story dealing with a dating service for the handicapped.

Katie was born in Arlington, Virginia, just outside Washington, D.C., on January 7, 1957. It was during her years at the University of Virginia that she was drawn to television news and spent her summers working in newsrooms. She graduated in 1979 with a B.A. in English and headed straight for an entry-level job at ABC News in Washington—getting sandwiches for the

Couric at the 2000 Republican National Convention

decision makers and exposure and contacts for herself.

Couric soon moved on to the Washington bureau of the fledgling Cable News Network. Couric has described her stint as an assistant assignment editor at CNN as a combination of graduate school and on-the-job training. She moved to the Atlanta headquarters of CNN as an associate producer and eventually became a political correspondent for its news program *Take Two.* Couric moved on to Miami in 1984 as a general-assignment reporter. But in 1987, she worked her way back to Washington by winning a job at NBC's WRC-TV as a general-assignment reporter.

It was at WRC-TV that Couric encountered a boss with doubts about her abilities. After her persistent requests to try anchoring, she was given a chance. As Couric recalls, it did not go well. "There

are some very basic mechanical skills you need to be a good anchor, and I was a disaster," she says. "When I asked the news director if I could try anchoring again sometime, he said, 'Perhaps if you go to a really really small market.'" Undaunted, Couric worked hard to improve her delivery and only six short months later was filling in for Garrick Utley on the weekend evening news.

Couric became firmly established on the national scene in 1989, when Tim Russert, the NBC bureau chief in Washington, approached her about a plum job as a deputy Pentagon correspondent. It was a good move for Couric—reporting stories for *Today,* covering the invasion of Panama, and demonstrating expertise in an area of journalism where few women were making a mark. Says Couric, "One thing about my Pentagon experience is that, since there aren't a lot of women covering the Pentagon, I think it elevated me in the eyes of a lot of people. You can't be an airhead and cover F-14s."

Her regular reports on *Today* gave her visibility and the chance to showcase her talent as an experienced journalist. It wasn't long before she was named the show's national correspondent based in Washington; along with that came the chance to be a substitute cohost of *Today*. The outbreak of the Persian Gulf War gave Couric the opportunity to cover a front-page story in a field in which she had expertise, credibility, and sources. Her journalistic expertise and her growing popularity in front of the camera came to a head in 1991, when she was named coanchor of the *Today* show.

Couric's combination of exceptional interviewing skills and hard-news judgment have led to many *Today* interviews that have themselves made headlines. In 1992, while interviewing First Lady Barbara Bush at the White House for the building's two hundredth anniversary, President Bush wandered into the interview area. Couric, completely unfazed, proceeded to conduct a twenty-minute impromptu interview with the president that many consider a defining moment of her career.

Couric's interviews have often been noteworthy for their groundbreaking content or because they were a "first": a 1996 interview with presidential candidate Bob Dole and his wife, Elizabeth, concerning Dole's stance on whether tobacco is addictive; Anita Hill's first television interview concerning allegations of sexual harassment against Supreme Court nominee Clarence Thomas; and General Norman Schwarzkopf's first interview after the Persian Gulf War, to name a few.

Couric, who has two daughters, Elinor Tully Monahan and Caroline Couric Monahan, knows what it is to balance work and family: "There are still difficulties with women achieving certain heights and balancing a family. I have been really lucky that I have two beautiful daughters that mean the whole world to me." Couric's personal life has brought her joy, but also tragedy. In 1997, her husband, Jay Monahan, a legal analyst for MSNBC, was diagnosed with colon cancer. He died the next year.

Couric turned her anguish into action. Since her husband's diagnosis, Couric has made colon cancer a focus of her work and has brought great public awareness to the need for early detection. She took this awareness to new heights when she allowed cameras to accompany her visit to the doctor for a screening test; it aired on the *Today* show. In 1999, along with Lilly Tartikoff and the Entertainment Industry Foundation, Couric launched a national campaign—the National Colorectal Cancer Research Alliance—aimed at increasing awareness of colorectal cancer; she promotes the campaign throughout the country.

Throughout Couric's career, her ability to overcome adversity and the confidence to be herself have paid off. Not only has Couric proved her early doubters wrong; she has rewritten the standard for women in the industry. ∎

Twenty years after graduating from college, I really do feel as if I have a front row seat in a world history class and in the school of life. I'm so grateful that I've been given the chance to occupy a chair on the *Today* show, and I'm ever mindful of the tremendous responsibility that goes with it. And let me tell you, I know just how hard it is to get here.

Journalism seemed a natural career choice for me. I've always loved to write and could do so quickly, and I'm blessed with an insatiable curiosity about people and things. When I first gave a thought to a career, my father encouraged me to give radio a try. So I got out the phone book and started calling stations in nearby Washington, D.C., asking if I could come in for an informational interview. With a lot of persistence, I landed a summer internship at an all-news radio station and watched everyone in action. The next summer, I worked in the news department of another station and, after my junior year at the University of Virginia, still another. By the time I graduated from college, I had a good deal of work experience under my belt.

My journey started in earnest at ABC News, where I was given the important tasks of answering the phone, making coffee, and fetching ham sandwiches for anchorman Frank Reynolds. From there I went to a fledgling little network called CNN, which at the time was mocked as "Chicken Noodle News" by some of the same network types who would kill to have a job there today.

Next up, I headed to the local CBS affiliate in Miami in the mid-1980s, the heyday of *Miami Vice,* where I covered a lot of stories about bodies in trunks. I moved on to Washington, D.C., for a two-year stint at the local NBC station. I was eventually hired to cover the Pentagon for NBC. And then, somehow, miraculously, I was picked to fill in on *Today.* The rest, as they say, is history.

So, having toiled for twelve years in the business in five different assignments prior to my current job, I can hardly be called an "overnight success." And considering some of the bumpier stretches in my career path, my good fortune amazes no one more than me. And maybe the president of CNN, who, after witnessing a particularly lame performance of mine at the White House, decreed that he never wanted to see me on the air again!

I'm often approached by students who are eager to pursue careers in journalism, and my advice to them never changes: get a good, solid liberal arts education, and focus on areas such as economics and government, foreign policy, and Russian history. Learn as much as you can, I tell them, and make sure that learning continues through your first, lowly jobs. Be patient and tenacious, because smart, dedicated people will eventually make themselves known. As I say, that advice never changes.

I hope I am a woman with the kind of values everyone has—a person who can be the viewers' eyewitness and ask the questions they would want to ask and feel the way they might feel.

This past January, as I stood in Times Square and rang in the New Year and the new millennium with Tom Brokaw, I was surprisingly moved. These are exciting times we live in. Relative peace throughout the world, a booming economy, an exploding new industry in the Internet, the feeling that this is a country of endless opportunity and vast potential. I can't think of a better time to be doing what I do. Now if I could only figure out how to cram eight hours of sleep into five and a half!

—KATIE COURIC

Nancy
Dickerson

■ LATE ONE NIGHT ON THE 1964 CAMPAIGN trail, President Lyndon Johnson stopped by the hotel room of NBC-TV correspondent Nancy Dickerson. Johnson had something important he wanted to discuss and was suitably attired: in his pajamas. Press Secretary Bill Moyers soon came to fetch his boss, but Dickerson had things under control. "I never took the proposition very seriously," she noted years later, "because LBJ was truly more interested in talking politics than sex."

Nonetheless, that encounter speaks volumes of the comfort zone Dickerson enjoyed with Washington's power elite. When she married wealthy businessman C. Wyatt Dickerson in 1962, consider the trifecta of high-powered pals who tossed her a party: then–Vice President Johnson, Connecticut Senator Abraham Ribicoff, and Supreme Court Justice Arthur Goldberg.

A fine professional line separates news and schmooze, and Nancy Dickerson deftly walked it without losing her balance. When she was first breaking into the business, a veteran newspaper columnist had advised her to "go everywhere, learn everything, meet everybody, and it will make you a good journalist." Dickerson followed directions well. She did indeed meet lots of people ("There were so many dates over the years I can't

remember them all," she once confessed), and she became a very good journalist.

She was the first woman hired as a correspondent by CBS News; she subsequently moved to NBC and became the first woman floor reporter at a presidential convention. In 1971, she became the first woman to have a daily news program on network television. In 1980, she formed her own independent production company, the Television Corporation of America. A documentary she did on the Watergate scandal, *784 Days That Changed America—From Watergate to Resignation,* won a George Foster Peabody Award. "It would be a great thing if this program could be shown in every high school and college in the country," said

U.S. District Court Judge John Sirica, who presided over the main Watergate trials.

Nancy Conners Hanschman was born in 1927 in Wauwatosa, Wisconsin. She graduated from the University of Wisconsin in 1948 with a teaching degree, majoring in Spanish and Portuguese. After two stifling years teaching in Milwaukee schools, Dickerson headed for New York in search of a new career. She couldn't even get hired as a tour guide at Rockefeller Center (to which, ironically, she would eventually return to broadcast the evening news for NBC) and in 1951 moved to Washington, where she got a job as a researcher for the Senate Foreign Relations Committee. Three years later, she heard that CBS was looking for someone to produce a radio show, *The Leading Question,* about the Washington political scene. She talked her way into an interview.

"They wanted a newspaper person, a man, who knew Capitol Hill," Dickerson said. "I'd never worked on a newspaper. Obviously, I'm not a man. But I did know Capitol Hill."

She got the job. As active as she was on the social circuit (her first dates in Washington were with two future senators: John F. Kennedy and Henry "Scoop" Jackson), Hanschman was an even harder worker. She took speaking courses at night during her early days at CBS and volunteered for all the holiday shifts. In 1959, she used her vacation time to go to Europe and file a series of radio reports that gained her visibility at CBS. A year later she wangled an interview with

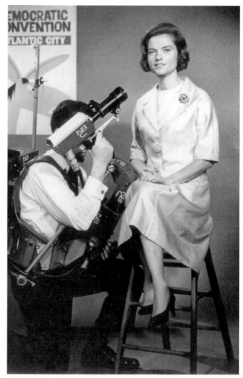

Dickerson broadcasting from the Democratic National Convention, 1964

media-allergic Speaker of the House Sam Rayburn of Texas, which broke news and led to her being offered a full-time correspondent's job. While CBS News gods Edward R. Murrow and Eric Sevareid welcomed her into the fold, Dickerson always felt she was something of a curiosity at the network.

"The men had a certain funny feeling about women going on the air," she said. "It was downright strange. I remember going on *Face the Nation* for the first time. The then–vice president in charge of news called me up beforehand and said, 'Listen, you're going to go on this program, and we've never had a woman on it before. *Now, don't giggle.*'"

She didn't giggle. Or cry. Or put on

makeup while asking questions. Rather, she held her own with the big boys and then went back about her business of racking up scoops (for example, breaking the news that LBJ had picked Hubert Humphrey for his running mate in 1964) and covering some of the biggest stories of the day, including the John Glenn space launch, Martin Luther King, Jr.'s "I Have a Dream" speech, and the downfall of Richard Nixon. Dickerson was especially wired into the Johnson administration. LBJ was so fond of her that he often opened press briefings with a hearty "Hi, Nancy" and, remarkably, got directly involved in contract negotiations when she was in the process of leaving CBS for NBC.

Dickerson was making her name when Washington was at its social high-water mark, when candlelit dinner parties in Georgetown mansions were still major political events. She displayed an almost Jackie Kennedyesque flair. She had the same high cheekbones and wore vicuna suits and a Dior camel-hair coat that she called her "foreign correspondent's coat." Dickerson, her husband, and their five children occupied two homes in the Washington area, one of which was Merrywood, the Virginia estate where Jacqueline Kennedy had grown up.

The Dickersons divorced in 1982, and seven years later, Nancy married Wall Street financier John C. Whitehead, a former deputy secretary of state in the Reagan administration. As a journalist-hostess, Dickerson had the cachet needed to reel in A-list guests, among them

Dickerson interviewing Lady Bird Johnson at the White House, 1964

Ronald and Nancy Reagan, Pamela Harriman, publisher Walter Annenberg, and assorted heavyweights dating back to the Kennedy administration.

Dickerson returned to television as a commentator with Fox News from 1986 to 1991. In January 1996, she suffered a stroke from which she never fully recovered, and she died in New York in October 1997. Long before then she had written her autobiography, *Among Those Present,* which among other topics tackled the proverbial question she was always asked about her groundbreaking tenure at CBS News: "Did I have to sleep with anyone to get the job?"

Nope, Dickerson insisted. The secret of her success involved a more mundane form of legwork. As she once remarked, "Being a reporter is really having a good pair of shoes to get you around. It's hard work, but it's exhilarating." ■

From the moment I started at CBS in 1954 through the entire six years I was a producer, I wanted to be a correspondent, but this possibility was so far-fetched that I never even asked.

Looking back, I see now that parts of my life fit together like a jigsaw puzzle, and one of the most important pieces fell into place when I met General C. V. Clifton, a dynamic Pentagon press officer who later became JFK's military aide. Together we concocted a plan for me to go to Europe in the summer of 1959 on a military transport, with the rank of general, provided that CBS News would carry my reports on women in the Army stationed abroad. The CBS brass in New York agreed, with the odd stipulation that I must not refer to the WACs as a "group of attractive women." (Networks always have been a strong bastion of male chauvinism.)

I went to several Army camps, saw a great many WACs and then went to West Berlin, where General Clifton helped me set up lines to New York for my first broadcast. Earlier in the day I had gone to East Berlin, and after I did a report on the WACs I followed it with a piece about the communist sector. At the time, Khrushchev was in the United States, and I reported that in East Berlin there seemed to be preparations for a Khrushchev visit, which was a subject of lively speculation then. After Germany, I flew to Vienna, interviewed our ambassador, and described the city, which had become a listening post in the Cold War. CBS was delighted with this report too and said they'd take any others. In Rome I joined a papal audience, and since His Holiness mentioned Khrushchev, I did another broadcast there.

By this time I had created a new career out of reactions to Khrushchev's adventures in the United States, and by the end of my trip to Europe I considered myself a foreign correspondent. A prophet is without honor in his own country; while CBS would not think of my broadcasting from Washington, in Europe I had acquired new wisdom, previously unapparent to them.

Back in the [U.S.] capital, I suggested every conceivable story idea that wouldn't infringe on the jurisdiction of a male CBS correspondent. I realized that the only way I could get on the air was to report news no one else had access to, so I went to House Speaker Sam Rayburn. He did not like television because the bright lights made his bald head look even balder; in fact, he once sat through an entire television interview with his hat on. But he had always been nice to me and he liked women; they adored him and flocked around him at parties. His attractiveness was undoubtedly similar to Henry Kissinger's, who explained it by saying that the greatest aphrodisiac of all is power. Speaker Rayburn was powerful and knew more about leadership than most presidents ever learn. Out of deference to him, the House used to reopen every year on his birthday, January 6, and on that night Scooter and Dale Miller, Texas friends, always gave a big party in the Speaker's honor.

The day before his birthday in 1960, I asked Mr. Rayburn if I could have an exclusive interview, and he told me to come back the next day. By now CBS was grudgingly beginning to believe that if I said I would produce a certain body, I would do it; so far I always had. But though they didn't know it, this was the one time I thought I might fail. However, since no one else could get the Speaker on television, they let me have a camera crew in great secrecy so the other networks wouldn't learn about it and try to horn in or complain about exclusivity and abort the whole interview.

We went to the Speaker's office, set up the equipment, and waited for him. When he arrived, he roared—literally roared—when he saw the cameras and lights. Then he tripped over a cable, and I wished I were someplace else—anywhere else. I said I was sorry. Then there was a dreadful long silence. I reminded him that he had agreed to an interview—or at least I thought he had agreed to an interview. In steely tones through clenched teeth he admitted that he had, but not with those unholy cameras. It was a royal scene, with half the Rayburn staff looking on.

Then I began to see the humor. (Fortunately, I can usually detect the ridiculousness in situations where I play an inadvertently comic role.) We did look pretty silly—he at his desk, pouting and grunting, sitting there with his hat still on; me, knee-deep in cables. Apparently the Speaker admired my guts. I was the youngest press person around the Hill and the only one courageous or foolish enough to ask him for a television exclusive. He liked the drama, too, as I kept insisting that I couldn't interview him without cameras and lights.

I asked him what was ahead in the legislative year, and he made a lot of news with his answers. I ended by asking him what he most hoped for in the coming year and he said, "To be back here." To which I said, and I couldn't have meant it more, "Well, I hope we're back with you, and now back to CBS News in New York."

The interview went off perfectly and we got rave reviews, but I never saw the program because I was celebrating the Speaker's birthday. It was a late party, and the next morning, when the producer of the CBS nightly news, Don Hewitt (now producer of *60 Minutes*), phoned, I was still asleep and didn't quite realize the significance of his remark "We want you on the air every night."

— NANCY DICKERSON

Phyllis
Diller

■ WHEN PHYLLIS DILLER MADE HER FIRST national television appearance, on *You Bet Your Life* in 1956, she seemed shy and demure—a far cry from the raucous quick wit audiences know today. That in itself should have come as no surprise: Diller was just starting out and, like most comedians, needed years to develop a trademark persona. What stood out as remarkable about that debut was that it took place when Diller was thirty-seven. She was learning the performer's craft at an age when most had either succeeded or stopped trying. And she was, of course, a woman, whereas all of the other prominent stand-up comedians at that time had names like Jack, Bob, or George.

"I was excited out of my mind," Diller recalls of her debut on Groucho Marx's popular quiz show. "I had bought a new dress." In the end, however, nervousness got the best of her, and the appearance "didn't cause a ripple." So Diller went back to performing at clubs, continuing to build confidence and break ground with her jokes about the pitfalls of housekeeping and motherhood, the reality of looking like an authentic housewife rather than the June Cleaver variety, and the indignities dished out by Fang, her unappreciative spouse. Along the way, her relatively mature age proved an asset.

"I feel compassion for some of the young female stand-up comedians today," she says. "What have they got to beef about—that their sixth-grade teacher was mean to them? By the time I did comedy, I had kids, neighbors, in-laws. I had lived. Plus I'd had failures in housekeeping and cooking. The audiences loved that because it took the onus off their own failures."

Her gender, too, counted in her favor. "It wasn't a guy complaining about his mother-in-law; it was a woman complaining about her husband," says Stephen Rosenfield, director of the American Comedy Institute in New York City. "That was a new perspective. She also created a unique persona. There was no one else like that, with the gloves, the makeup, the tiara."

Fang, the husband she so enjoyed maligning, never existed. Phyllis describes her real first spouse, Sherwood Diller, as handsome, morally supportive, and charming, with one little problem: an inability to provide for his wife and their five children. "The longest he ever held a job was for three years," she says, "at a bomber plant during the war—so of course they wouldn't fire anyone."

Lacking employment prowess himself, Sherwood recognized the promise of his wife's talents. Born July 17, 1917, in Lima, Ohio, Phyllis Ada Driver had learned as a child to use humor to deflect unkind comments about her long nose and uneven teeth. After moving to San Francisco and marrying Sherwood, she performed at community amateur shows. "My husband knew I was funny and that there was a lot of money in comedy," she says. "He nagged and nagged me to perform."

With her husband's help, she landed a two-week gig in 1955 at San Francisco's Purple Onion; it ended up lasting eighty-nine weeks. Later that same decade, her talents came to the attention of Jack Paar, who booked her for a series of TV performances on *The Jack Paar Show*. Within five years, she was playing Carnegie Hall and had refined her material enough that she could deliver a rapid-fire succession of punch lines—as many as twelve a minute—that enthralled audiences and allowed would-be hecklers few openings.

Bob Hope soon became a fan and helped Diller branch into movie work. She won a small role in *Splendor in the Grass* in 1961 and then costarred with Hope in *Boy! Did I Get a Wrong Number,*

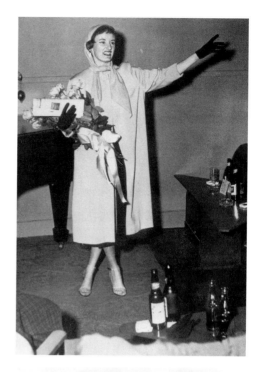

Top: Diller's opening night at the Purple Onion, March 7, 1955
Bottom: Diller and Bob Hope on the Christmas tour in Vietnam, 1966

Eight on the Lam, and *The Private Navy of Sergeant O'Farrell.* She also appeared in twenty-two of his TV specials and went with him to perform for American troops in Vietnam.

A household name in the United States by the mid-1960s, Diller further raised her profile by taking her nightclub act to Canada, England, Australia, and Bermuda. She became so widely recognized that at times she needed to travel incognito. "People couldn't tell it was her, but they looked surprised to see a woman in a nun's habit smoking cigarettes," says Ingrid Chapman, Diller's former road manager.

Diller wrote *Phyllis Diller's Housekeeping Hints* as well as three other books, all of which became best-sellers.

On Broadway, she received favorable reviews as the title character in *Hello, Dolly!* A classically trained pianist, Diller also performed as a solo artist with more than a hundred symphony orchestras from 1972 to 1982. The Friars Club made her a member in 1978, presenting her with a Piaget diamond-and-gold watch at her roast, attended by two thousand industry colleagues.

A reputation for professionalism helped to perpetuate her career. "Producers knew she would always be ready, directors knew she'd always be on time, and fellow performers knew she'd always be kind," says Corrine Hanley, Diller's former personal secretary.

Watching herself on a guest appearance on *Sonny and Cher* in the 1970s,

Left to right: Jimmy Stewart, Phyllis Diller, Mayor Sam Yorty, and Johnny Carson on *The Tonight Show*

Diller decided the time had come to rework a little material—namely, her face. Inadvertently, as a result, she became the first celebrity to admit to having plastic surgery. "I'm not devious," Diller says. "If someone asks me what I'm doing Thursday, I say I'm having a face-lift." The American Academy of Cosmetic Surgery subsequently honored her for "the tremendous breakthrough in acceptance of our field."

Today Diller lives in Brentwood Park, California. Since divorcing her second husband, Warde Donovan, in 1975, she has remained single. She continues to perform comedy at clubs around the country and, as always, writes most of her own material. In 1998, she lent her voice to the queen aunt in the animated feature film *A Bug's Life.* Her recurring role as wisecracking makeover artist Gladys Pope on the daytime drama *The Bold and the Beautiful,* seen in 150 countries, has reinforced her stature as an international star.

Ironically, after more than forty-five years of portraying herself as a complainer, Diller attributes her success in part to a stiff upper lip and goodwill to all—even when it's not reciprocated. "My mother told me, 'Never close the door behind you,'" she says. "If I had a bad experience with someone, that person would never know it, even if I were dying inside. It's called acting." ■

How I became the first female stand-up comic probably started someplace in childhood and had a lot to do with the gene pool and DNA. Let me tell you unhumbly, there is no such thing as a stupid comic. A comic is a bright, supersensitive human who may have felt abandoned in childhood.

You can be wealthy and abandoned at the same time. Robin Williams still shakes hands with his father and calls him "Sir." Jonathan Winters spent a lot of time alone; his father was a banker and his mother a busy radio personality. When only children have time to themselves, they develop absolutely startling imaginations. Both of these fabulous comics are geniuses as well as only children from rich families.

I was an only child (although not a wealthy one) and a late-in-life baby. My mother kept sending me away. She sent my dad out with me to sell insurance. People must have bought out of pity.

Another thing characterizes so many comics that it must be vital: I'd say 75 percent of them are musicians. One of the most important elements of all in comedy is timing. Music is mathematics—timing romanticized. Like musical talent, comic ability involves a keen ear, good listening, and a God-given feeling for "the right time."

As is true with a musical career, to reach the highest level in comedy—that of the comic—you must acquire enough skill to play solo. In 1955, when I became a comedian (not a comic yet), most of the men in the business were working in tandem. George Carlin had several partners. There were [Steve] Rossi and [Marty] Allen, Dean Martin and Jerry Lewis, and many other pairs. The real comics, the ones who could stand alone, were the seasoned older guys, such as Jack Benny and Bob Hope.

It took several years in the trenches for me to become a comic. But before I dive into that story, let me explain the three categories of funny women: comic actress, comedian, and comic.

A comic actress differs from a comic. There have always been wonderful comic actresses in the old movies, present-day movies, and television. Two of the most time-honored are Lucille Ball and Carol Burnett. A comic actress works ensemble with one or more people, and the material is written for her. A comedian, such as Carol Channing, Tracey Ullman, Lily Tomlin, Ruth Buzzi, or Kaye Ballard, may use props, dancing boys, costumes, song, and dance.

A comic, on the other hand, is the hard-core refinement of comedy. The person works "in one," alone, and is responsible for his or her own material. "In one" means in front of the first curtain. And if you don't think that is a lonely spot, try it. There, without ammunition, you'd rather face a firing squad.

When you are an unknown comic, you are fair game for everyone in the audience. Drunken men, even inebriated women, think they're funnier than you. Sitting in the dark with someone else up there in the bright light, doing setups, brings out the worst in audience members. When they yell out their ideas, ruining your timing, they are the geniuses called hecklers.

It is easier for a man to handle heckling than it is for a woman because, to become a successful female comic, you must preserve some semblance of civility. I never mixed it up with hecklers. I simply ignored them. It wasn't happening; I just went on with my act.

I started out with a hodgepodge of funny stuff—things that worked at parties and amateur performances. I sang, I played the piano, I talked, I used the great stuff in my prop box to create characters: a ninety-year-old woman, a Channel swimmer, an opera star, a gangster's moll. In my magic prop box I had shawls, combs, jabots, spectacles, swim caps, torn sweaters, books, berets, hats, feathers, anything to make the imagination soar.

But I realized that to get into the big time I must give up my crutches—my beloved props. Then, and only then, did I become a stand-up comic. This meant forgoing music in my act and relying completely on talk. When you have no ethnic accent or cadence, that is another disadvantage. There is a Jewish sound that is funny in itself; consider Jackie Mason. Likewise, the black sound makes a certain kind of material even funnier, and the Latino singsong made Bill Dana. As I didn't have an accent of any kind, my new focus became the material—more commercial material that went on and on in a funny story line. I also developed a rapid-fire style.

In 1958, I made the transition from the comfortable and wonderful *Tonight Show* with Jack Paar on NBC to the highly paid and hottest show of the week, *The Ed Sullivan Show* on CBS. That's when I graduated to stand-up.

Being the first notable female stand-up comic was a plus rather than a minus. People would say, "Whaddaya mean, a female doing stand-up? What is it? Get a stick. Kill it before it multiplies." In other words, they had to see it to believe it, it was such a breakthrough. By then I had them. This was seven years before Joan Rivers came aboard the stand-up ship. Then for the next thirteen years, it was Joan, Totie Fields, and me as the only female stand-ups. Later, comedy clubs started popping up like mushrooms after a rain, and lots of women grabbed the open mike to try their wings.

I was born to do what I do. I treasure the history of becoming known, the hardships, the ghastly situations, the legions of precious people who were the wind beneath my wings, the people who helped me, who propelled me along a path to greater acceptance and fantastic joy in my work. I thank my two most significant boosters, Jack Paar and Bob Hope, from the bottom of my heart and the top of my heart and both sides, including my blessed pacemaker.

—PHYLLIS DILLER

Linda
Ellerbee

■ IN A DELICIOUS BIT OF IRONY, LINDA Ellerbee got her start in television by being, well, outspoken. Working in 1972 as an Associated Press news writer in Dallas, Ellerbee had written a letter to a friend on her computer at work. Intending to print a copy of the letter, Ellerbee pushed the wrong button. The letter, critical of her boss's hiring policies, the city of Dallas, the local newspapers, and the Vietnam War, was instantly transmitted to television and radio stations throughout Texas and three neighboring states. Fired on the spot, Ellerbee was no longer writing news; she became the news.

Broadcasters read her letter on the air, and regional newspapers picked up the story. But out of an embarrassing moment came a job offer. The news director at KHOU-TV in Houston told her she "wrote funny." When asked if she would consider working in television news, Ellerbee replied that she didn't even own a TV set. But as a single mother with two small children, she needed a steady job. So television it was.

From this inauspicious beginning, Ellerbee has gone on to become a highly respected journalist, award-winning network correspondent, nationally acclaimed television writer, best-selling author, and founder of a successful television production company.

Born August 15, 1944, in Byron, Texas, Linda grew up an avid reader, filling her curious mind with information and facts. Ellerbee remembers that her mother "would push me to read, to stretch even when she didn't agree with what I read or where I stretched." Ellerbee left Vanderbilt University for Chicago, where her then-husband was enrolled in graduate school. Over the next decade, she worked in a variety of jobs: as a disc jockey at WSOM radio in Chicago, program director of a small radio station in San Jose, speechwriter for an Alaskan politician, and finally the AP job in Texas.

While it was her error that got her a break into television, it was her talent that got her noticed. In 1973, while she was reporting for KHOU-TV, an assistant news director for WCBS-TV in New York City saw one of her reports and offered her a job reporting for the local eleven o'clock news. After five years covering strikes, murders, fires, and riots at WCBS-TV, Ellerbee moved to the network level—to NBC as coanchor with Lloyd Dobyns of *NBC News Weekend.* Although Ellerbee and Dobyns got good reviews, the show failed to attract much of an audience and was canceled in 1979.

The Ellerbee-Dobyns team again won critical acclaim in 1982 for a pioneering nightly news program, *NBC News Overnight,* for which they had carte blanche to present the news any way they wanted. Ellerbee, in typically wry fashion, described the show as "the inmates being allowed to take over the asylum." Others saw it as exceptional television. Ironically, by the time the program won an Alfred I. du Pont–Columbia University Award as "not only the best post-midnight show on the air, but just conceivably the best-written and most intelligent TV news anywhere," the show had been canceled, provoking an outpouring of angry phone calls, letters, and protests in front of the network's corporate headquarters.

Ellerbee found television news a difficult workplace for women. "In the beginning we were dancing dogs," she says. "It wasn't how well the dog danced; it was that the dog danced at all. Their expectation of us was that we all screwed our way into our jobs and that, therefore, we didn't have a brain in our head." Ellerbee believed that her superiors

Seven-year-old Ellerbee at her cousin Shirley's graduation, 1952

expected women reporters to be as aggressive and ambitious as their male counterparts in pursuit of a story but to assume a more traditional subservient role back at the station.

Not buying into her bosses' expectations, Ellerbee let the world know it in her 1986 book *And So It Goes,* a humorously scathing tour of her experiences in television news. That same year, Ellerbee moved to ABC, where she wrote and anchored a prime-time historical series, *Our World,* for which she won an Emmy for best writing. After only one year, however, Ellerbee left network television for what she describes as the best thing that ever happened to her: she formed her own production company, Lucky Duck Productions, which has brought all of her experience and talent full circle. Lucky Duck's prime-time specials and weekly series are seen across the spectrum—

on HBO, A&E, MSNBC, Lifetime Television, MTV, ABC, and CBS.

In 1991, Lucky Duck began producing a news program specifically for kids, called *Nick News,* with Ellerbee as host and writer. It soon became the most popular children's news program on television, airing on Nickelodeon and close to two hundred stations in syndication. It has won three George Foster Peabody Awards, an Alfred I. du Pont–Columbia University Award, and two Emmys. For Ellerbee, the rewards have been sweet: "All those guys who really worried about what I might say to their audience—I've got their kids."

Ellerbee's success with *Nick News* might seem like an obvious transition as she has always placed great value on accurately portraying a story and giving it straight to the audience, an approach that works well with kids. "Colleagues sometimes ask how I 'dumb down' stories for kids. I don't. I never did it for adults; I'm not going to do it for a ten-year-old who, after all, is not dumber, only younger and shorter. I still believe the audience is just as smart as I am, likely smarter. They deserve my respect—and my very best effort."

A breast cancer survivor, Ellerbee also travels thousands of miles every year to deliver inspirational speeches. Never a fan of artifice, Ellerbee didn't hide the side effects of her cancer treatment earlier in her career, appearing on air without the usual camouflage of a wig.

Ellerbee interviewing Fidel Castro in Cuba, 1977

Ellerbee on the set of *Nick News Special Edition: Kids Pick the Issues*, 2000

Although Ellerbee has won all of television's highest honors and been able to make television "her way," Ellerbee says her richest rewards are her two children, Vanessa and Joshua. The rewards to Ellerbee's viewers have been rich as well: she still gives people the news straight up, well written, and on target—just as in the old days in Texas. ■

I've been called a maverick, irreverent, outspoken, a trouble-maker, and much worse. I don't mind, except when someone thinks it was intentional on my part, that I meant to be some standard bearer, pioneer, or even noble eccentric. What nonsense. For me, being different wasn't a choice. For you, it may be. I can't explain it any better than that. I've had a fine run as a television journalist, and often been able to do it my way. But make no mistake: there is a price. And if you would do it your way, you must be willing to pay that price too.

Begin here. When I first came into television news in 1973, I was confronted with the notion that the reporter should become part of the story. As in "Here I am walking up the courthouse steps. Here I am strolling the shore in meaningful conversation with A Very Important Person. Here I am tasting the blue ribbon pie at the local fair. Here I am walking the streets at night to see what it feels like to be a woman alone on dark city streets (pay no attention to that camera crew back there). Here I am in the cockpit putting on that cute little helmet. Here I am staring mournfully at the sea where the sailboat sank. Here I am riding the circus elephant. Here I am . . ." It seemed phony to me then and it still does. The reporter is not the story; the story is the story. The rest of that stuff is a charade perpetrated for the viewer by a management theory that reporters, not stories, are what sell the evening news. They're probably right, but I still tried not to do those things. Mostly I succeeded; not always. I rode the elephant once, but that was when I was a lot younger and dumber.

Something else. We were supposed to take our microphones and cameras and shove them into the face of the grieving mother and ask her how she felt about her son lying there dead. I couldn't stand that. In fact, I believe to put a microphone in the face of any living person on this planet who has just undergone immense personal tragedy and ask them anything at all is the act of a moral dwarf—and a clear indication of a shortage of a better idea of how to convey the sadness of the moment.

Then there is the all-consuming issue of appearance. For some years I have been on the air, I have been overweight. And for all the years I've been on TV, I've mostly dressed differently: I often wore what I felt like wearing, which was sometimes simple and workable and sometimes entirely inappropriate or just plain sloppy. My long brown hair was, more often than not, untamed to downright unruly. Okay, messy. Also, I wore glasses on the air. But wasn't I a journalist, not a model? Interesting question. When I was covering the U.S. Congress for NBC News in the mid-70s, I wore T-shirts and blazers, jeans and sneakers, or jeans and cowboy boots. This made some of the men covering the Congress unhappy. You see, they had to wear coats and ties; the congressional rule book said they did. However, since the men who wrote the book never envisioned the possibility of a woman in that job, they never bothered with a dress code for women. One of the few times sexism worked in my favor.

Though not with my employers. Seemed to me my employers mostly wanted something else—something really weird. They wanted me to look like this idea they had of "girl reporter," but then to go out and behave like a guy reporter. They wanted me to uncover what someone else wanted hidden, to be aggressive and strong-minded, to not take no for an answer, to argue and pursue and, when necessary, to be pushy in the act of getting the story. Then those same men wanted me, when I got back to the shop, to be mild-mannered, to be obedient. Obedience, like silence, is not what I do best. I soon realized one of two things would happen: they would make me crazy or I would make them crazy. I believe I made the right choice.

But I have paid a price for my choices. Talking back, loudly disagreeing, being thick-headed, arrogant, and sarcastic, looking "funny," misbehaving and/or simply ignoring my "superiors" while "going my own way" did not make me the favorite reporter or anchor of my bosses. Neither did just being different, even if I couldn't help it. Please understand. It's not that they didn't like me: some did; most merely didn't understand why I wouldn't play their game. I mean, it wasn't that hard, was it? Frankly, I often wished I could have done things differently; it would have made life so much easier for all of us. Especially for me. After all, there are women television journalists whose work I greatly admire who seem to fit in so much more gracefully than I, and without selling out either. That's why I am uncomfortable with the notion that I have been some kind of role model. I have been equally a failure.

I do not anchor a major network news program. I do not make seven million dollars a year. My name is not a household word. I have not been inducted into the Television Hall of Fame. I have never been invited to the White House socially. When I was on the cover of *TV Guide* and *People,* it was for having survived breast cancer, not because of my work. Neither the Secretary of State nor Jack Nicholson would recognize me on the street. Nor would most other people.

But I have a life, I like my work, I make pretty good money. And I am still here. It is enough. Better than enough. For me, I guess you could say the price was right. Besides, only dead fish swim with the stream all the time.

And so it goes.

—LINDA ELLERBEE

Diane
English

■ AMONG THE EARLY SIGNS OF DIANE English's genius in creating *Murphy Brown* was a dispute about the pilot episode with Gregg Mayday, then head of CBS comedy development. In a scene at Phil's Bar, Murphy is conducting a preliminary interview with a man who claims he had an affair with a female candidate for vice president. The bar is noisy until Murphy leans toward the man and asks if he really slept with her. The stage directions read, "Everything in the bar stops. Like an E. F. Hutton commercial." Mayday hated that moment. "I kept saying to Diane that it was wrong," he says, "that it didn't work in the style, the tone, the mood of the show." English insisted it was a guaranteed laugh and she was going to leave it in. She won, it worked, and Mayday now admits she was right.

Diane English was right not only that time but consistently so during *Murphy Brown*'s formative years, serving as head writer and executive producer for the show's first four years, then returning as executive consultant for the sixth and tenth seasons.

The comedy series is acclaimed as one of the greatest ever, but also one that took great strides, especially by presenting a type of woman not seen before on TV but one who represented a generation of women. No matter how different previous female leads had been from one another, one characteristic was shared by them all from Lucy (Lucille Ball) to Laura Petrie and Mary Richards (Mary Tyler Moore) to Ann Marie (Marlo Thomas): they were likable young women who faced relatively simple daily problems and, with their own twinkly spunkiness, overcame them.

A high-profile professional in her forties, Murphy Brown was flawed—she could be crotchety, deceitful, and even downright nasty (though only to the bad guys), and her problems ranged from alcoholism to unplanned pregnancy to angling to stay on top in her career. As gut-wrenching as Murphy's problems were and as hard to love as she could be,

English and Candice Bergen on the set of *Murphy Brown*

audiences took to her because she was real and complex, in a way her idealized predecessors had never been. English gave *Murphy Brown*'s fans not only plenty to laugh about, but a lot to think about as well.

The creative talent that flourished in *Murphy Brown* had been years in the making. Born May 18, 1948, in Buffalo, New York, Diane loved writing in elementary and high school. At Buffalo State College, she majored in education and minored in theater arts. Her mentor, theater director Warren Enters, taught Diane to write indirect dialogue, which she says may be the most valuable thing she ever learned: "how to make a point without going right to it, how to write two people in love when they're really in a supermarket talking about what kind of soap they're buying."

After graduation in 1970, Diane taught high school English in Buffalo for a year and then moved to New York, where she worked at WNET-TV, New York's PBS station, and wrote a column about television for *Vogue*. During that time, she met Joel Shukovsky, an advertising and design executive also working at WNET. The couple married in 1977, forming a personal and professional partnership that nourished their subsequent work.

English's first big success came in 1980 with a Writers Guild Award nomination for coauthoring the adaptation of Ursula Le Guin's *The Lathe of Heaven*. The production was Public Broadcasting's first full-length made-for-television movie.

Nine TV-movie scripts later, English, then living in California, was asked to create-write-produce the pilot for CBS's *Foley Square,* a sitcom about a professional woman. Though critically praised, *Foley Square* lasted only fourteen episodes in 1985–86. After that, the network put her in charge of another short-lived sitcom, *My Sister Sam.* She also created and produced the series *Love and War* from 1992 to 1995.

It was in 1987, however, that lightning struck when English and Shukovsky pitched to Warner Bros. a sitcom idea they'd been working on for years. All involved emphasize that Warner's and, subsequently, CBS's support for *Murphy Brown* came equally from their liking the idea and from their confidence in English.

English sharing a script with her four-legged friend

English's reputation, along with her willingness to fight for what she wanted, also became critical in the casting decision that brought everything together. English and Shukovsky had been considering a long list of female actors until someone suggested Candice Bergen, who'd done little television but had been praised for her acting in movie comedies.

A couple of long meetings with Bergen in New York convinced English and Shukovsky they'd found their Murphy. Skeptical CBS executives insisted that Bergen audition, which English considered an insult for a professional of Bergen's stature, but Bergen gamely agreed. When English, Shukovsky, and Bergen arrived at the CBS office in Hollywood, the executives kept Bergen waiting forty-five minutes before she read some lines—and she didn't do well. As the trio were being shown out of the office, English knew she had to act quickly. To Bergen and Shukovsky's surprise, she told them to wait outside, and she marched back in. When she emerged, she had convinced the executives to cast Bergen.

When the series began in the fall of 1988, its high quality was immediately recognized; shortly thereafter, its ratings matched. *Washington Post* TV critic Tom Shales repeatedly praised the series over the next ten years, calling it "golden television," "a comedy essential," and "perilously close to perfect." The series and its regulars received sixty-two Emmy nominations, eighteen Emmy Awards (including two for best comedy series), and the 1990 Golden Globe for Best

60 Minutes' Ed Bradley and Mike Wallace with English and her clowning *Murphy Brown* colleagues (Joel Shukovsky is behind Bradley)

Comedy Series. The series was twice named Best Comedy Series by the Television Critics Association and received a 1991 George Foster Peabody Award. English also received numerous individual honors, including an Emmy for writing, two Emmys for producing, two Writers Guild Awards, and the Commissioners' Award from the National Commission on Working Women for positive portrayal of women on television.

Aside from creating Murphy Brown, English may be best remembered for the story line she created in 1992 in which Murphy gets pregnant. Murphy's decision to have the baby as a single mother caught the attention of conservative politicians, then most contentiously promoting "traditional family values." When Vice President Dan Quayle attacked Murphy, the character, for as he put it "glorifying" unwed motherhood and "mocking" the importance of fathers, the series became front-page news.

In that dispute, Quayle was lambasted for attacking a fictional character as if she were a person. Perhaps that's the best evidence of how good Diane English is and why her creativity stands out in television history: sure it's fiction, but it feels so real. ■

EXT. OLD TWO-FAMILY HOME—BUFFALO, NEW YORK—1971—DAY

When I pulled the U-Haul truck into the driveway of the house I grew up in, the neighbors all came outside to watch. A moving truck. It might as well have been a spaceship. No one had ever seen one in the neighborhood before. No one ever moved out of the neighborhood—until now.

I don't know what compelled me to do it, exactly. I loved my family and my friends. But after a year teaching high school English, I knew that was not my future.

I loved to write. A beloved professor of mine at Buffalo State College—Warren Enters—knew that about me. While a voice in my head kept telling me "Teaching's a good job for a woman, and you get the summer off," my professor was telling me to move to New York and write plays.

I had written stories and poems in grade school. In high school, I wrote three-hundred-page comic parodies of novels like Hawthorne's *House of the Seven Gables.* When I got to college, the theater bug bit.

I enjoyed my year of teaching, but it wasn't my passion. Passion can be a dangerous thing. It could make you rent a U-Haul, put all your stuff into it, and drive to a city where you have no job, no contacts, and no friends. It could make you rent an apartment you can't afford and limit your diet to cereal and tuna fish. It could cause you to do without a phone for ten months because you can't afford the luxury. It could also send you to the corporate headquarters of CBS with all your little essays and skits and plays and tell the receptionist you're there to apply for a job as a comedy writer.

INT. CBS RECEPTION AREA—DAY

The receptionist looks at the Buffalo girl with a combination of amazement and pity, all the while trying to muffle the screaming laughter in her head.

RECEPTIONIST Would you like to take a typing test?

It takes a kind of blind, stupid confidence to be successful. And sometimes it takes passing a typing test.

Here's where being a woman paid off. In 1971, it wasn't yet cool to have a male secretary. Typing and filing and getting coffee were woman's work. But the secretary's desk was a great entry-level spot if you knew how to work it. I took a secretarial job at public television station WNET/13 in New York. I'm leaving a lot of not-so-interesting stuff out now, but eventually they decided to do their first television movie. They were having trouble with the script and were just ten days away from shooting. I took the script home and rewrote it. There's that stupid confidence. Then I handed the thing to the producer and asked him to read it. I don't know what I expected to happen. Certainly not this:

INT. NEW YORK HOTEL BALLROOM—WRITERS GUILD AWARDS—NIGHT

> PRESENTER And the nominees for Best Writing for a Made for Television Movie are . . .
> Roger Swaybill and Diane English, *The Lathe of Heaven,* PBS.

We didn't win. But that was the beginning. My husband, Joel Shukovsky, decided it was time for us to move to Los Angeles and start our own production company. When we told this to the keepers of conventional wisdom, they laughed in our faces.

Breaking through comes from a combination of talent, very hard work, and lucky timing. Take any of these things out of the mix, and it's the difference between *Murphy Brown* and *Foley Square. Foley Square* was my first series. It was about a thirtysometing DA who was struggling with the realities of her job and her personal life. It was critically well received, but the timing was wrong. Canceled after fourteen episodes.

I learned, however, everything about running a show on *Foley.* I was lucky enough to work with two seasoned producers who wanted nothing more than to see me blossom. They were Bernie Orenstein and Saul Turteltaub. I love them dearly, and I owe them a huge debt. Because when Murphy dropped into my head, I was ready.

In college, I struggled between wanting to be a journalist and wanting to be a playwright. It all got resolved one day on the Ventura Freeway while I was stuck in traffic, listening to Aretha Franklin belt out "Respect" on the radio. Suddenly I had this idea about a top-notch broadcast journalist— a woman who was brash and inconvenient, who was in love with her job and tried making her place in what had always been a man's world. The show would mix fiction and nonfiction, take place in Washington, and have a political edge. Oh, and she'd be a recovering alcoholic.

I hadn't seen a woman like this on television—well, ever. At least not in a comedy where the rule was that lead characters should have no real flaws. Sixty Emmy nominations and twenty Emmys later, strong, flawed women were "in." Every Monday night at 9 P.M. on CBS, millions of women were able to tap into their Inner Murphy. It was a gift and privilege to be able to create her, and she will always remain a highlight of my life.

Looking back over the last twenty years of working in television, I've formed some conventional wisdom of my own. One, follow your passion. Two, pay no attention to the man behind the curtain. He's a network executive and doesn't know any more than you do. Three, no whining, no blaming. Big success is not for wimps. It exacts a high price. You have to be prepared to work like a dog and make a lot of personal sacrifices.

And finally, thank your lucky stars for a few good men. I had quite a few in my life who nurtured me, opened some doors, and then shoved me through.

In fact, they're still doing it. Stay tuned. . . .

—DIANE ENGLISH

Pauline
Frederick

■ WHEN THE AMERICAN BROADCASTING Company hired Pauline Frederick as a radio/television correspondent in September 1946, she was thirty-eight years old, had six years of Washington newspaper experience under her belt, and had covered World War II from nineteen different countries as a part-time ABC employee. However, the network's executives had brought her aboard to lend a "woman's touch" to news stories, and Frederick found herself writing about such juicy fare as the boom in nylon stocking sales and a seminar on "How to Get a Husband."

No surprise, then, that when angry truckers staged a walkout in New York, ABC's assignment editor fretted over what to do. "I don't believe I better send Pauline to cover the truck strike," he said. "There might be violence." He opted to put a male reporter on truck duty and packed Frederick off to a meeting of foreign ministers taking place in the city. It was the best thing that ever happened to her. Frederick began doing more diplomatic reporting, an interest that never waned. She wound up covering the United Nations for seven years at ABC and another twenty-one at NBC before leaving network television in 1975 and closing out her career as a news analyst for National Public Radio.

"She was the first full-fledged woman correspondent and opened doors for women's acceptance in television and radio journalism," said Beryl Pfizer, an NBC News producer who worked with Frederick. "And besides, she was a heck of a person."

Befitting her role-model stature, Frederick is credited with a number of professional "firsts": first woman to win a George Foster Peabody Award for distinguished reporting (1954); first woman to moderate a presidential debate (1976); and first woman elected president of the United Nations Correspondents Association.

Pauline Frederick was born February 13, 1906, in the coal town of Gallitzin, Pennsylvania. She worked as a society reporter for several Harrisburg-area papers while in high school but entered American University in Washington with the intent of becoming a lawyer. When a history professor suggested she "leave the law to others," she decided to use her undergraduate and master's degrees in international law as the basis of a career in journalism.

Frederick elbowed her way into the profession in 1931 by phoning the wives of two foreign diplomats in Washington and boldly asking them for interviews. When one of the women asked where the article would be published, Frederick, who had no assignment lined up, coolly replied, "Why, that depends on the story I get."

Evidently she got a good story because an editor at the *Washington Star*

Landing in Calcutta with a press party on a special mission to the Far East

Interviewing General Ho Ying-chin, premier of China, at Kunming, 1945

bought both articles and offered her regular work. She also started contributing pieces to the North American Newspaper Alliance, which in 1938 led to a part-time job writing copy for ABC radio reporter H. P. Baukhage, who graciously advised her to "stay away from radio. It doesn't like women."

Frederick ignored those words and keep plugging away at ABC, cementing her foothold in the business when she got the opportunity to file overseas dispatches during World War II, among them reports from the Nuremberg trials. By the late 1940s, she was doing six morning radio shows and three telecasts per week for ABC. Her résumé would grow to include every major news story from the Korean to Vietnam wars, from the Cuban missile showdown to the Iran hostage crisis.

"I was just doing what I wanted to do," Frederick once told an interviewer.

But though she didn't give much thought to being a pioneer, she was not unaware of the fact that the early days of television were terra incognita.

"I got in that door because in those days the men didn't know any more about television than the women," she explained. "I went to Elizabeth Arden to learn about makeup and to Bonwit Teller to learn how to dress, and always got plenty of advice on how I should look. Management wanted me in navy colors with austere necklines; they insisted I lighten my dark brown hair; they told me to wear contact lenses instead of glasses; and they continually had my hair teased because they said I was too flat-headed."

One can gauge how novel Frederick was back then by the treatment she received from the media. *Newsweek* ran a miniprofile of her in 1948 under the headline "Spinster at the News Mike."

That same year a *New York Times* article described her as "a tall, lissome brunette of mellifluous voice, and photogenic figure," adding that "underneath her serenity, however, there is a fine percolating of ideas."

One idea Frederick continually supported was that the United Nations is a vital, often underutilized, diplomatic tool. There likely wouldn't have been a Bay of Pigs fiasco, she said, if President Kennedy had "believed in the UN." Similarly, she admitted after the Vietnam War was over that "there were many times when I couldn't believe it was my country violating every principle of the UN charter."

Frederick belonged to the old school of concise, no-frills reportage, so it figures that she married another hard-news-oriented journalist: Charles Robbins, managing editor of the *Wall Street Journal.* Five years after they married in 1969, she left NBC, having reached the mandatory retirement age of sixty-five. She then returned to her radio roots, courtesy of her affiliation with National Public Radio. In 1990, at eighty-four, she suffered a fatal heart attack.

Throughout her career, Pauline Frederick refused to accept the kind of special treatment that most, especially early in her career, felt befitted women. She would never let a male colleague carry her luggage, for instance. And in 1948, when the Army invited the military press corps to accompany a squadron of B-29 planes on a rugged mission to Uruguay, 135 reporters showed up, but Frederick was the only female. "If the men can stand it, so can I," she told her bosses at NBC.

It turns out that about the only thing she couldn't do as well as a man was retire. "You know," she remarked on one of her final days at NBC, "if a man is old, he's called interesting. When a woman is old and shows wrinkles, it's terrible. She's finished. It's a double standard." In the face of the double standards Frederick faced most of her career, it's testimony to her talent and determination that she triumphed nevertheless. ■

In the beginning, I worked very hard to be accepted in the largely male world of broadcast news. I tried every way I could to convince the powers that be that I was able to broadcast news. While writing for the North American Newspaper Alliance, I was doing interviews with diplomats in Washington, D.C. An NBC scout asked me to do an audition to see if I could do this same kind of thing on the air. I did these interviews, and while they weren't news programs as such, this did give me a little bit of experience.

I decided the next step was to broadcast news and this was very difficult because it was unheard of for a woman to want to enter this man's world. I remember asking a radio executive [not at NBC] what I could do to really get an opportunity to broadcast news. I didn't want to go out and cover fashion shows as they were having me do. He was sympathetic but couldn't grant the request because, he said, "When you are broadcasting something as serious as news about the United Nations, listeners are going to tune out." When I asked why, he replied, "Because a woman's voice does not carry authority." I always follow up this anecdote with the comment that I am truly sorry I didn't have courage enough in those days to tell him that I knew his wife's voice carried plenty of authority in his house.

But I guess I was just stubborn and determined. . . . I suddenly realized that I was being discriminated against just because I wore skirts. So, consequently, this made me a little angry and made me determined that, come what may, I was going to break that barrier.

I was later told that there were directives from higher up not to use me on the air unless I got exclusive stories. So from that time on, I really worked very, very hard to try to get exclusive stories from the United Nations . . . and that way have a chance to get on the air more often. There was discrimination against women certainly and it was very difficult for the male world to accept a woman doing hard news. Also, I think a serious psychological study of this whole problem would indicate that women particularly like to hear a voice representing authority on the air, which is the male voice, the father, the husband, the lover. They prefer that to listening to the female voice on the air. While today women may have it a little easier in that they are considered for these positions, I still feel that women do not have full equality in this profession. It's still more difficult for a woman to get a position in broadcasting and to advance than it is for a man.

Of course, at the very beginning I was somewhat of a curiosity because I was the only woman broadcasting news. But as I tried to be professional in what I was doing, I found I was being treated as a professional which I think is terribly important. I have always rejected the idea that there was women's news and men's news because it seemed to me that the important thing was the qualifications of a person to cover the news.

My expertise happens to be the United Nations. I try to grasp as well as possible complicated and large issues and then bring them to the public in a matter of a few minutes. Time is so important on the air simply because there is so little time available. It's necessary to get the heart of the story without using too many words. I remember one time when I first began in this field and I was asked to summarize all the activities of the United Nations for a week in just two minutes. I slaved over that and then one day I took out my stop watch and read the Gettysburg Address. It ran about one minute and 27 seconds. So, while I'm not saying I could be Lincoln, I do believe that if you work at it hard enough it's possible to say something briefly. I believe that it is my responsibility to say things as simply and directly as possible so the public is informed.

There have been so many satisfying stories that I have covered because I have been here through all the crises. I've been at the United Nations since the beginning so each one to me was the greatest opportunity, starting with the Korean War—when I was on the air day and night during the six weeks when there were crisis negotiations at the United Nations—then the Middle East wars, the Cuban missile crisis, Suez, Hungary, the Chinese coming into the United Nations. At the time they each seemed to be the most satisfying [story] I would ever cover, but then another crisis would come up and I proved myself wrong.

Since I was a little kid, I was always interested in international relations, and I chose the United Nations [beat] because this was the center of international activity. This seemed to be the one place toward which I gravitated all the time.

—PAULINE FREDERICK

Dorothy
Fuldheim

■ BACK IN 1970, WHEN AMERICA WAS STILL stuck in Vietnam, wise-guy antiwar activist Jerry Rubin came to Cleveland hawking his book, *Do It!* Like Bob Hope, the Duke of Windsor, and innumerable other celebrities in motion, Rubin made a stop at WEWS-TV to be interviewed by Dorothy Fuldheim, grande dame of the local press corps.

At five-foot-two, Fuldheim had a bird's nest of coiffed red hair and a weakness for big rings, shiny bracelets, and frilly dresses, which may be why Rubin— an incorrigible shock-the-establishment prankster—suddenly began brandishing a photo of a naked woman on the air.

That did it for *Do It!*

"Out!" bellowed Fuldheim, slamming down her copy of Rubin's book and banishing him from the set midsentence. "I threw Jerry Rubin off my program because his manners were bad and his arrogant attitude offensive," Fuldheim later explained. Cocky NFL quarterback Joe Namath made an even quicker exit: Fuldheim gave him the heave-ho before he sat down in the interview chair.

Nobody was allowed to trample upon Dorothy Fuldheim's professional turf or sense of propriety. A colleague once described her as a "steel fist in a velvet glove." That strength of character served her well in emerging as a pioneer

in radio and in compiling one of the most remarkable longevity streaks in broadcast history. Already known nationally for her public speaking, Fuldheim was a fixture on WEWS for thirty-seven years, from the day the station went on the air in December 1947 until July 27, 1984, when she suffered a debilitating stroke shortly after finishing a satellite interview with then-President Ronald Reagan.

During the in-between years Fuldheim did everything from coanchoring the evening news to cohosting a pioneer afternoon talk show; from filing overseas dispatches to contributing a long-running series of talking-head commentaries. The "Queen of the News" crossed paths with every president from Truman to Reagan,

In front of the camera for WEWS-TV

not to mention Albert Einstein, Jane
Fonda, Martin Luther King, and hundreds more luminaries. She received an
Overseas Press Club Award in 1955 for
landing exclusive interviews with several
"brainwashed" Americans just released
from prison in Communist China, was
named Woman of the Year by the Radio
and Television Broadcasters Association,

and eventually rose to guest-star status
herself, making the rounds of *The Tonight
Show, Donahue,* and *Nightline.* Her greatest accomplishment, however, was trailblazing in the trenches of local television,
helping to pry open the doors of equal
opportunity. As Barbara Walters has
noted, "Dorothy Fuldheim was probably
the first woman to be taken seriously
doing the news." What makes that feat all
the more remarkable is that she got her
start in television at the age of fifty-four.

Fuldheim's life bridged the print and
electronic media cultures. She was born in
1903 in Passaic, New Jersey, to an immi-
grant couple so poor that when one of their
infant sons died he had to be buried in an
orange crate. The family soon relocated to
Milwaukee, where her father, Herman
Snell, worked menial jobs. His method of
relaxation was to sit in on county courthouse proceedings, and he often took
young Dorothy along. "The power of

Dorothy Fuldheim welcoming Dr. Martin Luther King, Jr., to her show, 1964

DOROTHY FULDHEIM

Fuldheim interviewing Helen Keller

words," Herman would tell his daughter, "is greater than guns or cannon."

Dorothy became such a voracious reader that her brother and sister nicknamed her "Dictionary-swallower." She earned an English degree from Milwaukee Normal College (now the University of Wisconsin—Milwaukee) at age nineteen and briefly taught school before joining a local acting troupe. That, in turn, became a stepping-stone to a successful stint on the public lecture circuit. Steeped in the liberal politics of Depression-era Milwaukee, Fuldheim sought support for the post–World War I peace movement and later directed her arsenal of words at the looming Nazi threat in Europe. She estimated that she delivered some four thousand lectures, frequently before audiences of several thousand.

In 1918, Dorothy married lawyer Milton Fuldheim. They had a daughter, "Dorothy Junior," and eventually settled in Milton's hometown of Cleveland. Dorothy Fuldheim's renown as a public speaker grew to the point where, in 1943, she was offered a job as a commentator on WJW radio, where she also did weekly commentaries on ABC Radio Network. Four years later she began her long run at WEWS-TV. The station manager, she recalled, was "the only man in the country willing to give a woman the chance to anchor a news show."

Starting with her first no-frills, fifteen-minute newscast, Fuldheim exuded confidence and flair. She attributed her success partly to intelligence ("If there is one thing that really irks me, it's to be told, 'You think like a man.' I doubt if one's brain were removed from the body whether it could be identified as male or female.") and in part to unbridled passion. "It's ridiculous to hear an anchorman report a killing with exactly the same expression as if he were reporting a recipe to make applesauce," Fuldheim once wrote. "A broadcaster is a human being and should cease acting like a feelingless printing press pouring out the news." When the British actor Charles Laughton went one-on-one with Fuldheim, they lapsed into a few impromptu scenes from *Romeo and Juliet*. "She never required notes and conducted interviews from her enormous intellect," said Ohio Congressman Louis Stokes.

Fuldheim was still putting in nine-hour days at WEWS in her nineties. By then she had been widowed, remarried to businessman William Ulmer, and widowed again. It was by most accounts a melancholy private life. Her tombstone was inscribed with a quote from Ecclesiastes: "With much wisdom, there is much sorrow."

Dorothy Fuldheim would not have had it any other way, however. She always said, "Life will have to retire me." And it did. She fell ill on the job in 1984 and died four years later. But Fuldheim made no apologies for hanging on in the news business until age ninety-one. She was, after all, still armed and dangerous with the power of words.

"It gets my goat when people say it's remarkable how bright I am at my age," she once groused. "I was bright forty years ago. And the more I use my brain, the sharper it gets." ∎

Sometimes I am handed a surprise. The other day I got into a cab driven by a young woman. As I got out she said, "Say, Babe, I'm real proud of you."

I was a little startled and said, "Why?"

"You show those men that a woman can be just as smart as a man. You show them, Babe; we're rootin' for you. I told my old man, 'There's a woman for you.' So he says, 'Why ain't you as smart as she is?' So I says, 'Why ain't you President Johnson?' But I sure am proud of you, Babe."

Why she referred to me as "Babe" I'll never know, but I loved it. Hers was a spontaneous expression of admiration, and it meant a great deal to me.

Another day I was downtown shopping; across the way some window cleaners were on a scaffold washing the windows on the eighth floor. I heard, "Hi, Dorothy," and as I looked up, the window washers waved.

They felt quite free to express their opinion about my broadcast. "I heard you last night and you were all wet," one shouted.

Many letters I receive are devastating. One read, "Dear Miss Fuldheim, you have such lovely hands and eyes." I always know that when a letter starts out with such encomiums, something disagreeable is coming. This letter ended with "but I don't like your figure." I wrote back, "Dear Madame, neither do I." That ended our correspondence.

Another wrote me that she was so devoted to my program that when Lent came she could think of nothing else to sacrifice that would mean more to her than giving up viewing my show during Lent. I tried to hide that from my sponsors for fear that they might drop me during the long Lenten period.

I do not harass any guests—the purpose of their appearance is to give them a chance to present their point of view, and the questions must be spearheaded with that in mind. I don't set out to embarrass them. If the opinions they entertain are illogical or inaccurate, the viewer makes his own judgment. A great deal of research and background reading is necessary in order to be prepared to meet the various specialists in their own fields. When I said to the great astronomer, the late Harlow Shapley, "The expanding universe taxes my credulity," he answered, "The whole universe taxes mine; it is so vast and magnificently ordered."

When I interviewed Arnold Toynbee I asked him which period of all history he would have chosen to live in if the choice had been his. After a moment's reflection he said, "The Victorian Period, provided I had money and belonged to the upper classes." And I would have liked to have added another condition, to be a male. For in that period the female had to sit around and wait until some man showed an interest in her. Not to be married was a reflection on one's charm and sex appeal. No matter what a brute one's husband turned out to be, it was considered better than remaining a maiden aunt. A woman's greatest asset was her virginity. No one demanded chastity from the male; to the contrary, the more of a rake he was, the more desirable he was considered. The long and painful break from that period has been made, and as in all such social revolutions it takes society some time to recover its balance.

I am not the only person to affirm that the most remarkable human being I have ever met was Helen Keller. She is more awe-inspiring than any physicist's achievement, whether it was in releasing the power of the atom or in sending pictures from Mars. The world knows the story of how Miss Anne Sullivan, by touching her hand to water, spelled the word "water" in Helen Keller's hand so that she began to associate the feel of water with the figure Miss Sullivan traced. That's all she had, the sense of touch and of warmth and cold. How did she learn the concept of abstract ideas, such as love, hate, war, anxiety? Crossing interstellar space is no greater achievement than to be able to articulate words never having heard the sound of a voice, only feeling the lips of her teacher as they changed with different syllables. I was humbled in her presence. After talking with Miss Keller, I knew that nothing is impossible, that whatever one dreams validates its possibility.

So many of the people I have encountered are gone. They fall from the tree of life like leaves from a great oak in the autumn of the year. If I could make a chain of memory and carry it with me always, I would never be lonely. They walked, these hundreds of individuals whom I have talked with, across the stage of life—some with great lines, some with sad lines, but they were all gallant, for it takes gallantry to live. We all climb uphill in our journey and there are few resting-places. We are strangers to each other, really, for there is a place beyond which no one else can be part of our soul. We are like balloons floating in the air and only occasionally touching each other at the periphery.

Now, as I enter the sunset years, the radiance and the glow of spring are gone, but the days are richer because I am so cognizant of their fleeting quality. I have drawn a great many days from my supply of life, and I have learned that everyone's life is an adventure, whether noble, mean, pure, sinful, wise, or foolish. But I have taken the passion, the sweetness, the torment, the knowledge, the divination of great writers and poets, and I might add, "My cup runneth over," for if I have been flayed by life, I have also lived it; and in the noble words of John Cowper Powys in *The Meaning of Culture,* I can look up at the moon and cry out to fate, "If you can impose it, I will have the strength to endure it."

— D O R O T H Y   F U L D H E I M

Phyllis
George

■ THE FIRST LOOK TV VIEWERS GOT OF Phyllis George was in September 1970, when Bert Parks crooned the famous song and she paraded down the Atlantic City runway as the newly crowned Miss America. Suddenly, the crown slipped off her head; rhinestones scattered everywhere. And America also got to see the grace under pressure that became George's trademark, for she just picked up the crown and kept walking, smiling, and waving; her poise and bubbly charm never wavered.

Who seeing her then could have imagined that her most notable professional accomplishment would be in the rough-and-tumble, predominantly male arena of pro sports? As the first woman coanchor of a national pregame show and the first national woman sportscaster in a continuing role, George was a pioneer in broadcasting history and an influence on the way sports is covered. In the words of Fox Sports President Ed Goren, "If not for Phyllis, there might not be women sportscasters."

As a native of sports-loving Texas, George grew up an ardent fan. Born June 25, 1949, in small-town Denton, the oldest child of Bob George, a distributor for Gulf Oil, and his wife, Louise, Phyllis was popular in school and active in church and was considered a piano prodigy at

twelve. At home, she walked around with books on her head to improve her posture and dreamed of being Miss America.

In 1972, after she had achieved that goal and traveled the country for a year representing the pageant, George discovered she liked both the spotlight and taking on new challenges. She decided not to return to Texas, where she'd attended North Texas State and Texas Christian universities. Instead, she moved to New York and took acting, voice, and speech lessons, supporting herself with TV commercials and stints as the first woman cohost of *Candid Camera*. For a number of years, she also cohosted the annual Miss America pageant with Bert Parks, occasionally serving as a featured performer as well and once as a celebrity judge—all the time hoping to use the visibility she'd gained as Miss America as a springboard for the rest of her career.

Soon she got her chance. Bob Wussler, then the new vice president of CBS Sports, was shaking up the network's sports coverage, including broadening the audience base by adding more women. After meeting George—whom, ironically, he didn't know had been Miss America— Wussler made up his mind. "In my gut, I

Phyllis George with her *NFL Today* colleagues Brent Musberger and Irv Cross

thought Phyllis was pretty special," he says. "I thought there was a role for her, as somebody who could talk to guys and who knew something about sports."

George started in 1974 doing interviews aired during sports programs. Within a year, Wussler had decided to create a new Sunday football pregame show and named broadcaster Brent Musberger, former player Irv Cross, and George as coanchors. The combination worked beyond anyone's dreams. *USA Today*'s Rudy Martzke, an influential observer of sportscasting, calls the stars of the Emmy Award–winning *NFL Today* "perhaps the most popular sports studio team in history."

In addition to coanchoring, George made her mark with taped interviews, talking with individuals in sports ranging from football to tennis to horse racing and all the great athletes, from Joe Namath to Muhammad Ali, Terry Bradshaw to Chris Evert.

From the beginning, George knew she wanted to be known as more than "the woman" doing sports interviews; she wanted to create something distinctive and memorable. Her answer was to encourage athletes to open up and talk about themselves in personal as well as professional ways, as individuals with real-life concerns and ambitions. Human-interest stories about players are common now. But when George did them in the mid-1970s, they were new—though they came naturally for her and seemed to spring easily from the simple fact that interviewees were comfortable with her.

Sometimes what they said was star-

tling. In her famous interview with Dallas Cowboys quarterback Roger Staubach, the two first discussed the team and the year he was having, but then she asked, "Well, Roger, what about your straight, square image? Do you find that works for you or is it a burden for you?" Staubach looked hard at her and said, "Phyllis, let me say something. Just because I drive a station wagon and go to church on Sunday and have kids and a dog and am happily married, people think certain things about me. But let me tell you, I like sex just as much as Joe Namath. The only difference is, I like it with one woman—my wife." Staubach's uncharacteristic boldness in comparing himself with the notorious playboy Namath made for big news when the interview ran the next Sunday.

As popular as George's interviews came to be, when she first went on the air, not everyone was thrilled. She received both complimentary and critical mail, and she encountered both curiosity and skepticism from a few players and coaches. Even some old-timer sportscasters, she recalls, were reluctant to share information because they feared it would help her get more airtime. But she didn't take any of those negative reactions personally, and there's no question that her appearances increased female viewership.

Midway during her decade with the show, George married John Y. Brown, who shortly afterward—aided by his wife's campaigning—was elected governor of Kentucky. George then became another pioneer as the state's First Lady with her own career. For years, she balanced doing

the show in New York with carrying out her First Lady duties, including supervising the restoration of the governor's mansion, working with family crisis centers for abused women and children, and promoting Kentucky crafts. But when her second child, Pamela, was born (joining son Lincoln), she decided to give up sportscasting. She and Brown later divorced.

Since leaving CBS Sports in 1986, George has tackled a variety of new enterprises. In 1988, she anticipated the market for marinated chicken breasts and created her own company, "Chicken by George," which she later sold to Hormel. Her charitable activities include the Phyllis George Scholarship for outstanding students in radio and television at the University of North Texas and twenty years working with Save the Children, for which she received the group's 1994 Distinguished Service Award.

George has also continued to appear before the camera, including a short-lived stint as cohost of CBS's *Morning News* in the mid-1980s. From 1996 to 1999, she also hosted celebrity interview programs on cable network TNN. In addition, she has used one of the late-twentieth-century's biggest broadcasting phenomena to promote a cause long close to her heart: in 1992, she convinced QVC to let her sell quilts and other crafts on the air. *American Crafts with Phyllis George* continues to build appreciation for handmade crafts (a subject on which she has written three books) and has generated nearly $20 million in sales for mostly rural craftspeople around the country.

To her credit, George has never run from the Miss America image that launched her career. But also to her credit, she's proven that she's much more than just a pretty face. ■

In Texas, where I grew up, you live, breathe, and die for sports—football especially. I was a huge fan and had been a cheerleader in high school, but obviously I'd never played the game, and I wasn't an expert and didn't pretend to be. Still, in 1974, I found myself a pioneer woman sportscaster, interviewing athletes on national television in this male-dominated arena where there had been virtually no women before.

A lot of very nice people were saying to me, "Phyllis, you'll *never* be able to do that! Are you crazy?" I'd appeared on television as Miss America and as cohost of *Candid Camera*, and I wanted to do more broadcasting—though I never dreamed it would be in sports! Once I had that opportunity, I knew I better sure as hell make it work. I had to prove to myself that I could do it; equally, I had to prove it to the fans and the powers that be because, if I failed, it might be a long time before a woman would be given the chance again. I learned then never to say never.

It started when I was invited to a meeting with Bob Wussler, then vice president of CBS Sports. Wussler didn't even know I'd been Miss America, but we were represented by the same agency and someone thought we should meet. Well, something clicked, and for reasons I'll never understand, he decided to make this incredibly gutsy move of hiring me. It was just for a thirteen-week option, but I needed a job to pay the rent, and I was praying to God I'd get my option picked up after the trial period.

They told me my first interview would be with Dave Cowens, who played for the Boston Celtics, and it would run at halftime of the NBA game.

When I went to meet him after a practice, Cowens didn't even acknowledge that I existed. His attitude was, like, "What is this woman doing here? They sent a *woman*?" I had to say to myself, "You can't let him get to you, you've just got to do your job and hang in there."

I'd say, "Dave," and he'd grunt at me. And I'd say, "Dave," again, and he'd say, "Yeah."

Then the producer said, "Why don't you ride with Dave in his jeep to his home?" We were going to do the interview at his log cabin on the outskirts of Boston. Then, it started to shift a little so that part of his reaction was still what is this woman doing here and part was, well, she's a woman and there was a little bit of interest because it was so different.

When we got there, we sat in rocking chairs on his front porch, he had a beer, and, amazingly, by the end of that interview we had connected. He became incredibly willing to talk about his life, his feelings, and what he wanted to do when his playing time was over. It became less of a traditional sports interview, which usually resulted in a string of pat answers, and more of a conversation in which he really opened up.

Right then I started to carve out my niche. No one had told me what to do or say, and I had no role models or precedents to follow. I knew the male sportscasters asked athletes about Xs and Os and game strategies, and I did that too. But what I could also do that was distinctive was to focus on the human interest: I could ask about things that interested me as a fan about the personal side of these superstar athletes. I'm going to be spokesperson for the viewers, I decided, and ask things I think they'd like the answers to. People started saying I was the Barbara Walters of sports. Former player Irv Cross, who became my colleague, always claimed, "Phyllis can ask questions we can't."

After that interview with Cowens, we went back, edited the piece, and ran it at halftime. The switchboard lit up like a Christmas tree: "Who was that woman?" "I've never heard Dave Cowens talk like that; it was amazing." All positive. After that, my option was picked up.

Then Bob Wussler came up with an ingenious idea. We were at an affiliate meeting, and Bob was asked what he had planned for CBS Sports. "Well, first of all," he said, "I'd like to announce that I'm putting together a show called *The NFL Today* with Brent Musberger, Irv Cross, and Phyllis George." That was the first I've heard of it; I was under contract, so he could assign me wherever he wanted. Wussler put the three of us together on Sundays for a half-hour show of news and analysis, interviews, and predictions. We were like the Mod Squad of CBS Sports! With that, I became the first woman coanchor on a national pregame show.

From day one, it worked—who knows why. Chemistry is chemistry. You could have put me with two other guys and it wouldn't have worked, but with Brent and Irv it did. We could feel it. Also, we had nothing to measure it against because it had never been done before.

Wussler, to his credit, believed in the show and stuck with us. In the beginning, some coaches, fans, and players were saying, "What is this woman doing? That'll *never* work." (There was that word "never" again.) But I remained positive and persevered: kept showing up, doing my home-work, working hard, trying out new approaches with my wonderful on-the-road producer, Louis Schmidt of NFL Films—and they finally accepted me.

After a while, *The NFL Today* became a mainstay on Sunday. There were stories about people going to early church services so they could be back home in time for the show. With six minutes of commercials, the show came out to only twenty-four minutes, but it made us household names. I knew we had struck a chord with the American public, but I didn't realize how popular we'd been until I was living in Kentucky later on with my family and people would come up and say, "Boy, do you know how great you guys were? Will you ever go back?" People still ask that question, to this very day. That's how I know we created something really special.

For whatever reason I was selected, I feel incredibly honored to have been a pioneer in sports broadcasting. I look around at women sports reporters today, and they're good, they're *really* good. I'm so very proud of them, and I wish there were more.

When I was growing up in Denton, Texas, I dreamed of being Miss America. Now little girls grow up dreaming of being CEOs and senators and, happily, sportscasters. It's a privilege to be part of that history.

—PHYLLIS GEORGE

Catherine
Liggins Hughes

■ CATHY HUGHES'S LOVE OF RADIO BEGAN like that of most kids in the 1950s: her parents bought her a transistor radio when she was nine, and at night she hid it under her pillow and listened to everything from the Everly Brothers to the Platters.

Today, in an industry dominated by megacompanies owned by white males, this African-American female has parlayed her talent, drive, and business acumen into success as a radio baron—no matter how you measure it.

Radio One, her $2 billion enterprise, is the nation's largest black-owned radio company and among the top twenty revenue producers overall, according to Inside Radio, an industry monitoring group. Boasting two million daily listen-ers, the company owns fifty stations from coast to coast, including WKYS-FM in Washington and WERQ-FM in Baltimore, which have separately and together been the number one stations in each city. Never before in the history of radio has a black-owned company dominated two major markets at the same time; never before has a woman-owned radio station been number one in any major market.

In May 1999, Hughes, now company chair, and her son, Alfred Liggins III, president and CEO, took Radio One public, generating $172 million for further growth—the most money ever raised from an IPO by any African-American-led company. The move made Hughes the first black woman to head a publicly traded company.

Radio Ink magazine recognized Hughes as one of the most influential women in radio in both 1999 and 2000, and *Essence* magazine named her one of the top ten black female entrepreneurs. Radio One was named Business of the Year by *Black Enterprise* magazine in May 2000.

Yet nothing is more important to Hughes than serving as "The Voice of Black America," as Radio One is often called, and spreading her messages of empowerment and community activism. She knows how to use "the mouthpiece of the microphone," says Jesse Jackson.

"She has raised the right issues and has gotten the right results."

Born April 22, 1947, Hughes grew up in Omaha, Nebraska, with her accountant father and musician mother, and was the first black student in an elite Catholic girls' school there. At the age of sixteen, she became pregnant, but her despair turned to love with the birth of her son, who became "my motivation and my inspiration," she says. As a struggling single mother (following a two-year marriage to her son's father), she finished high school, took college courses in business, and monitored EEO and affirmative action programs on a Ford Foundation project.

Then, in 1971, she moved to Washington, D.C., to accept a job at Howard University's new school of communications, working with the dean, famed commentator Tony Brown. There,

Brown says, it became "a story of Cathy outworking most people and outthinking most people." After a couple of years, Hughes had so impressed Brown that he assigned her to WHUR-FM, Howard's radio station.

In radio, Hughes found her niche. Her sales and marketing skills turned the station into the university's first profit center in its hundred-year history, increasing the station's revenue from $250,000 to $3 million in her first year. By 1975, she had been put in charge of the station, becoming the nation's capital's first female general manager of a broadcast facility, perhaps the industry's first female general manager.

At WHUR, Hughes also made a major contribution to radio programming when she created the format known as "Quiet Storm," in which silken-voiced

Hughes hosting her own show in the early days at WOL-AM

Hughes in the studio today

deejays play hour after hour of love songs. This format is now the most-listened-to nighttime radio format in the country, presently heard in more than four hundred markets.

Showing the mix of creativity and business savvy that would mark her career, Hughes knew she had a winner with "Quiet Storm" and wanted to license the format. When the university refused, failing to see its commercial viability, Hughes vowed that next time she would be the one making the ultimate decisions.

Soon she created that opportunity. After a brief period running a local commercial station, Hughes learned that WOL-AM was up for sale. The offer she assembled with her then-husband included their own savings as well as loans from several sources, including a group of black D.C. investors. In 1980, she became the owner.

What Hughes wanted was an opportunity, but what she got was trouble. The building housing the station was a former drug den in a tough D.C. neighborhood; the previous staff had stolen or destroyed everything valuable; her marriage collapsed; and she lost her house and car. But Hughes refused to give up. She met with neighborhood toughs to keep the peace; brought in her own records to play on air; moved herself and her son into the station; and hosted her own talk show since she had no money to hire anyone else.

While Hughes believed the talk radio format would give voice to D.C.'s black community, advertisers were initially reluctant. Soon she built a listener following so strong that people wrote "I listen to WOL" on their checks and dollar bills. Advertisers paid attention, and in 1986 the station turned its first profit; the next year Hughes bought her first FM station.

The mid- to late 1990s were a particularly busy expansion period for Radio One. Federal caps on radio ownership had been lifted, enabling large companies and conglomerates to expand more easily, often by purchasing small stations, including black-owned ones, that could no longer compete. But Radio One was strong enough to buy many that were failing, thus keeping stations in African-American hands.

Hughes is known for using her clout to help community enterprises, just as she uses the airwaves to advance political and social issues. Her voice has urged listeners to help D.C. residents in need, criticized the *Washington Post* for placing a black

criminal on the first cover of its Sunday magazine, denounced utility companies for their shutoff practices, and supported favorite politicians. Her mission also involves providing opportunities for African-American and women broadcasters. Of Radio One's 680 employees, about 500 are black, and she prides herself on having several women general station managers.

While Hughes has turned over day-to-day management to her son, she remains involved in new-station development and community and philanthropic efforts. "My job does not tire me out; it energizes me," she says. "Maybe I'm on the same frequency as my stations. I just love radio." ■

The bell signaling Wall Street's daily opening of the stock market shot through my ears like a cannon. My eyes became blurry with tears, I could not breathe, and I grew paler with each second it took to find the ladies' room. The last time I had felt overwhelmed by joy to this extent, I had been seventeen and on the brink of becoming the mother of the young man who was engineering the morning's activity. A member of our underwriter's team rushed in to make certain I was okay, exclaiming, "Wow! Miss Hughes! You are the first black woman to ever take her company public. I'm so proud because I know it had to be real hard." Guess I've always believed that if you conquered "real hard" your reward would be "real good"!

In 1978, after major successes at Howard University's radio station as the first female general manager in Washington, D.C., media history, as well as taking another station to the number one position in ratings, building a facility from the ground up, and getting it on the air after twelve years of being dark, I found myself unemployed! I realized I could no longer trust my career to anyone other than myself; I had to own my own station.

WOL-AM, a 1,000-watter in D.C., was on the block, but I was around $1.5 million short of being able to make an offer. I gave up 5 percent of my company to secure an introduction to potential lenders and form my "business plan." I tried to convince thirty-two different male bankers that my company was a "sound investment and a good credit risk." They all said "no," asking questions such as "Are you planning to have any more children?" or "Is your husband going to be the president?" I pitched my thirty-third presentation to a new woman loan officer at Chemical Bank. I became the first loan in her portfolio. I'd known the law of averages would eventually come into play, but, more important, I learned the value of women having their own network.

At midnight on October 3, 1980, I took possession of my new station and thought I had entered the wrong building. The last DJ to leave said "Good-bye," instead of "Good night." In addition, furniture and phones were missing, there were no pens or pencils, and the last record was running out. Then a reality smacked us across the head like a gale wind in full rage: there were no records! I had just poured two years of my life and $1.5 million into what turned out to be an opportunity, not a business. Undaunted and fueled by the excitement of the moment, I went home, retrieved every album we owned, and played hits from our home collection all night.

In spite of this, I believed the worst was over until I was proven wrong. In the early 1980s, interest rates soared to a record high and I was paying 2 1/2 points over prime. My marriage fell apart, and I had to move out of my house. I lived in the radio station for a year and a half, cooking on a hot plate and taking "bird baths" in the station's public ladies' room. On the most dismal days, I would reflect on how minor my challenges were in comparison to my ancestors'. Through prayer and perseverance, they had prevailed and progressed, and if I used their strategy, I believed I would do the same.

New business owners are told that the first three to five years are the toughest survival period. By the time my company's debt storm had turned into an avalanche, I was down from forty-eight employees to eighteen. Investors and lenders were getting nervous and insisted that I drop my news-talk format and return to a music format, due to costs. In good conscience, I could not own a station that provided only entertainment to its listening family. The Washington, D.C., market needed and wanted "news and talk" from a black perspective.

I followed the example of our ancestors and substituted my own human resources for the lack of financial resources. I began hosting the daily four-hour morning news and talk format and, over the next two years, built a revenue base during those four hours that accounted for nearly 80 percent of the station's total revenue. It took five years of slowly adding news and talk before we were able to return to twenty-four hours of talk/news from an African-American perspective.

By our seventh year we were able to purchase our first FM station in Washington, D.C., as a companion to WOL-AM. I now owned a "combo" in the nation's capital. After a long and trying decade, we expanded into the Baltimore market with an AM/FM combo. Shortly thereafter, we bought our second AM/FM combo in Baltimore. With six radio stations within a forty-mile radius of one another, we became a real competitor, and we were finally viewed by lending institutions as a viable enterprise, worthy of increased credit.

Radio One, Inc., now owns fifty radio stations and a television station in the top fourteen media markets in the country. We are a publicly traded company with a market cap of nearly $2 billion. In August 2000, we closed a $1.3 billion acquisition of additional broadcast properties—the largest business transaction ever completed by African-Americans in the history of the United States.

Thirty-five years passed between the joy I experienced with the birth of my son and my first morning of public trading on Wall Street. Evaluating the last twenty-five years of my career, I thank God that the "real hard" produced a "real good" company that nurtures the very best minorities and women in broadcasting. I am proud of the growing number of media superstars who got their start with my company and am blessed that I was chosen to captain this ship on its historic journey. I now understand what my grandfather meant when he said, "Rough waters make for high sailing!"

—CATHY LIGGINS HUGHES

Anne
Ashenhurst
Hummert

■ ANNE HUMMERT IS CONSIDERED THE founding mother of mass-market radio soap opera. Though she didn't write the first radio soap opera, she created—with her husband, Frank, an advertising executive—the first successful dramatic radio serial, *Just Plain Bill*. Hummert's creative genius was to invent realistic characters to whom radio listeners would respond as "just plain folks," but she also had the business acumen to negotiate radio sponsors. Her copywriting and marketing abilities, coupled with her storytelling skills, propelled her to the top of her profession. In the 1930s and '40s, Hummert mapped out plots and characters for dozens of serial dramas and supervised a stable of scriptwriters. At the peak of her career, she was one of the highest-paid women in the country.

Hummert started out her career as Anne Schumacher, working as a stringer for the Baltimore *Sun*. She was born on January 19, 1905, in Baltimore to Frederick and Anne Lance Schumacher. Lacking family support for education, she worked her way through nearby Goucher College, earning the $200 annual tuition as the college's correspondent to the *Sun*.

Despite her workload writing for the paper, primarily on the obituary desk, while studying as a history major, Anne was a member of Phi Beta Kappa and graduated magna cum laude in 1925. By 1926, she was writing for the *International Herald Tribune* in Paris. Soon she married a fellow reporter, John Ashenhurst, but shortly thereafter she left him to move to Chicago with her baby son.

Anne Ashenhurst embarked on her broadcasting career as an advertising copywriter creating advertisements and jingles. In 1929, she joined Blackett, Sample, Hummert, Inc. in Chicago as an editorial and copywriting assistant to Edward Frank Hummert, a partner in the firm. By January 21, 1933, she had been named a vice president and partner herself. There, Anne also met Frank Hummert, who became her second husband.

It was a logical move from writing

advertising slogans and jingles to creating serials linked to specific products. Hard on the heels of Irna Phillips's pioneering 1930 soap opera drama, *Painted Lives,* Anne and Frank began creating their own radio soap operas. In 1932, their serial *Just Plain Bill* started as an evening radio drama on WGN in Chicago, and in 1933 it moved to daytime radio. *Just Plain Bill* became the model for many other soap operas, so-called because detergent companies were the main sponsors. The character Bill was a barber who had married above his economic class, so he provided a perfect voice to express a variety of social perspectives. As a result, both Depression-burdened poor and middle-class listeners and those who were better off could identify with him.

The Hummert team was particularly adept at creating radio serials coupled with catchy advertising jingles that they sold to manufacturers. WGN, the radio subsidiary of the *Chicago Tribune,* was a groundbreaker in the production of these serial narratives, airing programming carefully orchestrated by the Hummerts to support sponsors' products. Anne Hummert's soap operas, such as *Just Plain Bill, Helen Trent, Backstage Wife, Stella Dallas, Young Widder Brown,* and *Lorenzo Jones,* were all attached to advertising for household products. Listeners would stay glued to the radio set in anticipation of the evolving drama and in the process became a captive audience for the commercials as well. The characters' identities soon became synonymous with advertisers' brands, such as cleaning products, toiletries, and foods.

Backstage Wife, for example, was sponsored by Dr. Lyon's Toothpowder. It ran weekdays just before lunch and was carried on thirty-six stations by NBC. *How to Be Charming,* an advice program that ran Monday, Wednesday, and Friday after *Backstage Wife,* was a vehicle for Phillips Facial Cream. *Little Orphan Annie,* sponsored by Ovaltine, ran weekday evenings from 5:45 to 6 P.M. Brand names sometimes even figured in the titles, such as *Oxydol's Own Ma Perkins,* which aired mornings and afternoons every weekday. In the 1930s, the Hummert team also created the "Breakfast of Champions" slogan for Wheaties breakfast cereal, which is still used today.

The plot lines for the serials used surprise endings on Fridays to keep listeners hanging until the Monday show. The serials also followed a formula of histrionic dialogue, larger-than-life characters, sudden plot twists, and improbable resolutions—which continued into television soap operas.

The task of writing episodes for eighteen different fifteen-minute serials, totaling nearly a hundred episodes a week, each with attention-grabbing cliffhanger endings, was more work than even the brainy and hardworking Anne Hummert could handle. So a team of writers was hired to write the dialogue and back story for the characters and plot twists, based on outlines created by Anne and Frank. The couple also picked the actors and kept a sharp eye on the production process.

In the mid-1930s, the Hummerts moved to New York City and created Air

Anne and Frank Hummert discuss strategy at CBS, July 1948

Features, a broadcasting syndicate, which CBS later purchased. The couple continued this work until 1960, during which time they founded another broadcasting syndicate, Hummert Radio Features. By this time they were responsible for around forty drama serials for daytime radio. During World War II, Anne also consulted on radio production for the War Department and the U.S. Treasury.

The Hummerts dominated the business until the genre moved to television in the 1950s. Paid $100,000 each per annum, they were probably the highest-earning creative team in the United States, Hollywood excepted. However, when television edged out the radio

series, the Hummerts decided to retire and travel. After Frank died in 1966, Anne continued to live in New York on her own.

During the final decades of her life, Anne Hummert shared her broadcasting expertise with students at her alma mater, Goucher College. In 1978, she was the first artist-in-residence for the college's communications program, and she was active in alumni events until the early 1980s. Always a great walker, she was known to take daily three-mile walks well into her eighties. She died on July 5, 1996, at age ninety-one and is buried in Graceland Cemetery in Chicago. ■

Miss Borden, Mr. Thorn

Mrs. E. F. Hummert

AMANDA

In developing the present story-line, please keep the
scripts tight. Don't let's drag anything out. In
~~~ ~ to build up the show we shall find this approach
st one, I think. If we did every month a new
vely simple plot we should probably get in more new
rs, and hold them on with us by not moving too
in solving our plot problems.

Let me know when you need a new story line.

ASH

MEMORANDUM
October 20, 1944

Mr. Ludlum and Mr. Scopp

FROM   Mrs. E. F. Hummert

SUBJECT   AMANDA

I have listened to the show today, and I think that it is in
a deplorable state.

From theme to theme everything is wrong with it, with the
exception of the announcer, who is good.

I believe that Mr. Ludlum and Mr. Scopp both should get in
touch with Mr. Ricca, to have a clear understanding with him
as to what is wanted. Granted that the scripts are not good,
nevertheless there is no possible excuse for playing the
telephone scene as Amanda did, in a feeling almost of hysteria.
Furthermore, the actress who played the part of Bettina was
extremely bad, whatever her lines — and was so blatantly
obvious in her playing as to tip off a six year old child as
to what she was up to.

As far as Jimmy Meighan was concerned, there was no reason for
a tired man to wheeze and hem and haw and blow into the mike
to indicate that he is tired.

Furthermore, here is a DO, DON'T, and MUST. Never have any drinks
served on any of our shows, except tea. No strong alcoholic
beverages are to be served under any condition on any of these
shows.

Furthermore, in the playing of the theme, "Annie Laurie", Anne
Leaf is playing off the melody. In other words, you don't know
that it is "Annie Laurie". The whole show goes on the air at
a low level — much lower than the show before it. Furthermore,
in the playing of the theme, a new arrangement should be worked
out to give the effect of brilliancy, to make it sound as if
something is actually going on the air. Further, I have indicated
over and over, the same music of the theme should not be used under
the lead-in. Incidental music should be used under the lead-in.

Also, the chord, or effect used at the end with the spot, is very
logey and dull. Something loud and attention-getting should be
worked out here.

I have instructed Mr. Ludlum that it may be advisable to re-cast
Bettina at once, it he feels that it is necessary, and I have
asked him to get hold of Miss Leaf at once, in an attempt to
effect as much a change as possible before Monday. Mr. Ludlum
is just taking over this show.

16 5M 2-44 R&B

Also effective immediately, instead of calling the show
AMANDA OF HONEYMOON HILL, simply call it AMANDA. Leave out
all mention of HONEY MOON HILL. Will Mr. Scopp, Mr. Hoffman,
etc., please ask the newspapers to list the show as AMANDA.

The principal thing to tell Miss Hathaway is that she should
play her lines with strength and fire, but not with despair
and weeping. At present she sounds like the least self-possessed
person on the show, and this mitigates very much against the show.
She needs self-control and calm.

I should like this memorandum, in full, to be read to Mr. Ricca
so that he knows exactly what I am talking about.

ASH

Anne Hummert's staff memos

Charlayne
Hunter-Gault

■ WHEN CHARLAYNE HUNTER-GAULT FIRST encountered the media, she *was* the story. As one of the first two black students at the University of Georgia in 1961, she found that reporters and cameras recorded practically her every move as she made history in that previously all-white bastion of the Old South. But while her courage helped open higher education to all African-Americans, it was her passion to be on the other side of the story that motivated her. She wanted to be a journalist, and the university was the only place in the state to earn a degree in that field.

Hunter-Gault's pioneering role as a journalism student shaped her career. Not only did her studies prepare her professionally, but the experience of being covered influenced the kind of journalist she would become. In time she became an award-winning reporter acclaimed for using print and broadcast media to broaden public understanding of critical issues, especially regarding race. She did so by exploring issues through the personal stories of individuals caught up in historic events.

From the age of twelve, Charlayne wanted to be a reporter. Her role model: Brenda Starr, the comic-strip newswoman. Outsiders may have questioned this goal for a little black girl in the segregated South, where African-Americans were expected to stay "in their place." But Charlayne's family and community supported her and encouraged her to believe in herself.

Born February 27, 1942, in Due West, South Carolina, Charlayne Hunter was the oldest child of Charles S. H. Hunter, Jr., a chaplain in the U.S. Army, and Althea Brown Hunter. Throughout Charlayne's childhood and adolescence, the family moved around, following her father's postings. When he was overseas, Charlayne, her mother, and two younger brothers lived with Charlayne's maternal grandmother, a determined woman who read three newspapers a day. Her gentle manner and love of the news heavily influenced her granddaughter.

During her teen years in Atlanta, Charlayne was editor of her school newspaper and graduated near the top of her class from what was considered the top black high school in the city's segregated educational system. She was crushed to discover that the doors of UGA's journalism program were closed to her. As a result, she agreed to be a test case when a group of black leaders asked her and another student, Hamilton Holmes, to try to force Georgia to implement the Supreme Court's ruling requiring integration of all educational institutions.

While waiting for the integration order to be signed, she attended Wayne State University in Detroit, Michigan. Then, in January 1961, Hunter-Gault and Holmes arrived on the UGA campus in Athens. Riots ensued. From then until both graduated, they met with hostility at times and welcome at others. In her highly praised memoir, *In My Place* (1992), Hunter-Gault described her fears, but also the support of faculty members, administrators, and some white students, including a fellow journalism major named Walter Stovall, who became her first husband.

Hunter-Gault also became friends with journalists covering her story, especially Calvin Trilling, then a *Time* reporter, who wrote a book about the incident. Hunter-Gault says that Trilling "had a way of interviewing that was unobtrusive, that made you feel he really cared. I think it was because he listened more than he talked."

It was a model she would follow. "My experience at the center of the news,"

Hunter-Gault reporting from Baidoa, Somalia, with U.S. troops delivering food to a rural area paralyzed by war, December 1992

Hunter-Gault said later, "had transformed my Brenda Starr fantasy. Journalism might be as exciting, as mysterious, and as much fun as it was in the comics, but it also had the awesome power to help change things. By now, the [civil rights] movement had endowed me with a sense of mission that was bigger than myself, and I felt I had to lose my public self in order to find my place in that new world where *other* people's lives would be the focal point."

In the process, Hunter-Gault has worked at the nation's greatest institutions in journalism. When legendary *New Yorker* editor William Shawn offered her an editorial assistant job on graduation, she became the magazine's first black staff member. Then, after a year at

Doing the "Macarena" with Jesse Jackson during the Democratic National Convention, 1996

Washington University in Saint Louis on a Russell Sage Fellowship and a year at WRC-TV in Washington, D.C., as an investigative reporter and evening news anchorwoman, she returned to print journalism—this time as a metro reporter with the *New York Times,* where she stayed from 1968 to 1978. During that time, she established the paper's Harlem bureau and, by means of a scathing but solidly argued memo, convinced editors to use the word "black" instead of "Negro" to refer to African-Americans. Her investigative reporting gained particular attention, especially a series with Joseph Lelyveld on a twelve-year-old heroin addict that won the *Times'* Publishers Award in 1970. She received

two additional Publishers Awards for urban reporting. In 1971, her earlier marriage having ended in divorce, she married Ronald Gault, an investment banker; she has two children, a daughter from her first marriage and a son from the second.

In 1978, Hunter-Gault moved back to broadcast journalism as a correspondent for PBS's *MacNeil/Lehrer Report,* which soon expanded to the *MacNeil/Lehrer NewsHour.* Five years later, she was promoted to national correspondent and fill-in anchor. During her twenty years with this program, Hunter-Gault also interviewed such newsmakers as Margaret Thatcher, Norman Schwarzkopf, and Bill Cosby.

But it was her special reports that earned the greatest acclaim. Her coverage of Grenada after the American-led invasion in 1983 won her an Emmy Award. She received another Emmy for her story on Elmo Zumwalt III, who had developed cancer from exposure to Agent Orange in Vietnam; spraying of the defoliant had been authorized by his own father. While at PBS, Hunter-Gault also received a George Foster Peabody Award in 1986 for her documentary on the effects of apartheid on South African whites and blacks.

That documentary prefigured the next stage of Hunter-Gault's career. In 1997, she moved to South Africa, joining her husband, who had arrived a year earlier. Hunter-Gault became chief Africa correspondent for National Public Radio. Her series of reports on South Africa's transition to democracy as well as her stories on famine, civil war, and other struggles from all areas of the continent earned her a second Peabody Award.

That Peabody citation, as reported in *Broadcasting & Cable,* read: "Hunter-Gault demonstrated a talent for ennobling her subjects, and revealed a depth of understanding of the African experience that was unrivaled in Western media. Moreover, her reports illustrated the power of radio. Described and introduced with intelligence and passionate eloquence, her sub-

Hunter-Gault with *MacNeil-Lehrer* camera crew in Saudi Arabia where they covered Operation Desert Storm, August 1990

jects were given voice, and their personal stories moved from our ears into our hearts."

Now back on television as Johannesburg bureau chief for CNN, Hunter-Gault has clearly found her place as an influential reporter. But throughout her career, she has also created a place in the media for those who are often overlooked—and in the process has enlarged the understanding of all who see and hear her. ■

My whole effort throughout life has been consistent: to try to bring people on the outside into the mainstream. Early on, I tried to integrate the stories of black people and black life into mainstream coverage. When I opened the Harlem bureau of the *New York Times,* it was to do intensive coverage that would, hopefully, get into the mainstream so that Americans could truly appreciate our diverse place on the planet, our kind of global neighborhood.

In my own professional life, many different experiences—including the profound one of the civil rights movement in the South and then working in major institutions in journalism—helped to carve a little niche for me. I've never apologized for who I am and I have never been ashamed of, or shrunk from, covering those things that I know best. Now over time, the things that I know best have expanded to include many things that have nothing to do with race, color, or culture. But I cut my journalistic teeth writing about those things that I knew were happening to black people in Harlem, Atlanta, Los Angeles, and ultimately Africa—wherever I found them.

No matter what the subject or place, I genuinely try to tell stories through people. I think that's also my signature. I approach every story as one that is the most precious and the most interesting in the world—because, to the people I'm interviewing, it is. Obviously, there have been some high points. The Nelson Mandela interview two or three days after he was out of prison was a major high point. But I also believe that the pieces I did on some ordinary and extraordinary South Africans were high points too. Most recently, I was in Mozambique and interviewed a family. The wife had given birth to twins on the roof of the house and one of the infants died. When I asked the father, who was a minister, what that did to his faith in God, he told me that it deepened his faith in God, who could have taken all of his family, but took only one.

When I was in South Africa for the first time in 1985, white South Africans were intrigued because they couldn't figure me out. I was the same color as their "coloreds" [mixed-race people], but I was a woman and I was an American who was a foreigner. So it kept them off-balance most of the time. I could ask any question, and they would innocently give me an answer, even when it made them look ridiculous. I now grasp the other dimension to all of this: that the world is becoming increasingly dominated by people of color. There is a pride that people of color all over the world take in other people of color they can see who are achieving things, and they try their damnedest to help them in any way they can. But, as a journalist, I like to think that I relate to any person regardless of color.

I think the passion for what I do, regardless of the venue, is always present. There are parts of Africa that could be very challenging to get to because of the lack of infrastructure and the difficulty of making phone calls and reaching sources. Often, you have to get in your car and drive for miles until you find where you think the person is. However, that person may not be there when you arrive because you haven't been able to call ahead and make an appointment.

I was sitting just beyond a rock quarry recently in Zimbabwe where there had been some violence connected to the politics there. I had interviewed these people who had been beaten up and intimidated. Then we drove around to take some shots of a burned-down house. I realized what a really good and different story I had because just about everybody else was reporting about how the violence was connected almost exclusively to the land question and how the victims had been nearly all white. But I discovered that a lot of the violence was connected to politics and a lot of the victims, in fact most of the victims, had been black.

So there I was in Zimbabwe, where there was no place to sit but in the dirt. So I was just sitting in the dirt, dialing Atlanta, Georgia, on a satellite phone and talking about this different element of the story that I had uncovered in this rural area. It was a wonderful day. The sun was shining. Africa is so beautiful and green in so many places. I was sitting there thinking, this is just the Lord's work.

You have to have a passion that lets you appreciate moments like that, or you cannot do this kind of job. But if you have that passion, then the things like sexism, racism, poor infrastructure, difficulty in traveling, screwups that inevitably occur and could stand in your way don't matter. You can cope with all of that because ultimately the end product is something that comes out of your soul.

—CHARLAYNE HUNTER-GAULT

Kay
Koplovitz

■ As a fifth-grader in 1955, Kay Koplovitz served as class newspaper editor. Media had always fascinated her, as had science and sports. Twenty-two years later, Koplovitz combined those three interests in a way that changed television forever: she plotted the industry's course in a direction that enabled it to reach millions more viewers and give them access to entertainment and sporting events traditionally available only to ticket holders.

The technological foundation of Koplovitz's career was laid, almost by chance, during college when she heard astronomer Arthur C. Clarke deliver a speech about the theory of orbiting satellites. "I recognized that satellite technology could give broader coverage of news and entertainment," Koplovitz says. "I saw how powerful it was and that it was relatively inexpensive." She proved the theory by establishing the Madison Square Garden sports channel, which today is known as USA Network and reaches seven million subscribers. She went on to create the Sci Fi channel and later, as founder of Springboard and CEO of the Working Woman Network, to give women the tools they need to follow their business dreams. In 1998, *Broadcasting & Cable* magazine called her one of the four most powerful women in the television industry.

Koplovitz's path to glory had its beginnings far from the epicenters of the entertainment industry—in Milwaukee. The daughter of a homemaker and a sales executive, she got good grades in school and graduated Phi Beta Kappa from the University of Wisconsin with a communications degree in 1967. That led to a job as a producer for Milwaukee's WTMJ, the biggest TV station in the state. But while she enjoyed working in television, she could also see its limits. "TV was exciting and something I'd grown up watching, but there were just three networks," she says.

Still thinking about the Arthur C. Clarke speech she had heard years earlier and with the goal of someday establishing her own network, Koplovitz went to work in the communications department of the satellite company Comsat in 1968. "We did a lot to introduce satellite service to homes and businesses," she says. "Today everyone takes it for granted, but back then it was only for the military."

Koplovitz applied what she learned at Comsat when she joined the Madison Square Garden sports network, known as MSG, in the mid-1970s. With financing from UA Columbia Cable Vision, she transformed MSG, then a small local service with 125 sporting events a year, into a national powerhouse that broadcast 550 events annually. It became the second cable network (HBO was the first), the first to feature all sports, and the first to support itself via advertising. Marketed via direct mail and special events, the network launched with 750,000 subscribers and broke even its first year—an unusual accomplishment for an industry in which new ventures tend to stay in the red for years.

"This was not rocket science," Koplovitz says modestly. "What do people want to watch? They want sports." Of course, the logistical details were a bit more complicated. Fortunately, Koplovitz had been thinking about them since college.

"She knew more about the cable business, programming, and technology than any one person had a right to know," says David Stern, now commissioner of the National Basketball Association. As NBA general counsel in 1979, Stern met with Koplovitz to discuss what would become the association's first-ever cable-TV contract. "She was a very strong negotiator

but very fair," Stern says. "Working with her, I could see that she was always looking to improve upon the business relationship, the product, and the experience for the consumer." Koplovitz also became the first to negotiate national cable rights to Major League Baseball and National Hockey League games.

In her perpetual quest to widen the entertainment spectrum, Koplovitz established the Sci Fi channel, the first of its kind, with 10 million viewers in 1992. To ready for the launch, Sci Fi not only amassed a library of science fiction movies and small-screen series but bought the rights to broadcast the three *Star Wars* movies—the first time the trilogy had been seen in sequence, in its entirety, on TV. Sci Fi turned into one of the industry's fastest-growing networks. Soon after, Koplovitz also decided to expand the USA Network by launching channels in Latin America, Europe, Brazil, and southern Africa.

With the USA Network and the Sci Fi channel operating profitably, Koplovitz began to consider how to help other women realize their goals. Alarmed that female entrepreneurs were receiving only 1.5 percent of venture capital funds, she launched the Springboard initiative. This program seeks out women with high-growth-potential businesses and arranges for them to present their case before a panel of venture capitalists. As a direct result, women have received $100 million in venture capital since the program's establishment in 1997, and Koplovitz projects that that figure will rise to $400 million in the near future.

Koplovitz also initiated the Erase the Hate campaign, an effort to eliminate hate crimes and discrimination based on race, sex, nationality, religion, age, disability, and sexual orientation. "Kay's intensity in public service is equal to her intensity in business," says David Stern.

When Barry Diller took over USA Network in 1998, Koplovitz stepped down as CEO and soon after joined the board of Working Woman Network, a multimedia business resource for women. A partnership including *Working Woman* and *Working Mother* magazines, the National Association for Female Executives, the Businesswoman's Research Institute, and a number of business-content Web sites, the network helps women thrive professionally by giving them access to crucial resources: accounting, high-speed Internet access, mentors, educational programs, and business-research data. WWN currently serves more than 6 million women; Koplovitz became CEO in 2000.

In addition, Koplovitz—who lives in New York City with her husband, William C. Koplovitz, Jr.—is a member of the boards of numerous business and public service entities including Liz Claiborne, the Museum of Television & Radio, the Broadway TV Network, and the International Tennis Hall of Fame. She spends her spare time biking, hiking, playing tennis, and white-water rafting—reinforcing the love of sports that, via USA Network, she shared with the world. ■

Y ou just don't know when opportunity is going to knock.

I certainly didn't, in the summer of 1966, when I took time off from my studies at the University of Wisconsin to travel in Europe. Having worked two and three jobs during college to pay for tuition and necessities, I felt I owed it to myself to explore the world a bit. I was there to have fun and experience new cultures, and I had an undying curiosity about, well, just about everything. This curiosity took me to the London School of Economics, where I heard a lecture that changed the course of my life.

At that time, my student interests were divided between medicine and the media. My core course work was in biology, but my electives were in communications. Both appealed to me, but in my mind I was headed into medicine. Still, I continued to flirt with television. That probably explains why a lecture on geosynchronous orbiting satellites had the potential to blow me away. "On what?" you ask. That's right, geosynchronous orbiting satellites.

No doubt the topic wouldn't have been so compelling if it hadn't been explained by a master storyteller. We know him as a great science fiction writer, but he is also a knighted space scientist, and he was expressing his thoughts on satellites and their potential to revolutionize global communications. He forecast the change in human behavior that would result from truly open communications systems pertaining to governments, politics, peace, war, and people in general. His name was Arthur C. Clarke, famous for *2001: A Space Odyssey* and much more. To me, he was a beacon of light that brought compelling changes to my life. Good-bye medicine, hello television!

Wow! I was blown away to learn about the power to transmit news as it happens to a global audience. Not only news but sports, entertainment, just about anything people valued. And most important, I saw it as a tool of the people. Since childhood I have strongly believed in the power of a compelling idea and that, once the mind has internalized an idea, like freedom of thought, it's there for good and you can never, like Pandora, put it back into a box!

Well, my mind raced. I saw satellites transmitting news to all parts of the globe simultaneously. The crumbling of despotic governments could be aided by the free flow of communication to people around the globe. Arthur C. Clarke had liberated my thinking, and I would bring these thoughts forward in the master's thesis I wrote in graduate school. It was about the power of these geosynchronous orbiting satellites and what they would mean to the people in the free world—and to people behind the Iron Curtain and those laboring under repressive governments in lands near and far.

Now, I can't say that the Berlin Wall fell and Tiananmen Square changed the entire course of China just because of satellite communications. But I will say that these events were in part a direct result of Pandora opening her satellite box.

Sound lofty? It was. It was next to impossible to get any university to accept this thesis, but I finally found one: Michigan State University, where a professor of international law was convinced by my arduous arguments. My thesis was on its way.

It was still seven long years between publishing my thesis and the event that turned it into practice. That event was the "Thrilla from Manila," the Ali-Frasier boxing match on September 30, 1975. And it was still two more years before I was fortunate enough to launch—along with Bob Rosencrans of UA-Columbia and Joe Cohen of Madison Square Garden—the forerunner of USA Networks: Madison Square Garden Sports.

Back to the beginning. You never know when opportunity is going to knock. I've lived by the belief that a mind open to change is essential for progress.

There are many more examples of how this openness led to a course of action throughout my career. And it often reminds me of something my father would say to me frequently: "Success is where preparation and opportunity meet." My career has been living proof of that.

—KAY KOPLOVITZ

Geraldine
Laybourne

■ GERALDINE LAYBOURNE HAS WORKED AS A teacher, focus-group leader, children's media developer, and cable television executive. But what she truly *is* may be best defined as a conceptual architect: she looks at what exists, thinks of ways to connect elements to create new synergies, and then develops an integrative plan that she supervises a team to build. In the late twentieth century, that talent helped Laybourne succeed as an innovator in the medium of television; now, in the early years of the twenty-first century, she is an entrepreneur in the grand media convergence of television and the Internet.

A pioneer in creating high-quality television programming for children, Laybourne spent sixteen years at the Nickelodeon cable network. During that time her team made the network a creative and financial success and, in the process, changed the definition of programming for young people. As a result, in 1996 *Time* magazine named her one of the twenty-five most influential people in America for her approach that "didn't insult kids' intelligence or their sense of fun."

Laybourne's current mission as founder, chairman, and CEO of Oxygen Media is to create an integrated media brand that serves modern women by combining the best qualities of the

Internet and television. The vast integrated-media realm is uncharted territory for Laybourne, as for anyone at this point in time. But with her creativity, business acumen, and media expertise, experts are betting that if anyone can make it work, Laybourne can.

Her combination of artistic and business savvy has deep roots. She was born Geraldine Bond in Plainfield, New Jersey, on May 19, 1947; her father was a stockbroker and her mother a former radio producer. Young Gerry's first job was working in her father's office in the summer while she was in high school. She graduated from Vassar College in Poughkeepsie, New York, in 1969 with a degree in art history and then earned a master's

Laybourne (right) prepares herself for a signature Nick experience, June 1991

in elementary education at the University of Pennsylvania. Degrees in hand, she began teaching at a private school in Concord, Massachusetts, settling down there with her teacher husband, Kit Laybourne, who had long enjoyed instructing children in making media.

Laybourne loved teaching but felt compelled to find ways to reach a larger group of young people than she could within one classroom. In 1974, she cofounded a company that conducted focus groups to determine children's opinions about television and film. She and her husband also started a production company to create children's television programs. Soon they sold some shows to a new and little-known cable network called Nickelodeon. At that time the network had only five programs and a million subscribers—and was losing money, $10 million in its first year.

In 1980, Nickelodeon hired Laybourne as a program manager. Times were still hard for a while: Laybourne says that kids hated the channel and viewership was low. But Laybourne, using what she knew as an educator and what she'd learned about children from her focus groups, had ideas for how to fix it.

At the time there were only two types of programming for young people: educational shows, such as *Mr. Rogers* and *Sesame Street,* and cartoons and other shows that were pure entertainment, designed to capture children's

Slimed!

attention for advertisers of toys and other products. Laybourne saw an opportunity for something in the middle: interesting stories, whether serious or funny, featuring problems ordinary children face, along with game shows that were both challenging and fun. Laybourne's backing of such mold-breaking shows as *Clarissa Explains It All, Double Dare,* and *Rugrats* led to major successes.

"She turned what was a 'spinach' channel, something kids *should* eat," explains Robert Pittman, her boss at Nick and now an AOL executive, "into a 'pizza' channel, something kids *wanted* to eat."

Laybourne also expanded programming hours with the addition of "Nick at Nite," airing classic sitcoms such as *I Love Lucy* and *Bewitched* for baby-boomer parents to watch after the kids were in bed.

Her progress at Nick was rapidly upward: to senior vice president and general manager in 1986, and president in 1989. In 1993, she was also named vice chairman, MTV Networks (owner of Nickelodeon), and she sat on the operating and executive committees of Viacom, the parent of Nick and MTV.

Under Laybourne's leadership, Nickelodeon/Nick at Nite became the top-rated twenty-four-hour cable service and won many notable honors, including Emmys, Peabodys, and Cable ACE and Parents Choice awards. She further expanded the brand by launching and distributing Nick programming to countries around the world, developing theme park attractions, and creating movie, toy, and publishing divisions.

When Laybourne become president of Disney/ABC Cable Networks in 1996, she oversaw cable programming for the Walt Disney Company and its ABC subsidiary, as well as the operations of the Disney Channel and ABC's interests in Lifetime, A&E, The History Channel, and E! Entertainment Television. In addition, she played a role in the creation and management of ABC's Saturday-morning children's programming and was in charge of future programming for cable and other platforms.

Over the years, Laybourne—who, with Kit, has two children—has received numerous honors, including the Annenberg Award for Distinguished Lifetime Contribution to Children and Television, the Sara Lee Corporation's Frontrunner Award, and the Governor's Award from the National Academy of Cable Programming. She was ranked number one among the fifty most influential women in the entertainment industry by the *Hollywood Reporter* and has been inducted into the Broadcasting & Cable Hall of Fame.

Now, with Oxygen Media, her own company, Laybourne has both her greatest challenge and her greatest opportunity. With the help of partners Oprah Winfrey, Marcy Carsey, Tom Werner, and Caryn Mandabach, Laybourne launched Oxygen's twenty-four-hour cable network in 2000. Oxygen's network of Web sites operates in conjunction with the cable network, offering innovative means of communication and collaboration. Currently under development are new takes on talk shows, surveys, on-line chats, links to sites for related information, shopping, sitcoms, and movies. To find out what works, says Laybourne, "we have to try all kinds of stuff and fail—the same way we did at Nick."

With Oxygen, as throughout her career, Laybourne is not only the architect figuring how to make it work; she is the advocate, dedicated to work that makes a difference. ■

Since I started out in life as a teacher, I look at my experience as a series of lessons. Here are three.

Lesson one: Good ideas can make up for a lack of experience. Name some of history's most important scientists, and you'll discover that they did some of their most profound research in their twenties: Galileo was chair of the department of mathematics at the University of Padua before he was thirty. Sir Isaac Newton invented the reflecting telescope and calculus in his early twenties. And of course, Albert Einstein published the special theory of relativity before his thirtieth birthday. You get the picture.

When we first started Oxygen Media, we hired five twenty-year-olds to analyze and dissect the burgeoning Internet. They sat in a windowless conference room and literally drew maps of the Internet on the walls. My husband and I would come in on Fridays and absorb the information these smart thinkers had gleaned during the course of the week. The work they did laid the foundation for our company.

So my plea is this: listen to twenty-year-olds; and keep using your brain, no matter what your age.

An important corollary: make sure you are making mistakes. If you are playing it so safe that you aren't making mistakes, you'll know you aren't pushing your brain hard enough.

I learned this lesson especially at Nickelodeon. By watching our audiences, we quickly discovered that the green-vegetable programming we produced in our early years actually made kids feel inadequate. *Going Great,* for example, featured one inspiring kid after the other—cellists, artists, "brainiacs." It was as if we handed kids a checklist of things not to try because they'd compare themselves and come away feeling crummy. For our next effort, we discovered green slime, reverse psychology, and humor. We succeeded because we created a home base where kids knew we were on their side, standing firmly against AWFFULs—Adults Who Find Fun Unbearably Loathsome.

Lesson two: Passion for your work makes up for a lot of late nights.

I was on a plane recently, sitting next to a young man who, after asking me what I did, said, "You've had a successful career. Tell me, what is the easiest way to make money?"

"I have no idea," I replied.

He was furious. "Yes, you do."

"No," I blurted out. "If getting rich quick is your motivation, you will never succeed." (Both of us wished we were closer to our destination!)

The people whom I count as successful never set out to make money—not Oprah Winfrey, not Marcy Carsey, not me. They set out to follow their passions. I set out to make a difference in kids' lives. Now I'm working on making a difference in women's lives.

Whatever your passion, whatever gets you going in the morning, be it painting or singing, writing or medicine, research or law, children or education, entertainment or computers, history or politics, let your passion drive your engine.

Lesson three: Make the impossible the inevitable, and don't take no for an answer.

When I was growing up, anything that looked impossible looked interesting to me. I've made a career out of the most important lesson I can share: nothing is impossible. In the early 1980s, people laughed at our plans to improve the children's television landscape and turn it into a profitable business. No one outside the team that built it expected Nickelodeon to survive, let alone thrive.

Since June 1998, I've set my sights on programming for women and the possibilities created by the convergence of TV and computers. And it should come as no surprise that even after a strong run at Nickelodeon, I'm still met with a chorus of "That's impossible. It will never work." Well, we're proving them wrong.

Several years ago, when I was at Disney, we talked about how profoundly the Internet would change the audience and their demands on the media. One senior executive was disturbed and asked if there were any way we could stop it.

What we're doing with Oxygen Media is focusing on the possibilities of the new media and leading the way with making inevitable what many still see as impossible. What I see today is that the Internet is more about community, communication, and cocreation. It's about divergence and diversity. It's about people and their passions. It's about a different kind of storytelling—pluralistic storytelling. And there is no way to stop it.

When you've talked to people who have discovered community on the Internet and seen how it has transformed their lives, when you watch kids who are energized by the freedom and access to learning on the Internet, when you see how eager people are to create and interact, you understand the inevitability of the change.

At the beginning of the twenty-first century, the list of impossibles is daunting, and it will be up to us all to tackle them.

They say it will be impossible to turn every public school into a vibrant center of learning where children are valued and nurtured, regardless of race, ability, or creed; where every teacher is qualified and competent and takes home a paycheck befitting the most important job in our society: the care and instruction of our children. "Impossible," they say. Don't you believe it.

What about poverty and hunger in this, the wealthiest country in the world? How many times have you heard that the United States alone has the resources to feed every man, woman, and child in the world? So what are we waiting for?

Or hatred? In the 1950s and '60s, Congress and the Supreme Court took important steps to eliminate legalized discrimination in this country. How will we come to understand that embracing diversity is our country's backbone—our strength?

And what about getting guns out of the hands of juveniles and criminals? Is the notion that members of Congress can be pried from the grip of the NRA really impossible? A million moms don't think so, nor should you.

The list could go on and on. But here is my charge: You have the power to make the impossible inevitable. Bring your brains, your ears, and your hearts, and you can make it happen.

—GERALDINE LAYBOURNE

Shari
Lewis

■ FROM 1959 TO 1962, *THE SHARI LEWIS Show* was a staple of Saturday-morning children's programming. Lewis's puppet characters charmed youngsters, and her vision of teaching through play endeared her to parents and educators alike.

But animated series chased live children's performers right off TV in the early 1960s. Disappointed but undeterred, Lewis clung to her ideal that, to realize self-worth, children must not only listen but participate; she used her multiple talents to make the concept work in other media before orchestrating her television comeback in the 1990s.

Lewis's dedication to quality made her television's foremost early advocate of interactive learning and earned her a life-

time total of ninety-eight awards, including twelve Emmys, seven Parents Choice awards, a George Foster Peabody Award, and a John F. Kennedy Center for the Performing Arts honor.

Lewis's creative efforts also stand out because, whereas most children's entertainment featured a male character such as Mickey Mouse or Bugs Bunny in the principal role, she made her signature character, Lamb Chop, a female.

"Lamb Chop was the smart little girl," says Alice Cahn, who grew up watching Lewis on TV and eventually became head of children's programming at PBS. "She was exploring new things and asking questions about what's going on in the world. Kids could look at her and say, 'I want to be like her.' It made me feel smart that I got her jokes."

Born January 17, 1933, in New York City, Shari projected intelligence from a young age. She graduated from the High School of Music and Art at age fifteen with dreams of becoming a prima ballerina. Her mother, a musical coordinator for the New York City Board of Education, fostered her love of, and proficiency in, classical music and dancing. Her father, a professor and magician, saw to it that she learned vaudeville-type performing skills, including magic and joke telling. "It was acknowledged that I was going to be a performer from the time I was about two," Lewis recalled in a 1986 interview.

At age seventeen, when a broken leg halted her ballet dancing, Shari learned puppetry and ventriloquism from a family friend. For performances at synagogues around the country, she developed a Jewish-content act that included a girl dummy, Old Testament stories, and a menorah that lit magically. After appearing on the television show *Arthur Godfrey's Talent Scouts* in 1952 and winning with her puppet act, Lewis concentrated on developing new characters of the handheld variety.

"I've had hundreds of puppets. I start puppets, and if they talk to me, swell, and if they don't, I give them away," Lewis said. "Either a puppet is a facet of you or you have no right working with that puppet." Eventually she whittled her repertoire to three main characters: the saucy Lamb Chop, the adventurous pony Charlie Horse, and the Ozark-bred Hush Puppy.

Lewis then starred in *Shariland*, a live hour-long Saturday morning show on local New York City television that showcased her abilities as a singer, dancer, magician, storyteller, and ventriloquist. In 1957, her guest performance with Lamb

Lewis and kids on the set of WNBT-TV in the 1950s

Lewis and friends appear with a life-size Lamb Chop

Chop on *Captain Kangaroo* impressed NBC executives so much that they formulated a national series for her, *The Shari Lewis Show.* Lewis developed each segment with the goal of spurring young viewers to action. "Her message wasn't 'Look at me,'" says Mallory Lewis, the late star's daughter. "It was 'Join me.'" Lewis's songs often included phrases for viewers to shout back at the TV, and instead of simply telling stories, she taught kids to make up their own.

After the show ended its run in 1962, Lewis appeared in nightclubs as a singer and dancer, acted in stage productions, and guest-starred on TV variety and talk shows with her puppets. In between, she flew to England to star in a ten-minute children's segment broadcast before the evening news on BBC. The spots, which ran from 1968 to 1976, were such a hit that Lewis ended up singing with Lamb Chop at four command performances for Queen Elizabeth. "She was a favorite of the little princes Charles, Andrew, and Edward," says book publisher Jeremy Tarcher, who was married to Lewis from 1957 until her death in 1998.

With her U.S. television career uncertain in the 1960s and 1970s, Lewis looked into other forms of entertainment. She continued to perform in nightclubs and even collaborated with Tarcher to write the *Star Trek* episode "The Lights of Zetar" in 1968.

While she remained dedicated to her longtime educational goals, Lewis wisely recognized young people's changing mental landscape. In the 1980s, she wrote the *One-Minute Bedtime Stories* book series for children accustomed to the quick-cut sequencing of television. Her highly praised storybook, *A Perfectly Perfect Person,* instructed the reader to fill in personal traits—height and eye and hair color—to learn at the end that he or she was indeed "the perfectly perfect person."

To capitalize on the burgeoning home-video market, she produced *101 Things for Kids to Do,* which won five awards, including a 1987 *Ladies' Home Journal* citation as one of the year's ten best videos. She also drew on her classical music training to serve as a conductor with more than one hundred orchestras. For a gig in Japan, she and Lamb Chop learned Japanese well enough to give a TV interview without a translator.

While her dexterity gave her the ability to adapt to the changing media industry, her diligence astounded colleagues. "Virtually every moment of every day she was working on material or new ideas for a TV show or recording," says Jim

Lewis and Lamb Chop—in the 1960s and the 1990s

vehicle, *Lamb Chop's Play-Along,* which debuted in 1992 and continued for eighty-five episodes.

"She taught children without making them feel lectured to," said Golden. "She made them want to participate."

Lewis's next PBS series, *The Charlie Horse Music Pizza,* with costar Dom DeLuise, was a situation comedy in which characters taught basic music education. While working on that highly rated series, Lewis learned that what she thought was an upset stomach was something much more serious.

"The day after she was diagnosed with uterine cancer, she came to tape the show," says Mallory Lewis. "She gave a speech saying 'Sorry to screw things up, but I have to try this chemotherapy thing.'"

Six weeks later, on August 2, 1998, Lewis died. The sixty books, twenty-four home videos, twenty-one audiocassettes, and hundreds of TV episodes she left behind attest to her genius and the gift of self-esteem she imparted to young people. ■

Golden, who was Lewis's manager from 1982 until her death.

"I was talking to her on the phone one time, and I realized I was standing up—out of respect," said Alice Cahn, who worked with Lewis on her TV comeback

My father was Dr. Abraham B. Hurwitz, a professor at the Yeshiva University in New York City and also the official magician for the city of New York. His professional name was Peter Pan, the Magic Man, and he raised me as his son because he didn't have one, and so I was very fortunate. It changed my life. If Daddy had had a son, I would not be doing what I do today because he far preferred to work with boys. He just didn't have that raw material at home and so I was his victim and his student. I learned the things that he knew whether I wanted to learn them or not. And my mother was one of the music coordinators of the New York Board of Education. Ann Ritz Hurwitz had been a concert pianist and a very devoted teacher. Mother taught me the arts and Daddy taught me the variety arts, and I far preferred ballet and music to the *mishegoss* that Daddy did, which ended up being what saved me from having to get out of show business. . . .

Mother trained me in a lot of instruments, and Daddy insisted that I take a week's lessons in juggling, five . . . eight hours a day for five days because, he said, you never know what's going to come in handy. And he had me study with Spolladoro, who was one of the great puppeteers. I had to learn how to work marionettes—I hated marionettes, still do to this day. But Daddy insisted that I learn a great many things, and he of course was right, you never do know what's going to come in handy. I really didn't like magic. And I thought very little of the ventriloquism that I did because I was a ballet dancer. It wasn't until I tried to get into ballet companies—and found that I could get in but I couldn't get out of the chorus—that I said to Daddy, "Where'd we put the dumb puppet?" And three months after we took the dumb puppet out from under the bed, which was where we kept the dumb puppet, I won the Arthur Godfrey talent scout program. Papa was my talent scout. . . .

Daddy was a tremendous influence and Mother was a tremendous counterbalancing influence. It was like yin and yang. It was like the poet and the peasant. I got what was supposedly the high end of theater and the low end of theater, and I think my function has been to meld the two. I've always felt that that was a very real place that I filled that nobody else filled. There were no other ventriloquists who were as elegantly trained as I, in classical music, in quality theater. I mean I studied with Lee Strasberg and with Sandy Meisner—I studied with the best—and then to apply it to a craft of theater, that was my niche and has always been. I didn't do ventriloquism as a child; I scoffed at it. I didn't do it until I was about 15, and I haven't stopped since.

I did magic always, but I did it because it pleased Daddy. He had many things in mind besides my being a magician. He used magic to develop my skills, that was his interest. I remember being four years old, sitting with Daddy, and he taught me Sy Stevens, which is a very complex memory act, a mind-reading code. Really complicated. It's the epitome of the mind-reading codes used professionally. It was hard! And he taught it to me and gave me a dime every time I got it right. In that evening I learned it, and I earned $14. I learned two things: one, I could memorize anything; two, it's fun to know something that you're not supposed to know because it knocked out all the other magicians and that was very exciting. I tackle anything. I am willing to learn anything because I know I'm capable of learning anything. . . . It's because I was brought up to know that if I focused on anything I could do it.

—SHARI LEWIS

Ida
Lupino

■ IN THE EARLY 1950S, CELEBRATED MOVIE actor and director Ida Lupino was urged by a friend to consider working in television. She told him he was out of his mind. Like that of most people in Hollywood then, Lupino's initial curiosity about the new home-based medium was evolving into suspicion that it would steal audiences away from movie theaters.

She was right: it did. But Lupino followed, coming to view television work not as a betrayal of film but as a new and exciting opportunity. In time she received acclaim not only for her television acting but, much more remarkably, as one of the very few women television directors in the 1950s and '60s.

Sometimes called the "female Hitch"

(as in Alfred Hitchcock), this pioneering woman television director became best known, ironically, for her expertise with Westerns and action stories. Popular series for which she directed episodes included *Have Gun Will Travel, Gunsmoke, Sunset Strip, The Virginian, The Untouchables,* and *Thriller,* a mystery-horror show starring Boris Karloff. She also directed for *The Fugitive, Bewitched, Dr. Kildare,* and others.

She was the only woman to direct an episode of the long-running series *The Twilight Zone.* In addition, the producer of *Gilligan's Island* credited her for coming in to remedy problems in the pilot episode and creating the formula that made the series a hit.

As director of episodes in these weekly series, Lupino was praised for skillfully pulling together, in very short periods of time, large casts made up of both regulars and guest stars. Producers admired her as well for finding ways to make each episode fresh and interesting while meeting the demands of keeping certain elements constant.

She was also a creative tactician on the set, acclaimed for her use of a mobile camera at a time when filming was generally static. In 1987, her skill was honored in a retrospective of her TV work at the Film Center of Chicago. "The range

Lupino directs a scene from the film *Mother of a Champion*

hanged as an accomplice in the Abraham Lincoln assassination, and a bitter drama that Lupino also wrote and starred in about a declining actress who is hated by a woman living in her shadow.

Though she continued to accept occasional acting roles, Lupino always preferred directing. Once Alfred Hitchcock wanted her as the lead actor for an episode in his series. She said no, she'd prefer to direct it instead, even though the acting job paid $5,000 and directing only $1,250. Hitchcock grudgingly agreed.

Later in her career, Lupino became known for guest spots on series such as *The Mod Squad, Columbo,* and *Charlie's Angels.* She also starred with her third husband, Howard Duff, in a *Batman* episode, playing the evil Dr. Cassandra, who could become invisible.

All of her life, reinventing herself to take advantage of opportunities came naturally to Lupino. Born in London on February 4, 1918, she was descended from a long line of European performers. Her father was a well-known English comedian and headliner in musicals; her mother, also an entertainer, was billed as "the fastest tap dancer alive."

Little Ida became known in her neighborhood for her early attempts at drama. She often directed her cousins in amateur theatricals. In an early exercise in self-dramatization, at age seven she ripped up her clothes and ran from house to house begging, claiming she had been starved and beaten by her parents—till the neighbors caught on.

As Ida grew, she studied drama with her father and attended the prestigious

of her television work," said film scholar Barbara Scharres, "makes it clear that Lupino could handle almost any subject with great technical skill and highly imaginative use of the camera, as well as define what it was that interested her most in terms of a powerful struggle in any script."

Lupino's move into television had started with acting. Her debut, playing a woman who encounters a psychotic killer, was in a drama produced by Four Star Playhouse, a company headed by actors Dick Powell, Charles Boyer, and David Niven. In December 1955, Lupino was invited to join Four Star, and in her television directorial debut she directed a story she wrote about a woman whose solitary life in a mountain cabin is disrupted by bank robbers on the run from police.

Other directing jobs with Four Star followed, including a courtroom drama about Mary Surratt, who had been

Lupino directs the Western "The Only Man in Town" for CBS television's weekly series *Hotel De Paree,* 1959.

and crafted a new image for herself. She stopped peroxiding her hair, threw away her heavy makeup, and returned to her dramatic training. Finally she was given the lead female role in the successful drama *The Light That Failed* with Ronald Colman. Soon she was one of the screen's top dramatic stars.

Even then, Lupino itched to be behind the camera, directing the creative process. She got her chance when she and her then-husband, writer Collyer Young, along with a low-budget film producer, formed a production company. Lupino became the company's creative force, writing, directing, and producing six feature films.

Though not commercial successes, all were praised for tackling controversial subjects—such as rape, single motherhood, bigamy, and promiscuity—considered taboo by major studios. For this work, film scholars honor Lupino as an auteur and social realist whose films explored themes of female sexuality and independence. During that period Lupino was the only woman in the Directors Guild, and *Holiday* magazine gave her a special award for artistic courage.

Throughout her long career and until her death on August 3, 1995, Lupino proved herself worthy of her family's hereditary symbol: a red-hot poker, emblematic of their skill at firing up an audience. By doing so behind the television camera in the middle decades of the twentieth century, she pioneered a whole new role for women in broadcasting. ■

Royal Academy of Dramatic Arts. But her plans to be a stage actor were interrupted when, at fourteen, she was given a role in her first movie. After a few more English films, Lupino headed for Hollywood with her mother in 1933: Paramount had invited her to audition for the lead in *Alice in Wonderland.* Once there, however, she convinced the studio executives that she was too sophisticated to play Alice, and they began to mold her as a potential Jean Harlow.

By 1937, after acting in several light comedies, Lupino was determined to escape roles she felt wasted her talent and seek serious dramatic parts instead. She refused to renew her Paramount contract

I did not set out to be a director. I was only supposed to coproduce *Not Wanted* [her production company's 1949 movie] since we had this wonderful old-time director, Elmer Clifton, to make the picture. About three days into the shooting he got heart trouble. Since we were using my version of the script, I had to take over. My name was not on the directorial credits, however, and rightly so. This gentleman, as sick as he was, sat throughout the making of the film. I'd say, "Elmer, is it all right with you if I move the camera, if I do this, and so forth and so on?"

Our editor on this picture happened to be Alfred Hitchcock's editor for *Rope* and *Spellbound*, William Ziegler. I would run to the phone every five minutes and say, "Bill, listen, I want to dolly in and I think I'm reversing myself." On the first picture he helped me out, and he would come down to the set.

On the second film we got Bill again. The picture, *The Young Lovers*, was based on my original story about a young woman dancer who contracts polio, and I cowrote the screenplay. I'd run to the phone again, but this time he'd say, "Uh-uh, you're on your own. I'm cutting right behind you. You can't afford for me to come down on the set." So that is how I became a director. . . .

I had to find my own style, my own way of doing things. I wasn't going to try to copy anybody. But certain directors, like Charles Vidor, Raoul Walsh, or Michael Curtiz, couldn't help but rub off. And Robert Aldrich, God knows it was a delight to work for him in *The Big Knife.* He's not only a fine technician, but he certainly knows the actor. He digs down into your role and pulls things out you weren't aware were there. . . .

[Walsh] used to let me watch him in the cutting room. I wouldn't bother him, but I'd ask him certain things, you know, about "lefts-to-rights" and "rights-to-lefts" and "over the shoulders." . . .

I felt [that making *Outrage,* the story of a rape victim, in 1950] was a good thing to do at that time, without being too preachy. . . . I just thought that so many times the effect rape can have on a girl isn't easily brought out. The girl won't talk about it or tell the police. She is afraid she won't be believed. . . .

I suppose we were the New Wave at that time. We went along the line of doing films that had social significance and yet were entertainment. The pictures were based on true stories, things the public could understand because they had happened or had been of news value. Our little company became known for that type of production, and for using unknown talent. Filmmakers was an outlet specially for young people—actors, writers, young directors. . . .

Then [for television] I was asked to direct Joseph Cotton in *On Trial,* a series presentation on the trial of Mary Surratt who was hanged as a suspect in the Lincoln trial. It was shot in three days, with three or four days to prepare. I sat up all day and night doing all the research I could on the assassination of Lincoln. Television—there's nothing rougher, nothing rougher. And from then on it became like a snowball. They'd book me in advance because they had to have answers in advance and I couldn't direct movies again until 1966, with *The Trouble with Angels*. . . .

[Successful directing] is a matter of chemistry. A combination of a good script that is possible to shoot in the time allotted, a producer I am completely simpatico with, good actors and my cameraman. The night before shooting and during that very first shot I always have butterflies in my stomach. But once I get the first few shots in the camera, well then, the stomach starts to settle down.

Communication with my actors is also very important. Being close to them. I understand their problems. . . .

The producer who started me [in television] began me in Westerns. He had seen [my movie] *The Hitchhiker* and the next thing I knew I was directing *Have Gun Will Travel* with Richard Boone, *Hong Kong* with Bob Taylor, *The Fugitive* with David Janssen, *Manhunt, The Untouchables*. Who me? I thought. Here I'd always done women's stories and now I couldn't get a woman's story to direct.

—IDA LUPINO

Penny
Marshall

■ IT WAS PENNY MARSHALL'S FINAL APPEARANCE on the television comedy series *The Odd Couple,* and her recurring character, secretary Myrna Turner, had a problem. Her boyfriend, Sheldn ("they left out the 'o' on the birth certificate"), had unceremoniously split and she wanted to seem more alluring to win him back. Under Tony Randall's tutelage, she tried to substitute a ladylike titter for her normally hacking laughter and to glide across the room like a lady—"bust pridefully erect"—instead of pacing along with slumped shoulders. In both cases she failed. Jack Klugman arranged for a belly dancer to teach her how to shimmy, but even Al Molinaro, Officer Murray Greshner, could follow the instructions better than Myrna could. All seemed lost until Sheldn (played by Marshall's then real-life husband, Rob Reiner) reappeared, having returned from a singles weekend where he had met dozens of women; but none had compared to Myrna, and he wanted her just the way she was, "unproud bust" and all.

The episode, a favorite among *Odd Couple* fans, not only highlighted Penny Marshall's growing talent as a physical comedian but also seemed to lay to rest personal doubts that had plagued the actor at the beginning of her career. She had worried that she wasn't pretty or

vivacious enough for show business and that she had gotten the *Odd Couple* job only because her brother was the producer. But, like Sheldn, the audience loved Penny Marshall for her lack of affectation, her originality, her inability to be anyone but herself. And the episode demonstrated that Marshall had star quality—something her brother had recognized before she did. At the end of the show, Myrna announced to her boss that she was resigning as his secretary to get a better job. Penny Marshall did, too.

Marshall went on to star in *Laverne & Shirley,* earning a higher salary than Rob Reiner, who played Mike Stivic in *All in the Family,* the number one show on television in the mid-1970s. Marshall's numbers kept going up when she began directing films, becoming the first female director to have a movie gross more than $100 million.

Although Marshall, born in Brooklyn in 1942, came from a show business family, nothing in her early childhood hinted at the blockbuster success she would later achieve. Her mother was a dance instructor, her father an industrial-film maker. As a girl, she appeared as a dancer on *The Ted Mack Amateur Hour* and *The Jackie Gleason Show*, but later she headed off to the University of New Mexico with a vague goal of becoming a secretary. After graduating and entering into a brief marriage that produced a daughter, Tracey, Marshall realized that a role in an amateur theater production in New

Mexico was the most fun she'd had in a long time. She moved to Hollywood, took acting classes, and eventually won small parts on *The Danny Thomas Hour* as well as several other shows.

When she got the part of Myrna Turner in *The Odd Couple*, Marshall became a familiar character actor but not yet a household name. Several appearances as a supporting character on *The Mary Tyler Moore Show* elevated her profile, but it was her *Laverne & Shirley* role as Laverne De Fazio—a plain-talking working-class woman prone to brawling—that turned her into a full-fledged celebrity. Laverne, loud and uninhibited, and her best friend, Shirley (played by Cindy Williams), reserved and fussily feminine,

Cindy Williams (left) and Marshall star as Shirley Feeney and Laverne De Fazio on *Laverne & Shirley*.

The real-life mothers of *Laverne & Shirley* series stars Penny Marshall (center left) and Cindy Williams (center right) join their daughters in "The Second (Almost) Annual Shotz Talent Show" episode of *Laverne & Shirley*.

made a memorable comic duo as beer-factory workers sharing a basement apartment in Milwaukee.

"She was brilliant as Laverne," says Peter Ross, a former ABC programming executive who is now president of

Warner Bros. Television. "What Laverne De Fazio presented to the public was an ordinary blue-collar schmo. Penny brought a physicality and accessibility to that role. . . . Her relationship with her father and best friend seemed real."

Swinging on a vine while wearing a leopard-print nightie in a lingerie show or preparing to "Ready, set, sleep" as a volunteer in a sleep-lab experiment, Marshall revived the tradition of physical comedy unseen on TV since Lucille Ball had stopped making sitcoms. When Williams left the show, Marshall carried it by herself for a while, but soon she decided to leave, too.

By the mid-1980s, she was beginning to make a name for herself as a director, a transition she didn't consider particularly daring despite the notable lack of women in that profession. "We [sitcom actors] have been around," she explains. "We worked very hard for a number of years, so we're responsible, reliable people."

Marshall's first feature film, 1986's *Jumpin' Jack Flash,* starring Whoopi Goldberg, went nowhere fast. Her next venture, however, skyrocketed straight to the stratosphere. *Big,* with Tom Hanks as a thirteen-year-old boy trapped in a thirty-year-old's body, enchanted the country and garnered an Academy Award nomination for its lead actor.

Suddenly Marshall was again at the top of her game, this time as the hot new director in town. Next, she directed Robert De Niro and Robin Williams in the well-received medical drama *Awakenings,* and in 1992, she made her second film

that grossed more than $100 million: *A League of Their Own,* starring Geena Davis, Madonna, and Rosie O'Donnell. In making that film, based on the true story of the All-American Girls Professional Baseball League, Marshall unearthed a chapter in women's history that might have otherwise been forgotten—a time during World War II when young men had been in such short supply that women had been recruited to play ball before paying audiences. The movie poignantly portrayed the birth and demise of these teams, which were scrapped as soon as GIs began returning home to take charge of the diamonds once again.

Marshall's success in the director's chair has continued. In the late 1990s, she directed the Whitney Houston film *The Preacher's Wife,* following that with *Riding in Cars with Boys.* Though in constant demand for feature films, Marshall has not forgotten her small-screen roots, making several TV guest appearances, including a memorable turn as a baby-sitter with a criminal past on *The Simpsons.* Along with Rosie O'Donnell, she has also appeared in a series of Kmart commercials, work that other Hollywood directors might not have even considered. But Laverne—oops, Penny—has said that it suits her just fine. She did, after all, start out in a beer factory. ■

By the time I moved to Los Angeles, [my brother Garry Marshall] was a hotshot television comedy writer, along with his partner, Jerry Belson. Garry asked me what I wanted to do with my life.

"I don't know," I said.

I had gone to the University of New Mexico as a math and psychology major, but instead of getting a degree, I ended up with a husband and a baby girl. Of the three of us, only the baby decided that we were meant for each other. However, I had to leave her in New Mexico with my ex-husband's family while I went to California to try to look for a job. My previous work experience had been achieving the goal that I had set for myself in my high school yearbook: secretary.

"Think," said Garry when I arrived on his doorstep in Los Angeles. "When was the last time you were happy doing something?"

"When I was sitting on the Parkway fence watching the boys play stickball," I said.

"We're looking for a career here, Penny. Think more. When were you happy doing something? Anything?" he persisted.

I thought for a moment and came up with this: "In New Mexico I was in a production of *Oklahoma!* where I played Ado Annie. I made the audience laugh and that made me happy. Does that count?"

"Yeah, that's acting. That's good."

But I thought to be an actress you had to look like Elizabeth Taylor, and I told Garry I wasn't pretty enough. But he said all I needed was some training, so he helped me enroll in Harvey Lembeck's acting class. Those damn classes were hard, but I stuck with it and finally got a call for my first job: a Head & Shoulders shampoo commercial. I went down to the set and was told I was to play a character with limp, stringy, dandruff-specked hair and that my costar, an up-and-coming actress named Farrah Fawcett, would play a character with thick, bouncy hair without a speck of dandruff.

While Farrah and I were having our makeup done, the director put two stand-ins on the set so the crew could light the shot. Farrah's stand-in had a sign around her neck that read "Beautiful Girl" and my stand-in had another that read "Homely Girl." When Farrah saw this, she quickly ran over with a pen and crossed out "Homely" and replaced it with the word "Plain." It was a nice try but my self-esteem had already sunk as low as buried treasure. When I got home, I called up Garry.

"Well, how did the commercial go?" he asked.

"Today I went from homely to plain," I said.

"You're on your way," he responded.

"But all they want is perky and pretty and I'm neither."

"Don't worry," he said. "You are pretty and you don't have to be perky if you don't want to be."

In between scratching, sneezing, and bleeding, he was a pretty nice brother. I used to come home crying all the time, thinking that I would never make it as an actress and should probably turn right back around and get on the next Greyhound for New Mexico. Working as a secretary looked pretty good compared with the rejection that went along with being an actress.

But my brother kept encouraging me and gave me a small part in his movie *How Sweet It Is.* I was cast in a scene set in the Louvre in Paris where a tour group of girls took turns smiling in front of the Mona Lisa. I really got the part because I was the only actress Garry could convince to put real wire braces on her teeth and smile in front of the painting.

But slowly I started getting other small parts on television, some of which did not require orthodontia, until Garry gave me my big break when he cast me in his TV show *The Odd Couple.* I was Oscar Madison's constantly whiny secretary, Myrna Turner. At first I thought Garry hired me just to be nice.

"No one's that nice," he said. "You're good. You aren't perky, but you're good."

And a few years later Garry, along with writers Lowell Ganz and Mark Rothman, created *Laverne & Shirley* for me and Cindy Williams.

During *Laverne & Shirley* I spent a lot of time learning what was going on behind the camera, and now I work behind it full-time as a director, a job I like even more than playing Ado Annie. I'm thankful that Garry encouraged me to go forward and make a life for myself in show business, but I must confess there were days on *Laverne & Shirley* when being a secretary looked mighty good and peaceful.

Over the years Garry has sort of been my muse because when I started out in this business I didn't have many women directors to look to for inspiration. Now that I think about it, my muses were all men. I guess the Seven Dwarfs got to Hollywood before the Nine Muses, and there's been a testosterone imbalance ever since. But I think I've managed to win over most of the dwarfs by now, too.

— PENNY MARSHALL

Mary Margaret
McBride

■ IN THE THICK OF WORLD WAR II, WITH almost everything in short supply, the U.S. government put out an urgent request for scrap paper and received help from an unlikely source: radio host Mary Margaret McBride, who donated more than three million of her fan letters to the cause. Not to worry; there were plenty more where those had come from. McBride received as many as five thousand letters a week. If planes had been made of papier mâché, she could have outfitted her own air force.

Mary Margaret McBride was the Oprah Winfrey of the pre-TV generation: a soothing, trustworthy media maven who commanded a legion of loyal, predominantly female followers. In her prime, some six million listeners, mainly housewives, tuned in to McBride's midday broadcast, a forty-five-minute pastiche of cooking tips, folk wisdom, and live interviews with the likes of Harry Truman and colorful plumbers. McBride's easygoing demeanor was so uncontrived that she would frequently broadcast from her Manhattan apartment, swaddled in her silk pajamas and Asian housecoat, waxing poetic about "mashed potatoes that have been hand-beaten with cream and butter until they are fluffy as a cloud."

American Mercury magazine noted

that her "seemingly aimless technique is really a rich mixture of experience and skill." But the middle-American charm was genuine. Mary Margaret McBride was born on November 16, 1899, in Paris, Missouri, to a poor, religious farm family. She took an oath of temperance at the age of eight and apparently never violated it. Years later McBride would refuse to do alcohol or tobacco commercials on the radio, insisting on pushing only those products she actually liked and used, such as Fannie Farmer candy or the appropriately named Sweetheart Soap.

In 1906, McBride enrolled at Williams Woods College, a private boarding school in Missouri. A great-aunt who was one of Woods's biggest benefactors paid Mary Margaret's tuition with the aim of grooming her to become part of the school's administration. But McBride yearned to be a writer. Knowing that her great-aunt would cut her off financially, she nonetheless transferred to the University of Missouri to study journalism, working her way through college as a part-time reporter with a local newspaper. After graduation, McBride took a job with the *Cleveland Press,* then moved to Manhattan. Following a brief stint at the *New York Evening Mail,* she began a lucrative freelance career in 1924, churning out a long string of magazine articles, plus a handful of travel books and cookbooks.

The Depression dried up many writing markets. Feeling the pinch, in 1934 McBride auditioned to host a new women's program about to debut on WOR radio. "I was the only one of fifty applicants who made no salary demands," she said later, explaining how she had been hired.

It turned out that the job required some acting ability. WOR made the thirty-five-year-old McBride adopt the on-air persona of "Martha Deane," a quintessentially perfect grandmother with superhuman homemaking skills. The show was a hit, but McBride felt like a fraud. On May 26, 1934, just three weeks into her new role, she broke character and confessed to her audience that she not only wasn't a grandmother, she wasn't even married. Her audience rallied behind her, and the show snow-

Eleanor Roosevelt joins McBride on the air in 1947.

balled in popularity. McBride soon dropped the protective cover of her "nom d'air," Martha Deane, and forged her own way under her own name—ultimately earning fame and fortune as "The First Lady of Radio." From 1934 to 1960, McBride was a pop culture staple, courted by all the major networks. She moved from WOR to CBS to NBC to ABC and back to NBC. Her spot on the radio dial changed, but her huge ratings didn't.

The *New York Times* once described McBride as "an amply proportioned woman with a hearty, sentimental approach to life" who "larded her programs with recipes for invariably weight-gaining dishes." But it wasn't all about the secrets of lip-smacking barbecue sauce. It was also question-and-answer sessions with Queen Elizabeth, book and movie reviews, listener letters, and homespun commentary. In short, the Mary Margaret McBride phenomenon foreshadowed the talk-show tornado that would sweep through radio and television, and that has yet to show any signs of abating.

In her mind's eye, McBride envisioned her typical listener as a young married woman who had left her job to raise a few children but who had not lost interest in the outside world: the progenitor of today's soccer mom. "So I try to talk about people who do things, the world at large," McBride said. "I try to give her the vicarious thrill of going places and meeting people. When I describe a restaurant where I had dinner . . . I try to look at it as she might . . . and to share her enthusiasm."

McBride prepares for the fifteenth anniversary show of her first broadcast, 1949.

It was the technology revolution that derailed the McBride train, for photogenic and animated she was not. On September 21, 1948, NBC launched *Mary Margaret McBride* on TV—and it landed with a thud, like a stuffed squash dropped from a third-story window. Three months later she was gone. The *New York Times* called her the first "fatality" among the ranks of radio stars who would fail to make the transition to the tube.

The mega-audiences slowly drifted away from the radio, too. But the host kept hosting, kept rowing her gravy boat of good cheer. From 1960 until her death in 1976, McBride downsized her career, syndicating one radio show and broadcasting another from the studios of WGHO in upstate New York. Ironically, the homemaker supreme never married or had children. She married her microphone and remained faithful through the years. As the poet Ogden Nash once quipped, "There have been many bridesmaids, but only one McBride." ∎

I believe that in every life there is one miracle and that radio, my third career in New York, was my miracle. I was middle-aged or nearing it (depending on the charity of the estimator) when it happened to me, and I needed a miracle desperately. I had been jobless and broke for nearly four years.

Then, surprise—a telephone call from my literary agent, Carol Hill. "WOR wants you to audition for a woman's program," she told me calmly, after the amenities were over. I shrieked in quick disbelief.

I thought to myself, "I'm not what they want in radio." I knew that the only contribution I could ever make to anything would be as a reporter. That was what I'd been trained for—interviewing people, observing, setting down what I saw, heard, tasted, smelled. When it came time for my second audition, I knew what I would talk about: life on the Missouri farm where I was born, myself as a little barefooted girl running down to the barn on a hot summer morning to have Papa fill my cup by milking straight from the cow into it; the one-room country school to which I traveled on an ancient bay farm horse behind my brother; Old Home Place on which my mother was born and where we lived when my little brother, Buford, was drowned in the Salt River.

[The producer] told me he had interviewed 50 women for the job and had chosen me because he believed I had the common touch. I wasn't sure exactly what he meant, but I was ready to do my best. It was then that he unfolded his idea that I should be a very simple but wise and kindly old character who had devoted her life to her large family. She would speak colloquially and dispense philosophy in great helpful chunks.

I was a little disconcerted by these instructions, but not enough to back out. I said I'd try, and in an effort to keep my word, I gave myself a family of six sons and daughters, married them all off, and added an astronomical number of grandchildren, upon whom I bestowed the favorite names I had been saving up since childhood for a real family.

Since I'm a very forthright person, this experiment couldn't have lasted. When I blew up that day and committed mass murder [by revealing on air that "Martha Deane" and her extended family were fictitious], my producer was furious—and fearful, too, about what might happen to the program. He really believed I'd committed radio suicide. "You've done a terrible thing," he scolded. "The only hope is that nobody in authority heard you."

Always I was consumed by the fear that someday they would find me out. Radio was too good to be true—that I should have this job year after year, that sponsors should wait in line to get on the program, that I should actually be paid for a chance to perform for the public that ordinarily wouldn't have been drawn to a person with my lack of histrionic ability and training.

I did have fun and I wanted my guests to be happy, too. This was partly self-interest, since if they weren't at ease they didn't talk well. Many of the broadcasts in the 20 years were done from my own home, and often we were alone, the guest and I, with the microphone between us and the engineer hidden behind a screen over in a corner. Quite often we would both forget that we were on the air, which was what I was working for.

The celebration of my tenth anniversary was planned by NBC at Madison Square Garden. It was to be an occasion for recruiting women for the war services. As I walked on, I heard a roar of voices and the next thing I knew 25,000 women (and a few men) were on their feet applauding and cheering. Fred Waring introduced John Golden, who in turn introduced Mrs. Franklin Delano Roosevelt. She made a moving plea for women volunteers. (She also said two sentences that I cherish to this day: "I always rejoice when a woman succeeds. And when one succeeds superlatively, as you have done, Mary Margaret, it helps us all.") Yankee Stadium was chosen for my 15th anniversary party—extra policemen, special subway trains with banners on the sides reading "to Mary Margaret McBride's Yankee Stadium." The official police count that day showed 54,000 persons checked in.

I do have to acknowledge that life has defeated me in one particular period. I wanted to be a great writer and now I never shall be. The trouble was, I suppose, that I wanted to be a writer but I didn't especially want to write, and anyway, I had nothing of consequence to say. So I was far better off as a day-to-day talker than as a would-be creative writer, breaking my heart trying to reach the stars. I touched a good many lives in the years, and I hope I alleviated some loneliness and awakened a few to the horrors of cruelty and injustice. If so, I am reasonably content.

—MARY MARGARET MCBRIDE

Judy
McGrath

■ When *Forbes* magazine wants to understand post–Generation X kids, they ask Judy McGrath. As president of MTV Group, McGrath is an authority on what young people think. She's the hip, music-loving "executive veejay" who is widely credited with this popular cable network's resounding creative and financial success in its nearly twenty years in business.

Under McGrath's direction, MTV has grown from a maverick cable channel into a well-established global brand that has come to symbolize a culture, a style, an attitude, and a vibrant musical landscape. From its beginning, she has helped bring the creativity of music, with its passion, originality, and energy,

to television. Along the way, McGrath has put together a uniquely talented group of programmers, producers, and writers who have, under her leadership, made and continue to make MTV a cutting-edge, award-winning network for young people and the young at heart.

Analysts estimate that since taking over the reins, first as MTV president in 1993 and now in her present position, McGrath has tripled MTV's revenue, establishing it as one of the top five most profitable U.S.-based networks, along with ESPN, HBO, NBC, and ABC. MTV reaches more viewers aged twelve to twenty-four than any other cable network. Overall, 73 million viewers aged two and older watched in the month of February 2000 alone. And the channel's global scope is vast, reaching 323 million households in 139 countries.

Under McGrath, MTV stays on top by constantly evolving to keep pace with viewers' changing tastes. Not only did she bring the network back from a slump in the mid-1990s by revamping its programming, but she has boosted program variety. Under her leadership, the network added *Total Request Live*, the live music video countdown show hosted by the wildly popular Carson Daly, which attracts throngs of screaming fans to MTV's Times Square studio on a daily basis; introduced sassy animated series such as *Daria*; and tried out new settings and story lines for perennial favorites such as *The Real World* and *Road Rules*.

For her ability to connect with the younger generation, McGrath has been called "the cool mother teenagers crave." But her success also derives from her possession of another trait valued by the young: she listens, and she really, really gets it.

McGrath credits her accomplishments to being a self-styled voyeur. "I do lots of scientific and unscientific research," she says. That means not just reading the reams of reports and statistics her staff collects but watching and listening on a more personal level—especially to the eighteen- to twenty-two-year-old interns the network hires each year.

She keeps an ear cocked to what musicians are saying, the ideas of her colleagues, the buzz in the industry. Her conversation is peppered with statements such as "I was thinking about what Beck said" and "I always look to music to tell me what's really going on."

McGrath has spent most of her career at MTV. Born July 2, 1952, in Scranton, Pennsylvania, to parents who were social workers, she earned a B.A. in English from Cedar Crest College in nearby Allentown.

A lifelong lover of rock and roll, she worked at a radio station in her first job, then held positions as copy chief of *Glamour* magazine, senior writer for *Mademoiselle* magazine, and copywriter for National Advertising in Philadelphia. Through what she calls "an old-girls' net-

McGrath with Ricky Martin and her MTV colleagues

work" in journalism, in 1981 McGrath joined Warner Amex Satellite Entertainment Company, MTV Networks' predecessor company, as copywriter for on-air promotion. In that job, she made her mark with contests such as "Devo Goes Hawaiian" and "One Night Stand with Journey." She then moved up the ranks at MTV, becoming editorial director, then executive vice president and creative director, and president in 1993. Married to a former banker, she has a seven-year-old daughter and sits on the boards of the New York City Ballet and Rock the Vote.

In addition to her innovations in regular programming, McGrath has introduced special programs that delve into important social and political issues for today's youth. The network first moved into political news coverage with its award-winning 1992 "Choose or Lose" political awareness campaign, then tackled the issue of tolerance around the world with its "Free Your Mind" program.

McGrath with singer Sarah McLachlan

Under McGrath, the network also launched the Emmy Award–winning "Fight for Your Rights: Take a Stand Against Violence" campaign in 1998. As part of this effort, MTV partnered with the American Psychological Association to create a show entitled "Warning Signs," exploring the psychological patterns and factors associated with suicide and violence. The show also addressed how to recognize clues that someone is about to explode and how to find help. Together with the APA, MTV hosted more than six hundred antiviolence public forums in schools and community centers across the country. In addition, MTV, along with the U.S. departments of Justice and Education and the Recording Industry of America, produced and distributed more than half a million enhanced CDs and guides on ways young people can take a stand against violence.

As both president of MTV Group and chairman of Interactive Music, McGrath also provides leadership for the MTVi Group, MTV Network's industry-leading music Internet operations, which include mtv.com (the number one music entertainment Web site), vh1.com, and sonicnet.com.

Perhaps the key to McGrath's accomplishments with MTV is her understanding that music is not just people listening to songs but that those songs generate a distinctive world. As she says of rock and roll when she was growing up and hip-hop today, "It belongs to sort of a new generation and it's real and it has a huge array of personalities, male and female. It's a culture."

Her ability to see the big picture takes on new dimensions especially, she admits, when she visits Washington, D.C., and "can't help feeling a little political and patriotic." Suddenly, she says, "I want to get on a soapbox and remind everyone that we built this country on rock and roll. By that I mean this country was founded on love, freedom, and the pursuit of happiness." Conceding these may not be "rock-and-roll values exclusively," she emphasizes that they are "the values that young people have always believed in."

Considering how well McGrath listens—and uses what she hears—it's no surprise that other executives listen to her so carefully. ■

Every time I try something new and radical, I run into a new prejudice, and it's annoying the hell out of me. I guess the most radical thing I've done over the last few years is get a private life. I got married and adopted my daughter, Anna, a little over five years ago.

Since then, I've become aware of a new prejudice—well, it's probably related to an old one—an ugly little myth that parenthood somehow diminishes your enthusiasm for your job. I hear it about women who take time off for their first baby. "Well, when she comes back, she probably won't have the same drive and energy"—that sort of thing. A variation on the theme is that when you become a parent, you lose your desire for everything else, particularly pop culture. Sexism is probably at work here because I don't think the same things are said about men who are parents.

Well, it's not fair and it's not true. If anything, raising Anna has rejuvenated me. In fact, raising Anna is a lot like running MTV. You have to live in the now; you have to be creative and spontaneous; you have to be supportive. Also, open-minded. Just last week Anna was singing to herself a snippet of the latest Britney Spears, "Oops, I did it again," and without missing a hip-hop beat, she segued right into "and that's Elmo's world!" for a big finish. Some would say, divine retribution; I say, the kid's got talent.

Another great thing about Anna is she reinforces my belief that you have to respect young people. That is the number one reason I work at MTV. And that's the number one thing I want MTV to always be: a place where young people are respected. So that if you're young, chronologically or psychologically, you know you have a home there.

In fact, my muses are the younger women in this business, the ones who haven't made it to any "best lists" yet, but who are doing most of the creative and business work. They're like the people who watch and work at MTV. They're not bound by the status quo; they're not jaded by commerce. They're smart and they're outspoken and they're inventing the future. Which is why I'm in love with them.

For our part, we at MTV try hard to maintain a culture that is truly sympathetic and nurturing to the creative process. Doing creative work is hard and involves risk, and some failure; it goes against what's usually considered to be "normal business practice." So we have to be a place where people feel comfortable testing new ideas, and if they fail, try again. It's the only way to continue delivering on our promise to offer our audience the most creative television there is.

Some people think of MTV as a hopelessly adolescent channel, a little off-kilter. But whatever it is, the good thing is that it keeps us tight with our audience. They trust us because we love them. They listen to us because we speak their language, we play their music. That puts us in a unique position to put something meaningful in front of them, now and again, about social issues, politics, the world they live in, the issues they care about.

And it's helped us grow MTV into one of the most recognized brands in the world. Hopefully, when you hear the word "MTV," you will think about music, attitude, creativity, and risk-taking. For all of us who work here, we take it as our mandate to protect and continue to nurture this amazing asset. We don't want to exploit it; we want to protect it because we have an emotional investment in it.

I hope everyone gets the chance to feel this way about what they do. Sometimes I look back and think, how did I end up with one of the best jobs in the world? I love young people, I love music, I love all that good creative energy that hits me every time I walk off the elevator and towards my office. I'm lucky like that.

You know, a long time ago, I got over the idea that we will have a crystal clear picture of where MTV is going and adopted a sort of tolerance for uncertainty—just like I'm not quite sure what my daughter, Anna, might next say or do. And that's even more the case as we all continue to move into this still-not-fully-tapped world of the Internet.

I guess that's the beauty of it: that we can't be quite sure about what to expect, and that can be a good thing, as long as you have a strategy, some guiding principles, and a little love for what you do. All this makes me wonder who will be on the future list of the "50 Greatest Women on the Web." Maybe Anna will be one of them.

—JUDY MCGRATH

Edythe
Meserand

■ IN 1926, WHEN COMMERCIAL BROADCASTing was in its infancy, seventeen-year-old Edythe Meserand was offered a job at a company called "NBC." Her response was "Oh, God, I can't stand biscuits"—confusing the then-better-known National Biscuit Company with a new company sharing its acronym, the National Broadcasting Company, which had just been created by the union of radio stations WJZ and WEAF in New York City. Once Meserand learned the difference, she accepted the job and went on to contribute significantly to radio's Golden Age of the 1930s and '40s as a pioneering news executive and cofounder of the first organization to support women in the industry.

During that time she helped define what radio news and publicity departments could and should do, especially as sources of breaking world news and as a service to their communities. She also produced some of the first radio documentaries, several of which won George Foster Peabody and Freedom Foundation awards. She blazed trails for women in the formative years of broadcast journalism, both through the example of her own career and as one of the founders and first national president of American Women in Radio and Television (AWRT).

Born November 29, 1908, in

Philadelphia, Meserand started out writing news releases in NBC's press department. What was happening on radio then *was* news, and newspapers published detailed schedules of programming and reported every new development. "People would stop working or make connections in order to hear certain programs," Meserand remembered. Being at the source enabled Meserand to make important connections and to begin to see the power radio could have.

After five years, Meserand moved in 1931 to WGBS (soon WINS) radio and became the first "Musical Clock Girl." From 6:00 to 9:00 in the morning, she played records and gave the news and the time every half hour. When WINS became one of the ten stations of Hearst Radio, she was made publicity director for the group. Then, in 1937, she moved to WOR radio, where she stayed until leaving the profession in 1952.

During her years at WOR, both Meserand and radio found their niche, as World War II created a massive hunger for news and radio became the place to get it quickly. Stations' publicity and news functions—until then handled together—were separated as the war approached in order to handle the increased news demands. Meserand went with the news and was named assistant director.

Then, Friday afternoon before Labor Day weekend 1939, she was about to leave the office for an out-of-town weekend with the young lawyer she was engaged to marry. The news came over the wire that England had just declared war on Germany. "It was the turning point of my life," she said. "I knew what radio meant and that it was going to be more important than my personal life. I went up to Master Control when the bulletin came and never came out for a day and a half while I manned the telephones, trying to get information. My parents and the poor boy, meanwhile, were calling the police and every hospital to see what had come of me." The marriage never took place, but Meserand had found her mission.

During the war years, Meserand—the only woman on WOR's executive staff—produced all special features. Most notable was the program considered the first true radio documentary, which Meserand created about V-E Day 1945, the day the war in Europe ended with victory for the Allies. While America slept, she recorded the program during Europe's daytime hours as the continent celebrated; she then broadcast it for her listeners when they woke up the next day. Her other war-related features included General Douglas MacArthur's homecoming and a meeting with Madame Chiang Kai-shek.

Meserand as the "Musical Clock Girl" at WINS in the 1930s

Meserand (front right) at an AWRT banquet, early 1950s

After the war ended, Meserand continued to produce documentaries on issues such as civil defense, mobilization, and the atomic bomb. But she also turned to investigative journalism, producing consumer-oriented programs marked by creativity and thorough research.

The idea for one of these was born as she waited nervously to speak at Ohio State University and a companion offered her a barbiturate to help her calm down. Meserand declined but created a series, *Name Your Poison,* about the harmful effects of medications. During her ten months of research, she not only worked with the FDA and New York's health department and legislature to collect masses of data but sent reporters to pharmacies around the city to try to buy

pills supposedly available by prescription only. Another series investigated food safety, from the finest dining establishments to Lower East Side dives, and included interviews of people with food poisoning from their hospital beds. Meserand herself got into the act, visiting restaurants to slip silverware and glasses surreptitiously into sterile bags and taking them to a lab for bacterial analysis.

Meserand also produced a weekly roundtable political discussion with newspaper reporters and was an innovative producer of religious and ethnic programming. She put a Jewish seder on the air for the first time; convinced Harlem's Father Divine to broadcast a fiery sermon; and spent days and nights with a Chinese

Meserand at WOR/WOR-TV, New York, during her tenure as first national president of AWRT, 1952

family for a program on Chinatown. In 1951, she produced a documentary on the Catholic Holy Year, for which Pope Pius XII awarded her a medal.

Service to the community defined Meserand's professional mission, but she also took it personally. She created the WOR Christmas Children's Fund to provide gifts for needy and hospitalized children and worked with the Fresh Air Fund. In 1951, for her fifteen years of service to children as a broadcaster, *McCall's* magazine gave her its first Golden Mike Award. That same year, Meserand and the other women in radio and television who'd been working to found a national trade organization to help them professionally realized their dream with the founding of AWRT.

When General Tire and Rubber Company bought WOR in 1952, Meserand retired from broadcasting and moved to upstate New York, running her own advertising agency for a time. She lived there until her death on June 2, 1997. In her later years, Meserand often criticized the direction radio had taken, feeling it had abandoned the hard news that showed the medium at its best and bemoaning the fact that she had never had the resources to buy a station.

Meserand's pioneering legacy as a serious newswoman in the industry, however, is clear. AWRT gave her its 1982 Achievement Award for exceptional service to the organization, her community, and women in the industry, and in 1997 she was one of eight newswomen inducted into the Women's Press Club Hall of Honor. As famed newscaster Pauline Frederick said in tribute to Meserand at an AWRT dinner honoring her in 1976, "What you did . . . has made it possible for our sex to participate increasingly in this vital area of communications. May the 'newcomers' never forget that *you* did it first!" ■

In the first days of radio, NBC at 711 Fifth Avenue was the height of glamour. . . . It was a time when you dressed to attend a "first night" of a radio series, when red carpet was spread from the special elevator reserved for the VIP or guest star, right to the curb; when NBC hired an elocution teacher to train the announcers . . . in what became known as the NBC Voice. . . .

Yes, the NBC Voice carried through right down to the lowliest of staff and was imitated by young and old alike. To this day, every now and then my sister will tease me if I suddenly revert to it.

It was a time when you rubbed shoulders with the top brass and they knew you by name. It was the glamour period when you dressed for dinner and the theater, a time when your social prestige was measured by the number of speak-easy cards you carried, when all the hotels had big name bands, and your social life included the very sophisticated night clubs all over the city, particularly the Cotton Club in Harlem. It was a time when most of the talent of the entertainment world was getting started and being recognized and enjoyed.

It was a time when I stood in awe in the control room, listening to the far-off voice of a young monsignor named Francis Spellman, translating the first broadcast from the Vatican in Rome; and the thrill to be present when the first two-way transatlantic broadcast [took place] between Merlin Aylesworth, president of NBC, speaking from the New York City studios, and Marconi aboard his yacht, the *Electra*, in the Mediterranean.

A time when there were so many fine newspapers in NYC . . . and they and the others throughout the country had full radio sections, not only with listings of programs, but full-page feature stories about the personalities and the programs on the air.

It was then that NBC hired two fine artists to do portraits of the stars, especially for these feature stories. . . .

And it was because of the popularity of these radio sections that Johnny Johnstone selected me to be the contact person with the radio editors throughout the country, setting up interviews, photo setups, etc. It was on one of these assignments that I suffered one of the most embarrassing moments of my lifetime.

NBC had engaged the great Madame Schuman-Henk as musical advisor. The radio editor of the *Telegram*, Jack Foster, was first in line for an interview. It fell on the same day that we had a date . . . so I took particular pains with my makeup, such as it was, for I never used anything more than powder, a bit of rouge and lipstick. We approached the lady at the appointed hour, I made the necessary introductions, and just as the interview was about to begin, Madame Schuman-Henk asked in a deep-resounding voice: "How old are you?" Very meekly, I answered her 19. She then turned and said: "Go in there and wash your face." She had her own dressing room. I did not argue, believe me, I did as I was told, dying a thousand deaths, while Jack sat and smirked. When I came out, shaking in my boots, she smiled, put her arm around me and said: "Now you look like a nice little girl." The interview was a success; I was limp. . . .

So many names, so many wonderful people who were willing to share their knowledge and learn together to bring the best possible to the new media. Names that are all but forgotten now, but who pioneered in the broadcasting field. I'll just mention a handful of them. Merlin H. Aylesworth, known as "Dean," the first president of NBC; George F. McClelland, executive vice president of NBC, who was the father of the commercial program; Margaret Cuthbert, director of public affairs for NBC; and Bertha Brainard, program director of NBC and the person responsible for such delights as the Metropolitan Opera broadcasts, *The Rise of the Goldbergs,* and so many, many others.

It's been a very full fifty years. I would not change one day of it, including the heartaches, the disappointments, the mistakes, and the frustrations, for the rewards far outweigh all of them.

—EDYTHE MESERAND

Mary
Tyler Moore

■ As a seven-year-old, Mary Tyler Moore liked to perform at family get-togethers. She taught herself to tap-dance and would emulate Betty Grable, twirling a black umbrella like a parasol while singing "On the Boardwalk in Atlantic City." Her mother and father's applause on those occasions was "like finding the light switch in a dark room," she noted years later. Her gratification stemmed not just from the nod to her talents but from the approval shown by her usually undemonstrative young parents.

The American public, however, would feel different. Television viewers fell in love with her almost immediately, beginning when she was in her mid-twenties, playing housewife Laura Petrie on *The Dick Van Dyke Show.* America's affection and respect for Moore grew as she played Mary Richards, an optimistic, happily unmarried TV producer who helped give shape to the emerging ideal of an independent woman, on *The Mary Tyler Moore Show.* Mary Tyler Moore remains America's sunny sweetheart, the girl we'd want for a daughter, the woman we'd want for a friend, the coworker we could count on to stand up for our rights.

Born on December 29, 1936, Moore began her career as a professional dancer after her family moved from Long Island, New York, to the Los Angeles area.

Married at eighteen and a mother at nineteen, she had a supportive husband (salesman Richard Meeker) who arranged his work schedule so he could drive her to auditions in the family's only car. Her first break as an actor came when producers of the *Richard Diamond, Private Detective* series cast her as Sam, the sultry voice of an answering service. The camera showed only Moore's legs, and the producers excluded her name from the credits to create an air of mystery. Resentful that her compensation was not rising along with the show's popularity, she left and created her own buzz by revealing her "Sam" identity to casting agents all over town. It was a move that hinted at her future ascent as a decision maker in the industry.

Moore and Dick Van Dyke promoting *The Dick Van Dyke Show*

After a few small guest roles on shows such as *77 Sunset Strip* and an audition for a role with Danny Thomas, Moore learned that Thomas had recommended her to *Dick Van Dyke* producer Carl Reiner. When Reiner auditioned her, he knew instantly that he'd found his Laura Petrie.

Over the years, many have pointed to Laura Petrie, with her capri pants and form-fitting dresses, as the first TV wife with a palpable though wholesome sexuality. Perhaps more important, though, is Moore's portrayal of a wife as a nearly equal partner in a marriage—a major accomplishment in the 1960s. "She bridged the transition from old-fashioned Father-knows-best American wife to a more powerful, independent woman," says Robert Thompson of Syracuse University's Center for the Study of Popular Television. "Laura had intelligent opinions, and she didn't always bow to Rob's views. She had arguments with Rob. They made decisions together."

When *The Dick Van Dyke Show* ended in 1966, Universal Studios gave Moore a multipicture contract, planning to position her as "the next Doris Day." She received good reviews for her performance as Miss Dorothy in *Thoroughly Modern Millie* with Julie Andrews, but her next project, playing Holly Golightly in the stage version of *Breakfast at Tiffany's*, proved devastating. At that time the most expensive ($350,000) musical in Broadway history, the show opened and closed

Performing with guest star Gene Kelly on *The Mary Tyler Moore Hour*, 1979

within a matter of days. Next she starred in the movies *Change of Habit* with Elvis Presley and *What's So Bad About Feeling Good?* with George Peppard.

In the late 1960s, Moore suffered a miscarriage and learned she had Type I diabetes, requiring several insulin injections a day. Fortunately, she was also on the verge of the greatest opportunity of her career. Having admired her performance in a TV special with Dick Van Dyke, CBS executives offered Moore her own half-hour situation comedy: the show would be named for her, and she would have the authority to choose the setting, writers, and costars.

In response, she and her second husband, producer Grant Tinker, formed the production company MTM in 1970 and built a show about Mary Richards, the TV producer with brains, heart, and ambition. For the first time on television, the plots centered around the kind of problems a real working woman might encounter: having to fire a colleague or—in a groundbreaking episode—successfully arguing for a raise upon learning that a man in the same job was paid more. "Mary Tyler Moore did for the career woman what Lucille Ball did for physical comedy," says Ann Hodges, a critic for forty years with the *Houston Chronicle.*

After 168 episodes and twenty-nine Emmy awards, the *Mary Tyler Moore Show* left the air in 1977. The show had turned into a mother lode of spin-offs as new MTM series were created for featured characters: *Rhoda, Phyllis,* and *Lou Grant.* In the 1980s, Moore sold her

Cast members of *The Mary Tyler Moore Show* on the twentieth anniversary show, 1991

interest in MTM, but she continued her career in front of the camera.

In 1980, Robert Redford cast her in his film *Ordinary People* as Beth Jarrett, the mother of a boy who commits suicide. Her powerful performance as a woman victimized by her own emotional rigidity—a character that Moore has said reminded her of her father—won her an Academy Award nomination.

Another uptight, but less serious, character, that of Ben Stiller's domineering mother in the 1996 movie *Flirting with Disaster,* endeared Moore to a new generation and reminded the old one of her comic versatility. In between films,

Moore has continued to appear in television series and made-for-TV movies, including the reunion movie *Mary and Rhoda,* which Moore executive-produced and which landed in the top-ten ratings.

Today, Moore lives in Manhattan and upstate New York with her third husband, cardiologist Robert Levine. In addition to her continuing professional work, Moore has directed significant amounts of her attention and enthusiasm to charitable work for such causes as diabetes, youth antiviolence, and animal welfare. She may have found, in her parents' approval, the light switch that sparked her career, but to her fans, she is the light. ■

Ever since childhood, I'd wanted to dance professionally. Fortunately, my young adulthood in the late 1950s coincided with the heyday of musical variety shows, both as specials ("spectaculars" they were called) and as weekly hour shows. Most of them were on NBC, and the broadcast studio in Burbank eventually became my second home.

It all came about after my mother became friendly with her neighbors Margie and Bernie Rich. Margie had been a dancer and was Debbie Reynolds's best friend. Bernie was an associate producer on *The Eddie Fisher Show.* It was a one-hour variety show that alternated every week with *The George Gobel Show.* They were hit shows. With a little sleeve tugging, Margie was able to arrange an audition for me to join the chorus of *Eddie Fisher.*

I got that job, and soon I was also appearing on *The George Gobel Show* in its opening commercial spot. George would enter center stage, music up, audience cheering, and take a Chesterfield (the show's sponsor) from his pocket and place it in his mouth. Enter me, dressed in a glitzy, beaded leotard and heels so high it's amazing I didn't topple over. I "showgirl-stepped" (a kind of knees-high prance) over to him, carrying a four-foot-high cigarette lighter that serviced his need of the moment. It didn't take much rehearsing, but they would call me in for three days' work just because they liked me. They liked all the dancers.

Before long I found myself being used by the choreographers of most of the shows—Bob Hope, Dean Martin and Jerry Lewis, and Jimmy Durante. I always kept a high profile, hopeful of being given something extra to do—standing next to the star as a part of the glamour group that surrounded him when he sang a song, perhaps being given a line of dialogue or a solo spot in one of the dance numbers. The potential could lead anywhere, if movie lore was to be believed. Most of the girls seemed happy with their lot and didn't leap up, as I did, when the director said, "Okay, girls, we need someone to . . ."

During one rehearsal, Jimmy Durante asked us (there were six dancers) if we would help him out and consider being driven by chauffeur to the home of Dr. Stroub, who owned the Santa Anita Racetrack. We were to perform our number that night at a big party. "You'll be taken good care of, goils," he promised. Well, it sounded so glamorous and Mr. Durante was so sweet to us, always, no one could refuse him. Besides, it sounded unorthodox and exciting. "Dress nice, goils. The limos will pick you up at nine."

It was the first time I had ever been in that sleek black vehicle of the rich, and it was thrilling. When we drove through the gates of the Stroub home in Pasadena, and I took in the number of limos just like ours parked around the home that resembled a palace, my palms got a little sweaty. The house was immense, all white with a Mediterranean, multileveled, tiled roof. Fabulously dressed people wandered about as if it were all normal.

The guests ate under a lavishly decorated tent brimming with flowers, something I had never seen before. We dancers dined in the kitchen, a room large enough to contain the two-bedroom apartment that I lived in with my husband and young son.

It was show time. We were wrangled to an enclosure just off the small stage area. Jimmy Durante was introduced, and he performed his monologue and several songs. Then we were introduced and high-stepped our way to our positions surrounding Durante. The audience, as always, adored him. They were quite taken with our presence, too. There aren't many performers who bring six backups along for just one song.

When we finished, we were asked to follow Dr. Stroub into the library of the house. There, he removed six crisp $100 bills from a silver box, and handed one to each of us along with his thanks. I had never seen a $100 bill, much less held one that belonged to me.

On the way home, my friend Mina, who had danced in the show with me, said that she felt like an innocent hooker. She suggested that we go to her neighborhood hangout to celebrate the extraordinary event, and I agreed. Why not pretend to be for one minute? Still wearing our costumes, we got some looks, but no one approached us as we sipped our Cokes. When the check came, I asked her to pay. I didn't want to let go of my talisman.

Although I was dancing in the chorus a lot and it was helping to pay the bills, it was also an ego cruncher. The directors and actors would laugh and flirt with the dancers, but when the latter got in the way, they were told to sit in the corner and be quiet. That $100-a-night-job at Dr. Stroub's was something of an anomaly: dancers generally live hand to mouth, the work is hard and underpaid, and they are thought of as charming, gifted monkeys. I crumbled because I couldn't stand being treated as one of the babbling herd. I still have a problem with that. Making a career of it would have killed me spiritually before it did physically (which happens in ten or fifteen years, anyway). That, plus the attention and consideration given to the stars, fed my insecurity. A yearning for respect, more than a need for artistic fulfillment, drove me to pursue a career in acting, a career more fulfilling than I ever could have imagined. However, beneath the confident surface of the successful actress you've come to know beats the heart of a failed dancer.

— MARY TYLER MOORE

Jane
Pauley

■ "MAYBE YOU'RE WONDERING HOW I GOT here. Well maybe I am, too." Those words, spoken simply and candidly, began Jane Pauley's self-introduction to Tom Brokaw, Gene Shalit, and the universe of viewers who tuned in to see the new cohost of the *Today* show in 1976. Literally untried and untested, the twenty-five-year-old Pauley had bested hundreds of hopefuls to replace Barbara Walters on the struggling show. And most critics expected her to fail. Not only did she not fail, but she proved that she has that intangible something broadcasters desperately seek: staying power.

Pauley herself has said that her career has succeeded in large part due to flukes and lucky breaks. But it was her intellect and ability to connect with people that sent her to the top. From a novice at a midwestern television station to a household name, Pauley's broadcasting career has spanned more than thirty years. That's thirty years of overcoming critics who predicted her downfall, first because she was too young and then because she was too old. Whether her longevity can be attributed to a record string of lucky breaks or not, there is no doubt that there is something truly special about her.

Born Margaret Jane Pauley in 1950 in Indiana to Richard Pauley, a food products distributor, and Mary, an office clerk

and homemaker, she was raised on solid midwestern values. Even as a child, she possessed an obvious intelligence and a knack for absorbing new information quickly. She joined the debate team in high school, eventually becoming a state champion and developing a lifetime interest in current events.

After graduating from the University of Indiana in Bloomington with a degree in political science, Pauley landed her first broadcasting job as a news reporter at WISH-TV in Indianapolis just weeks after graduation. "She was something special. She just lights up, responds to the people in the studio and beyond the camera. It's a gift that few people have," said news director Lee Giles, who had hired Pauley in part to comply with FCC equal employment opportunity regulations.

Within eighteen months, Pauley was noticed by the major markets and moved to Chicago to coanchor the five o'clock and ten o'clock newscasts at NBC affiliate WMAQ-TV. The move marked two firsts for Pauley: she became the first woman to anchor a Chicago evening newscast, and she went her first round with dissenting critics. Pauley was harshly described as a "corn-fed Catherine Deneuve" by *Time*, and despite her optimism in the face of her opponents, WMAQ's ratings fell and she was relegated to only one newscast a day plus occasional special reports.

In 1976, two major events were taking place on early-morning television: Barbara Walters had left the *Today* show in a highly publicized move to ABC, and *Good Morning America* on ABC had become a serious rival. Pauley auditioned for the vacancy and won the coveted spot by earning higher viewer approval than more experienced competitors such as Betty Furness and Candice Bergen.

Despite her youthful appearance, Pauley was confident. "I knew I was not going to set the country on fire and that there would be unkind criticism," she said. "But they're not going to be around as long as I intend to be."

Today won its ratings back, and the camera continued to love Pauley. Through rumors of replacements and changes of cohost in the early 1980s, Pauley persevered and was hailed by *Mademoiselle* magazine as "the woman America loves to wake up to."

By the late 1980s, the increasing matu-

Pauley early in her career

rity that Pauley had previously predicted would help her seemed to be working against her. NBC brought in the younger Deborah Norville, an anchor from the network's *Sunrise*, who soon was viewed as an equal to, and possibly a replacement for, Pauley. After some soul-searching, Pauley decided it was time to move on. "Going to the network and telling them I was leaving was a big step for a late-blooming baby boomer like me. It made me feel like an adult," Pauley admitted in 1990.

After Pauley's departure, in 1991 she was given her own show, *Real Life with Jane Pauley*, a prime-time feature news program that lasted only nine months.

But Pauley bounced back in 1992 as the cohost of *Dateline*, an instant hit that became the model for future TV news-magazine formats. By 1996, *Dateline* was airing four nights a week, making Pauley the first female to cohost four hours of prime-time news programming and again launching her into millions of American homes. The year 1997 marked Pauley's

Pauley with Neal Shapiro, producer of _Dateline,_ after she received a 2000 Gracie Allen Award

twenty-fifth anniversary in the industry, and _Dateline_ was still going strong in the Nielsen ratings.

Despite remaining at the top of her game and winning numerous awards for her work, including Emmy Awards, a Gabriel Award, and two AWRT Gracie Allen Awards, Pauley laughs off the notion that she is an American icon. "I can't imagine being an American icon! Besides, if I were an icon, I might find myself being poked fun at in Garry's strip," referring to her husband of twenty years, Garry Trudeau, the creator of the satirical _Doonesbury_ comic strip.

Not a surprising response from the humble woman from Indianapolis who brought new meaning to her father's advice to "aim high but be careful." Pauley not only surpassed her father's expectations ("He thought I should aspire to be a receptionist") but has risen through the ranks of broadcasters and stayed on top for thirty years.

Pauley, who was once trying to prove she wasn't too young and then trying to prove she wasn't too old, is now happy where she is: at the top. "I've never felt more committed, more competent, more confident," she says. "And having arrived at this point, I'm inclined to think it should last a very long time." ■

I went to Chicago on assignment recently and booked myself into the hotel where, twenty-five years ago, I had stood at the window, overlooking the Chicago River as the sun came up, and contemplated how my life was on the verge of something big. I skipped so many of the preliminaries that most of my colleagues write about because after three years as a general assignment reporter in Indianapolis I was catapulted into the anchor chair in the second largest television market in the country. There I stayed for 365 days before I was vaulted into Barbara Walters' recently vacated seat on the *Today* show! I was still twenty-five and did not know what had hit me. I was not one of those five-year-plan people who had it all worked out, so for many years all I could do was give the credit to good luck and very good timing.

After a decade or so I began to take some credit myself—while still feeling lucky—but no more than all the other broadcast newswomen of my generation whom I've named the "Class of '72" (give or take). We all have the FCC to thank for the affirmative action mandate that pried doors open that had been virtually closed to women for so long.

Then, one day in 1975, I got a phone call at my desk at WISH-TV in Indianapolis and then another and another. Unbeknown to me, I'd been included on a reel of women reporters and anchors that had been circulating around the industry and was suddenly being courted by Philadelphia and Atlanta and ultimately Chicago, to which I flew secretly one night after work to audition at WMAQ, one of NBC's owned and operated stations. That was the night I didn't sleep at all, because though my confidence was several months premature, in fact, I'd nailed the audition and just knew it. My intuition is my best asset.

I discovered my second best asset at the age of fourteen, when, heartbroken, I'd failed to make varsity cheerleader. I had the good luck to attend an otherwise ordinary suburban public school that then had a powerhouse speech and debate team—one of the biggest in the country—owing entirely to the dynamic and ambitious coach, Harry Wilfong, whom we all call "Uncle Harry" to this day. He got me in his beams and didn't let go until I was governor of Hoosier Girls' State and a state champion in extemporaneous speaking.

I parlayed my "expertise" in current events and politics into a degree in political science at Indiana University, not entirely sure what I intended to do with it. Still, I was in a big hurry to do something because in my sophomore year I plotted a path to graduate a semester early so I could be involved in the coming presidential election campaign. Improbably, I was the Indiana John Lindsay for President coordinator in the spring of 1972 before his campaign failed. Over the next eight months as a low-level staffer at the Indiana Democratic State Central Committee (a job I owed to my very Republican father, who, to my mother's everlasting chagrin, wangled an introduction to the state chairman, whom he met at a Presbyterian men's conference) I met all the local reporters—print and broadcast. And by election day I wasn't working in politics, I was reporting it as the newest (and only female) reporter at WISH-TV.

I had never seen a TelePrompTer, had to be told how to hold a microphone, mistook a camera lens for an ashtray, and managed to get the date of the election wrong, over and over again, in my first "man on the street" assignment. Still, I must have had "something." At the time he took a chance on me, without any journalism experience and without a degree in Radio/TV, News Director Lee Giles warned his boss, the general manager, that if they hired me, "we'll never keep her." He was right. And I'm still wondering what's going to happen next.

—JANE PAULEY

Jane
Cahill Pfeiffer

■ On September 13, 1978, the National Broadcasting Company announced the appointment of Jane Cahill Pfeiffer as its first-ever female chairman of the board. Reporters from every type of media were climbing over one another to get an interview, even just a few words, with the entertainment industry's newly crowned queen. Of course, they thought, this rising star must be dying to share her secrets for success and to pose for pictures in her new power chamber as a symbol of the first woman to break into the highest executive ranks.

They were mistaken. "Since her appointment, Pfeiffer has consistently turned down countrywide press requests for interviews," reported the *New York Times*. "She remains reticent about being photographed." It wasn't that Pfeiffer is shy; indeed, she has a gift for communication. It wasn't that she had no plan; she had come to the job with clear-cut goals. The reason behind her recalcitrance? Simply put, she felt she was there to work, not to show off. Pfeiffer's strong work ethic, dedication to quality, and no-nonsense attitude had enabled her to rise steadily in her twenty-year career at IBM, which preceded her tenure at NBC. In her move to television, she saw no reason to change her approach.

Although her stay ended after barely two years, Pfeiffer left a lasting mark on the network. "Jane brought the news up to another level," says Bob Blackmore, a former NBC executive vice president. Pfeiffer lured top-drawer CBS news staff and initiated extended, prime-time coverage of serious topics such as the SALT treaty. And, via the *Live from Studio 8H* series, she put a spotlight on highbrow culture such as opera, ballet, and classical music. Perhaps most important, she proved that a woman can blaze a trail in a man's world without making gender an issue. "She wears her femininity like a Brooks Brothers suit: She is comfortable with it, it is of fine fabric, but it never gets in the way," *Savvy* magazine wrote of Pfeiffer in 1980.

Actually, at one time in her life, it looked as though she would never wear any kind of business suit. Born into a devoutly Catholic family, Jane Cahill lost her father, marketing manager John J. Cahill, in 1940, when she was just seven years old. Her mother, Helen Reilly Cahill, went to work for the government as a dietitian and eventually became director of dietetics for the Veterans Administration. "My mother encouraged both my brother and me to do whatever we set our hearts on," says Pfeiffer. "I was going to be a nun." So after earning a B.A. in speech and dramatic arts at the University of Maryland in 1954, she entered a California novitiate, but she decided after a while that "it wasn't what I was cut out for."

The following year, IBM, then an $825 million company, hired Jane Cahill as a systems engineering trainee. She rose quickly through the ranks, growing with the company as it developed into a $23 billion superpower.

As part of her work at IBM, Pfeiffer applied for, and won, a White House fellowship, making her the first woman in the White House intern program. Upon her return from Washington, IBM promoted her to vice president in charge of government relations. "I was very involved in IBM's look to the outside," she says. After moving into communications, she significantly raised the company's cultural cachet by arranging for it to sponsor television series such as *Face the Nation* and *IBM Presents,* which featured such programs as educational dramas about Eleanor and Franklin Roosevelt and Clarence Darrow.

In 1976, as Pfeiffer was recovering from thyroid cancer, she received an offer

Pfeiffer with daughter Nancy and son John in Vero Beach, Florida, 1992

from the White House. President Jimmy Carter wanted her to be the next secretary of commerce. Partly because of her health—as well as her reluctance to leave the Greenwich, Connecticut, home she shared with her husband, IBM executive Ralph A. Pfeiffer, Jr., whom she had married in 1975—she turned down the job.

But an even more exciting opportunity arose when, her health restored, Pfeiffer was recruited by NBC President Fred Silverman (whom she knew from her television work at IBM) to help him run the network. She accepted and, as the second in command at NBC, received annual remuneration of $425,000, reportedly the highest salary for any woman in a publicly owned corporation at that time.

Pfeiffer immediately went to work putting her high ideals into practice. She upgraded the network's news coverage, recruiting CBS newscasters Roger Mudd and Marvin Kalb as well as strategists Richard Salant and William Small to NBC. The *Studio 8H* series she created debuted with Zubin Mehta conducting the New York Philharmonic Orchestra's tribute to Arturo Toscanini and continued with other high-quality programming.

Distinguished commentator Bill Moyers met with Pfeiffer when she proposed that he create a weekly NBC news series. Moyers fondly recalls that Pfeiffer "was always a delight to deal with because she was so open and direct, so full of enthusiasm, so willing to listen to new ideas."

In 1980, a gap suddenly grew between Silverman and Pfeiffer, and she resigned from the network. Expressing no ill will or regrets, Pfeiffer launched a career as a consultant in management organization, communications, and government relations. She retired and moved to Florida in the late 1990s and now serves on the boards of several corporations (including International Paper, Ashland Inc.) and the University of Notre Dame, works on a variety of charitable concerns, and spends time on golf (as a member of the LPGA tournament's advisory board) and family activities (she has ten stepchildren from her marriage to Ralph Pfeiffer, who died in 1996).

To this day, she has never voiced concern about how being a woman may have affected her corporate career. "I certainly felt there were times when you were watched more or more was expected," she says. "But it was never a real issue. If you worked hard, they didn't care too much about whether you were a male or female." ∎

On the Indian River in Vero Beach, Florida, 1999

On her career and the business of running a TV network:

I have always found competition exciting. It's the American system, and I think it's a good one. Competition brings out the best in a business and the best product for the public.

I can't emphasize this enough: We have to be profitable. This is not a foundation and it's not PBS; fundamentally it is a business. . . . We should be sensitive to the creative process, not captive to it.

We believe we can do something valuable by aiming higher. We are not going to forcefeed quality or oversell it. Audiences today have an infallible sense of what is authentic and what is contrived. We are not, nor do we want to be, public broadcasting. We are commercial broadcasting, and we intend to be very successful in the competition for audience and for profits. But we know what we can be proud of, and we are determined to have more of it.

In order to be successful in a corporation you need to be energetic physically and mentally, to care genuinely about other people, to have a sense of humor, and to be willing to assume responsibility.

Being inside the business is far different from looking at it through daily newspaper columns. Television's problems are not disposed of by its reviews, and television's priorities are not ordered by its critics. Our success hinges on certain realities, and those realities impose a firm discipline on the way you operate.

On the industry:

If we are going to have all the choices of home entertainment that I think we're going to have within five years—if I can sit down at night and decide whether to watch a movie or a rerun of a football game or whatever my special interest is—then the networks are going to have to be prepared to provide unique things that can't be provided other ways.

Hit comedies like *All in the Family* and dramas like *Little House on the Prairie* have certainly shown all of us that substance and popularity are not mutually exclusive. The kind of programming they represent will never go out of style.

If we've learned anything at NBC . . . it's the right answer to Hollywood's old question: Do you want it Tuesday or do you want it good? We want it good.

Television is too large a presence in our national life and too influential a force in American thought to escape responsibility for the quality and totality of its service.

We will never know [the miniseries *Holocaust*'s] total effect on some 220 million viewers world-wide, and its extended appeal from NBC's rebroadcast. . . . But if ever we doubt the positive power of television and of a single program, we would do well to remember the tidal wave of emotion left by the broadcast of *Holocaust* in West Germany. Perhaps more than anything else, it was responsible for the vote this summer [1979] that overturned the statute of limitations on the prosecution of Nazi war criminals.

When it is said that network television tries to be all things to all people, that is very true. And I do not feel it is a disparagement. But we must recognize that we have a responsibility to reach all people, and that includes those who want a SALT debate, a symphony orchestra, or a serious drama. We must try harder to stretch our boundaries. America is not just one audience. It is many.

Network television cannot afford to be half a step behind its changing audience. It must keep pace with the people's desire to be good citizens. That means programs that take into account their capacity to think and feel, that broaden their cultural enjoyment and their understanding of an increasingly complex world.

The influence of television as a social force must be exercised with great care. Television some-times gets pushed out in front of other institutions and is asked to do what they cannot. This calls for wise judgments but must not prevent us from developing programs that help people recognize and understand the hard realities and pressing issues of our time.

—JANE CAHILL PFEIFFER

Irna
Phillips

■ DAYTIME DRAMA FANS IN THE YEAR 2001 might think of Susan Lucci as the "Queen of Soap Opera," but if it hadn't been for Irna Phillips, Lucci might never have had a chance. Not only did Phillips establish the genre by writing the first soap opera for radio, but she created a number of the most successful and enduring soap operas of all time. Some, including *As the World Turns* and *The Guiding Light,* have survived into the twenty-first century.

A master of her craft, Phillips pioneered the use of broadcasting to tell ongoing stories with her 1930 radio drama serial, *Painted Dreams.* Her star rose steadily from there as she wrote many of the radio soaps that followed. Phillips was also able to remain successful for so long because she effectively transformed her work from radio to television.

Phillips's talent for plotting and character development set her apart from her competitors and created the models that soap writers still follow today. Her captivating characters and cliff-hanger plots assisted in creating the modern mass-market consumer who linked the dramas with the household products—primarily detergent, hence "soap operas"—made by the series' sponsors.

In her heyday in the 1930s and '40s, Phillips was renowned for her ability to create stories quickly and in mass quanti-

ties: during one period, she was simultaneously writing scripts for several daily serials and a weekly program. Her methods were just as entertaining as the final product. She dictated dialogue to her secretaries, changing her pitch and tone for each character. When her workload reached a level even she could not handle, she hired assistant writers to block out dialogue based on her story outlines.

It's not surprising that Phillips's own story mirrors some of the rags-to-riches characters she created. Born in Chicago, Illinois, on July 1, 1903, Phillips was the youngest of ten children. Her father died in 1910, leaving her hardworking mother to keep the family together and put food on the table. Nevertheless, the equally hardworking Irna graduated from both the University of Illinois, receiving a degree in education in 1923, and the University of Wisconsin, where she earned a master's in public speaking.

In 1930, after a period of teaching high school English and drama, Phillips made her debut in radio as an actor and writer. Soon her writing skills were more in demand than her acting, so she concentrated on creating story outlines and dialogue. Her *Painted Dreams* ran on WGN radio in Chicago in 1930. Showing an early hint of her business acumen, Phillips decided to take her talents elsewhere when WGN refused to sell her serial nationally.

At NBC, where she landed next, she created the serial *Today's Children* with writer Walter Wicker, furthering her reputation as a cutting-edge content developer. Broadcast on WMAQ starting on

Phillips poses for the camera, circa 1930s

June 20, 1932, this soap was the first to focus on young adults.

Phillips often used her own family experiences to inspire characters and relationships. The most visible example was the Moran family cast of *Today's Children,* led by Mother Moran, who Phillips admitted was based on her mother. The cast included three generations of family and their friends, allowing the show to examine intricate family interactions.

In 1937, Phillips created *The Guiding Light* and *Road of Life.* The following year came *Woman in White,* followed by *The Right to Happiness.* Dozens of other long-running serials followed.

Phillips's eye for the future also helped her find a place in the changing communications landscape. At the beginning of television's ascendancy, she adapted some of her radio dramas for the new medium. *The Guiding Light* was the first serial to succeed on television, although it also remained on radio until 1956. *The Brighter Day* was broadcast on NBC Radio starting in October 1948; the television version, starring Hal Holbrook and Patty Duke, began airing on CBS Television in January 1954. The radio and television versions ran parallel until 1956, when the radio version folded. *As the World Turns,* a series Phillips created specifically for CBS television, premiered in April 1956 and continues today.

Phillips relied on basic human motivations to drive her story lines: the self-preservation instinct, for instance, or sex appeal or family loyalty. She shaped dramas around her characters, exploring their actions and motivations. She also introduced the concept of dramatic characters who held professional jobs: doctors, lawyers, nurses, and ministers.

A well-organized manager, she mapped each program on paper with a grid for each daily episode projected up to six weeks ahead. Phillips is credited with inventing the tease ending that propels listeners to tune in for the next day's program. She also used organ music to enhance the dramatic mood.

Phillips knew that the audience for daytime radio dramas was primarily women, so she tried to use her stories to expand the worlds of these viewers whose lives during that post–World War II period revolved primarily around the home. Her characters were generally strong women, many of them single working women, whom she hoped would help her viewers see themselves as potential professionals too. At a time when there was a growing American interest in psychology, she often used amnesia, nervous breakdowns, and mental health problems as plot devices. She also wrote story lines featuring crime and juvenile offenders just as these issues caught mainstream press attention.

Though unmarried her entire life, Phillips had an adopted son and daughter. Katherine Phillips, her daughter, followed in her mother's footsteps, creating the TV serial *A World Apart,* which featured a successful woman television writer with two children. Just as Irna had modeled a character on her mother, Katherine dramatized events from her mother's life. Unfortunately, this show's success did not mirror that of Irna's. *A World Apart,* starring Susan Sarandon, premiered on ABC in 1970 and was canceled fifteen months later.

For the rest of her life, the elder Phillips stayed busy writing movie scripts, serving as script consultant for soap operas, and assisting her daughter with projects. Irna Phillips died in Chicago on December 23, 1973, at the age of seventy-one—the real, undisputed "Queen of Soap Opera." ∎

I was the youngest of a family of ten children, and since childhood I had admired the tact and homely wisdom with which my mother reared her fatherless brood. The character of Mother Moran in *Today's Children* is based almost entirely on my mother. Mother, with the sturdiness befitting a pioneer, kept the family together. You can quote me with the old one, "I owe all my success to my mother."

■ ■ ■

My big break came in 1930. I went to Chicago to try out as an actress with WGN (radio). The station manager told me my voice was not pleasant, that it was too low for a woman, but he signed me up anyway to do a program called "Thought for the Day." I got a release from my teaching contract, took the job with the station, and was promptly fired a couple of weeks later. But soon after that, the station asked me if I'd be interested in writing and performing in a family drama that would in effect be a continuing story, to run for ten minutes every day.

■ ■ ■

There were six characters on *Painted Dreams*. I took two of them and another woman (Irene Wicker) took the other four, plus an Irish setter named Mikey. She was an expert at imitating barking dogs and I became one. We never had to do male voices—the men were all offstage. Male characters weren't introduced on the air until two years later, on another serial I wrote called *Today's Children,* which was on WMAQ in Chicago.

■ ■ ■

But I finally had to give up acting to devote full time to my work as a writer. You might say I never stopped acting though, because I dictate all my scripts. That allows me to play the parts of all my characters and give them dialogue that sounds like real, colloquial speech. My working process arises from four themes that drive my daytime serials: appealing to the instinct of a woman's self-preservation, to sexual drive, to the family instinct, and some combination of the three. Each program is mapped on a huge piece of cardboard, with squares representing the daily episodes for a month or six weeks in advance. In a square, a word or two will be jotted down as a reminder of the course of the story. The whole process works so smoothly that we rarely have to make script changes.

■ ■ ■

We wrote three daily scripts completely plus a half-hour weekly show. I dictate to two secretaries, acting out the roles of the characters, changing my voice for whoever is speaking. Now I lay down the story line and three assistant writers block in the dialogue.

■　■　■

I avoid tape recorders—I dictate to another person, to get that essential human contact, that other person's reaction to my dialogue, that raised eyebrow that tells me a word or a phrase doesn't sound right. Dialogue that's typed or written out often sounds stilted when it's spoken by actors. That's why writers wedded to the typewriter find working on television serials so incredibly difficult.

■　■　■

Daytime dramas should be flexible so that you can rewrite an outline if it doesn't seem to be working out in the performance. I'm usually about three weeks ahead on my outlines, but I have no objection to changing horses in midstream on a moment's notice. And of course another advantage of a live show is that it gives you a "first night" charge of excitement that you just don't get with tape or film.

■　■　■

Characters have to be multidimensional. The story has to come from the characters to the point where your viewers will get to know a character so well they can predict his or her behavior in a given dramatic situation.

■　■　■

I believe soap opera has become a part of our culture because, unlike the worlds of Tennessee Williams and Doris Day, we deal with life as most of us know it. These stories deal with the human experience in all of us, not only women, because none of us can live in a world of reality 24 hours a day. We all escape in one way or another. There are no heroines. We don't solve problems—it is a matter of adjusting to them.

■　■　■

I attempt at all times to reflect life. . . . If my stories are sensational, then so is everyone's life. Every one of our lives is a soap opera, if you want to call it that.

—IRNA PHILLIPS

Cokie
Roberts

■ YOU MIGHT SAY THAT COKIE ROBERTS WAS destined to become a widely respected political commentator, capable of holding her own with the male pundits on the Sunday-morning talk shows. After all, as she was the daughter of a politician, Louisiana congressman Hale Boggs, Roberts's childhood was a primer on the politics of Congress and the ways of Washington. "My parents knew that if they wanted to have any opportunity for family life, they'd have to involve us in politics," says Roberts. "There was never any sense of 'the children shouldn't be here.' Lyndon Johnson and Sam Rayburn would come to the house and we'd argue with them about civil rights, Vietnam, everything." Yet Roberts's success as a woman in the world of political reporting and commentary was anything but preordained—it was earned.

Roberts's preeminence as one of the best-known and most successful political correspondents—as chief congressional analyst for ABC News and coanchor, with Sam Donaldson, of *This Week with Sam Donaldson & Cokie Roberts*—is beyond doubt. Her ability to cut to the core of issues makes her a standout in the competitive arena of political punditry. But her early attempts to break into television news were not encouraging. As a young woman looking for work in New York, Roberts was repeatedly told that women weren't hired to deliver news because they were not authoritative enough.

Those early setbacks did not deter her. Not only did Roberts enter the field, but she rose to the top, where she has thrived in the predominantly male world of political reporting and analysis.

Bob Franken, then congressional correspondent for CNN on the same beat as Roberts, found her "tough as nails. Formidable competition. A combination of humanity and toughness." While the toughness is readily apparent, the humanity also shines through and endears her to viewers.

Mary Martha Corinne Morrison Claiborne Boggs was born in New Orleans,

Reporting from Vatican City, Rome, 2000

Louisiana, on December 27, 1943. Cokie (as nicknamed by her older brother, who couldn't pronounce "Corinne") was the youngest child of Hale Boggs, a Democratic congressman, and Lindy Boggs, her husband's political partner and manager of his congressional office and most of his reelection campaigns. In 1972, after fourteen terms in Congress, then–House Majority Leader Hale Boggs was on a flight over Alaska when his aircraft disappeared. Lindy Boggs assumed her husband's seat in Congress and went on to serve two decades herself.

Growing up, Cokie, her sister, Barbara, and her brother, Thomas, spent part of the year in Washington and the rest in their father's congressional district in New Orleans. Politics was the order of the day—discussing issues at dinner, visiting the Capitol, watching her mother coordinate inaugural celebrations of Presidents Kennedy and Johnson.

After graduating from Wellesley College with a B.A. in political science in 1964, Cokie returned to Washington and got a job with WRC-TV, as an assistant producer and television anchor of the program *Meeting the Minds*. Two years later, she married Steven Roberts, a New York–based journalist with the *New York Times*. Cokie left her job in Washington and moved to New York to begin life with her new husband, reflecting later that "it absolutely never occurred to me or my husband that he might leave his job and come here. It was not in our worldview."

But her early attempts to break into journalism in New York indicate how difficult it was for women to gain a toehold.

Cokie Roberts uses the latest technology at the 2000 Democratic National Convention.

"For eight months I job-hunted at various New York magazines and television stations," she says, "and wherever I went I was asked how many words I could type." Roberts eventually found a producer's job at WNEW-TV.

Over the next decade the *New York Times* transferred Steve to Los Angeles, then to Athens, Greece, and finally to Washington in 1977. Cokie worked at each destination, as a producer in Los Angeles and a CBS News stringer in Athens.

In Washington in 1978, Cokie was encouraged by friends Linda Wertheimer and Nina Totenberg, both NPR reporters, to apply for a reporting job at NPR, which was known for hiring women as broadcasters and managers—though not necessarily for the best reasons. Recalling that period, Totenberg says, "For what they paid, they couldn't find men." Roberts got the job, and the trio gained a high degree of credibility and visibility on the political beat. Roberts thrived in her new role and remained at NPR as a congressional correspondent for ten years.

Roberts quickly built a name for herself in radio for her balanced political insights and her on-air delivery, qualities that made her attractive not only to radio but to television. While working at NPR, she was asked to appear on public television as a contributor to the *MacNeil/Lehrer NewsHour,* which turned into a regular spot. She also covered congressional hearings and floor debates with Wertheimer for the weekly PBS show *The Lawmakers.*

In 1987, Roberts began making guest appearances on ABC News' *This Week*

At the 2000 Democratic National Convention

with David Brinkley, which eventually led to a permanent seat on the show. Roberts, however, was hesitant to give up radio completely. When ABC News offered her the Washington correspondent's position and a regular spot on *This Week,* Roberts worked out an arrangement that allowed her to continue as a news analyst for NPR. Then, when Brinkley retired from the show, Roberts was offered cohosting duties alongside Sam Donaldson, and the show was renamed for the two.

Among the many awards Roberts has received for her work is the Everett McKinley Dirksen Award for her coverage of Congress. She is the first broadcast journalist to receive this prestigious award.

In 1998, Roberts, herself a mother of two, wrote *We Are Our Mother's Daughters,* a book that asks the question "What is woman's place?" Roberts answered with a celebration of the unique and special roles women play in the world, in one another's lives, and especially within their families. Although her roles are many, Roberts's public place is having a prominent seat at the table of political broadcasting analysis. ■

Looking back over the course of the last thirty years, I am most proud of the totality of the work that I have done, particularly the work explaining the intricacies of the workings of Congress and the political system. There's nothing sexy about it. It's just trying to inform people, in a way they can understand, about a lot of complex things.

My life's been filled with good fortune. I had no anticipation of ever being anywhere near as successful as I've been.

That doesn't mean there haven't been roadblocks along the way. When I got out of college in June 1964, it was legal to say, as people did with no hesitancy, "We don't hire women to do that. Women are not authoritative enough to deliver the news. People will not pay attention to them." By the end of the summer, all of that was illegal. But, none of us knew it and neither did most of the people doing the hiring. It took the women at *Newsweek* and CBS and the *New York Times* to bring lawsuits. Those women really did make a difference for all of the women because news organizations came to understand that they were in legal jeopardy if they continued to say what they had always been saying. But, in all the places I worked in the early years, I was always the only woman there and the only woman in the room.

For a long time I was the only woman doing this kind of political analysis. Sitting there with the big boys and discussing politics, a woman has to be very careful not to be pushy and aggressive. You have to let viewers get to know you before you start to assert yourself too much. Otherwise, you're considered a pushy broad. Now, that's a hard line because you have to get in there enough so that they know that you really have something to say. I was lucky because a lot of people had heard me on National Public Radio and felt I had something to contribute, so they wanted to hear me on television. You can't be a wallflower, but on the other hand, you can't just jump in there, interrupt the guys, and be part of the mix. For a while you have to say just a few things, hold your tongue, and wait until everybody thinks, "Okay, she's one of the gang now."

In my case it's been an advantage to get older because what I do requires people having some trust in you. I'm not out with a microphone on the street, I'm sitting in the studio telling people about why things are happening. Somebody's got to trust me to know what I'm talking about, so age does help a little bit that way.

But the question of how many wrinkles we're allowed to acquire is really a big question mark. A few women who came before our generation, Barbara Walters being the best example, have been singular women, and they somehow, with incredible determination, hard work, and talent, got to where they are. But they did it all by themselves.

Now there is an entire generation of women, and we came in all together. We came in with the law on our side, and we've been working our way through the workplace for the last thirty-plus years. We do not know how long we'll be allowed to stay on the air as a whole generation. Many of us are now in our mid-fifties, and some are edging into their sixties, so at the moment it's looking pretty good because it would be hard to fire everybody at once. I think that might attract some attention. But clearly, looks make a difference for men and women on television. Do they make more of a difference for women? Sure they do, just as they do everyplace else on Earth. Does it mean that you have to pay more attention to how you look when you get up in the morning and go out? Of course it does. I don't know how it's all going to play out. I'm a person terrified of anesthesia, so I've never had any kind of surgery, but I'll never say never.

Women in journalism often pay attention to issues affecting children and issues affecting families. We've certainly been more interested in women as politicians and women as voters. Once women get elected, we tend to cover them dealing with issues of children and family so that it all plays together. One of the reasons that female viewers want to see correspondents who are female is that they expect us to be covering some of these issues. Women are more concerned with educational and health issues. So I think that the softer issues, for want of a better word, are ones that women are more interested in. But they are the ones that people are more interested in as well. These topics were not covered as well by news organizations until there were more women reporting on them.

Both my daughter and my daughter-in-law are in broadcasting. They are highly accomplished young women whom I now watch going through this process, and it's a wonderful way to measure how the world has changed. They are doing it thirty years later.

It's a completely different world for women than it was. These young women work very, very hard. They work on very difficult subjects. But the idea of people coming to you to ask you to do things and not ever thinking about the fact that you can't do it because you're a woman—it's a completely different world.

Sometimes we older women complain that young women aren't grateful for the battles we fought. But that's what we worked for: to make them equal in the workforce to men (and, please God, someday that minorities will be equal in the workforce to whites). The fact that these young women are not grateful is probably the most natural thing on Earth.

— COKIE ROBERTS

Eleanor
Roosevelt

■ FOUR-TERM FIRST LADY. LIFELONG SOCIAL activist. First U.S. delegate to the United Nations. Chair of the United Nations Commission on Human Rights. Author of a longtime syndicated column and four books. Pioneer radio commentator and television talk-show host.

Eleanor Roosevelt did it all, and then some—which is why President Harry Truman called her "First Lady of the World." She holds the distinction of being the first First Lady to have her own radio show and the first to use the media to promote social causes dear to her heart. Radio may have been just one of her many efforts, but it was one that would project her directly into the homes of millions of Americans.

After her husband, Franklin Roosevelt, was elected president for the first time in 1932, Eleanor used her national platform to make some startling changes in the way the media operated. On March 6, 1933, she became the first First Lady to hold a press conference, forever changing how the role of the president's spouse would be perceived by the media and the public. She took her innovation a step further by holding press conferences specifically for women reporters—and then making sure those journalists were given sought-after scoops. These exclusive news-gathering events provided

unprecedented access for women journalists at the White House and prompted news outlets to hire more women reporters so they could have representation before the First Lady.

Eleanor's creativity and initiative in support of her causes were evident long before she arrived at the White House. She was born on October 11, 1884, to a distinguished family in New York City, but her early life took a tragic turn when her mother, Anna Hall, died when Eleanor was only eight and her beloved father, Elliott (a younger brother of Theodore Roosevelt), died when she was ten. The young girl lived in England with her strict Grandmother Hall for a time and attended Allenswood girls' school

Roosevelt (standing) and members of the press at a "female only" press conference for female reporters

near London, where she was influenced by the school's director, Marie Souvestre, a stalwart defender of the downtrodden and of unpopular causes.

At age seventeen, Roosevelt began a career in community work while whirling through the coming-out parties and dances typical of her social class. Soon she hatched a plan to marry her distant cousin, Franklin Roosevelt, who she believed had a spontaneous personality similar to her father's. She was successful, and the two wed on March 17, 1905, and lived in New York City while Franklin finished law school. Over the next eleven years, they had six children: Anna Eleanor, James, Franklin Delano (who died in infancy), Elliott, Franklin Delano, and John Aspinwall.

Throughout their marriage, Eleanor

campaigned for her husband and supported him when he took office, first as New York state senator, then as governor of New York, and then for four terms as president of the United States. When Franklin was stricken by polio and paralyzed in 1921, Eleanor took on additional responsibilities, traveling far and wide as her husband's liaison, acting as his eyes and ears around the nation and the world.

Yet she always maintained a full schedule of her own as well, especially working for such social reforms as civil and human rights and educational and health care for all, as well as international issues such as the promotion of peace and the plight of refugees.

Her use of the broadcast media, along with her appearances in print, were her means of reaching millions of people in a national audience. In the early years of World War II, realizing the importance of radio to rally support for the Allied cause, she made the first Radio Free Europe broadcast. During 1941 and 1942, she hosted a weekly radio public affairs and interview show called *The Pan American Coffee Bureau Series*. Her topics included the rising cost of living, freedom of speech and the motion picture industry, American children during the war, and the duty of American women to maintain morale during wartime.

In addition to her own broadcasts, Roosevelt was a master of using the media to spotlight issues and situations of oppression regarding women, African-Americans, poor rural Americans, and unskilled workers. She knew that wherever she went, cameras and microphones would follow. In Washington, D.C., where segregation prevailed in the 1940s, she visited—with journalists in tow—

neighborhoods and institutions such as hospitals and children's homes where black citizens lived and were served. NBC Radio broadcast nationally her address on civil rights issues to the National Urban League in 1936, as well as her presentation of a medal to African-American singer Marian Anderson at an NAACP convention in Richmond. In 1949, she wrote to RCA Chairman David Sarnoff, asking for his support for radio spots showing the inequalities in housing and employment experienced by blacks in New York City.

And just as Roosevelt used broadcasting to call attention to causes, she continued to write her popular syndicated weekly column, "My Day," which was read by millions across the country. In the column, which she began writing in 1935 and continued until her death nearly three decades later, Roosevelt frequently wrote on the plight of the most oppressed, but

Ruth Crane Schaefer (left) goes on-air with Roosevelt (right), October 1953.

Roosevelt with journalists at her second press conference for women, March 13, 1933

also featured snapshots of White House life and her experiences as First Lady.

Following her husband's death in 1945, Roosevelt continued both her activism and her broadcasting. In 1948–49, she presented, with her daughter, a fifteen-minute daytime talk show. The *Eleanor and Anna Roosevelt Show* ran on ABC Radio several times a week for thirty-nine weeks. Anna, based in Hollywood, commented on fashion and entertainment; Eleanor discussed world affairs, taping the program from wherever in the world she might be.

In the spring of 1950, with son Elliott, Roosevelt created a short-lived Sunday television discussion show for NBC-TV. Mother and son also produced a radio series, which aired from October 1950 until August 1951. *The Eleanor Roosevelt Show* featured Roosevelt as host interviewing such guests as Albert Einstein and the Duke and Duchess of Windsor. During 1951 as well, Roosevelt recorded Voice of America broadcasts to be aired in Europe.

When Eleanor Roosevelt died in New York City on November 7, 1962, of a rare form of tuberculosis, she left the world better for her many efforts—including her creative use of media. ∎

I do not happen to be one of the people who are fortunate enough to have a great deal of time to watch and analyze what television is now presenting to the public, but I did find that many of my contemporaries get a great part of their information from television programs and that many of their interests stem from what they have seen and heard on television.

I have, as you know, reached 75 and know many of the limitations that come with age. TV can supply many pleasant hours as well as much information. No matter what one's age, one can develop new interests, and TV will help older people to develop these interests.

As our senior citizens find themselves growing older, they realize that because of their physical difficulties they are no longer able to have the personal contacts with others and they cannot have the experiences which give validity to their taking part in home life and social contacts generally. Through TV they can often see something which the rest of their family perhaps has gone out of the house to come into personal contact with—a ball game, an inauguration, a convention, the arrival of an important foreign visitor, a thousand and one happenings that other members of the family may not even have an opportunity to see at all, or may only see for one passing moment. In watching TV the senior member of the family is probably seeing everything there is to see. So when the family comes home and discusses a topic, the elderly member does not need to feel left out of the discussion because TV provided full participation in the actual situation.

I think this is one of the significant contributions which keep older people from feeling cut off and diffident about the validity of what they may think or feel in discussions with younger people.

Many older people are alone a great deal. In their late years they may choose to live alone rather than to find themselves in the environment of a young family where they feel they may be a burden or where they find themselves exhausted by the life that of necessity must stir around them. Even if they live with younger people, they may find themselves often left out of the young activities. So they live alone and they are lonely, for the best that can happen to older people is that they will have family and friends who will come in to see them occasionally. They must learn to live with themselves. Physical handicaps may keep them from doing many things which before occupied much of their time, but if a sense of loneliness comes over them they can turn on the television, see people and hear them talk, listen to beautiful music, often watch a show as well as if they went to a movie or theater far away.

The old, like the very young, crave identification and remembrance. A child will often demand attention just for the sake of feeling that he is an individual and that you know him as an individual. Old people do the same thing just out of a sense of wanting so desperately to be recognized as people and not to be shoved aside without much thought and treated as though they were pieces of furniture. If they have something interesting to talk about, something that perhaps gives them a little closer touch with the experiences of younger people, they cannot be ignored. So we must think of all these things which bring the life and interest to our older citizens, things which keep them cheerful and undemanding.

People who are lonely are apt to make family and friends feel guilty that they cannot be with them more often. Yet the life that younger people lead today makes it difficult for them to find time to drop in on an older person who is no longer active in the same fields.

TV, I think, has made it possible for older people to learn to live alone happily, and that is one of the greatest contributions that can be made to people who have lost their life's partners and must live for a considerable number of years perhaps with serious handicaps and restrictions. If they have been intellectuals all their lives, as long as their eyes hold out they can read and that will help wipe out loneliness. But eyes suffer too with age, and television is probably a good change when one finds the need to give one's eyes some kind of variety.

Just because TV has such possibilities for reaching the lives of older people and, of course, of the younger people too, particularly of children, it seems to me that the responsibility of those who work out programs is very great. They should have in mind their most constant audiences—children and older citizens and housewives. The older citizens are the ones who are most apt to reflect at length on what they have seen or heard and to use it for good or ill in their contacts, whatever they are, with other people. If they find that they know what the younger people are talking about and that they have a contribution to make, it will add immeasurably to their happiness. They will sift programs they see through their own experience and this may be a valuable help, for the stations can use the reflections and reactions of the older people to the programs they devise and produce. It will give the older citizens an added interest, for they will feel they are taking part in improving or increasing the value to others through sending in their thoughts on certain TV programs.

TV can be used also to give older people an opportunity to help in different projects for different organizations if the organizations advertise on TV when they can use senior citizens in one capacity or another. This would bring happiness to the older people, for it would make them feel that they could be useful. They could even be told of situations in which their influence in the community could be used to advantage, and this would give them great satisfactions.

Whether programs are good or bad or offer opportunities for work or service . . . there is no question in my mind but that to our older citizens television is one of the blessings of our period of history.

— ELEANOR ROOSEVELT

Marlene
Sanders

■ ASKED ONCE TO NAME HER CONTRIBUTION on behalf of women, Marlene Sanders replied, "Just being there, being visible on television and serving as a role model." No one would quibble with the importance of Sanders's visibility as a pioneering woman in TV news or her status as a role model. But for generations of women broadcasters, Sanders did much more than just being there: she spoke up and took action.

In the early 1970s, when Sanders had the most to lose professionally, she risked her career to join a small band of women in the media trying to improve working conditions, pay, and opportunities for women. The group, in spite of the damage it could be done to their careers, held meetings network management to voice their ands for more equal treatment of women. This risk and their tireless efforts paid off as they slowly began to effect change, paving the way for future generations of women to receive better treatment.

Born January 10, 1931, in Cleveland, Ohio, young Marlene didn't like being told that boys didn't like girls who were "too smart." Sanders remembers that as a child it "made me so angry I couldn't stand it! I knew that the traditional role was not going to be enough for me. . . . I was going to be a great something—that something kept changing."

A speech major at Ohio State University, Sanders had to leave school when she ran out of tuition money. After working to save up enough money to travel to Europe, Sanders studied at the Sorbonne in Paris for a summer and returned to the United States with a new commitment: to pursue an acting career.

But after three years of casting calls and only one appearance off-Broadway, Sanders began to rethink her plans. While working as an assistant producer in 1955 in summer theater, Sanders met newsman Mike Wallace, who helped her get a job as a production assistant for WNEW-TV in New York City on *Mike Wallace and the News*. That entry-level position led to a job doing some writing and booking for the interview program *Nightbeat*.

After working next on a late-night talk and information program called *PM East,* Sanders moved to radio at WNEW in New York, as the assistant news director and the only woman broadcaster at the station. Sanders produced, wrote, and anchored weekly half-hour documentaries, one of which, *The Battle of the Warsaw Ghetto,* won Sanders her first Writers Guild of America Award.

ABC News had only one female correspondent when Sanders joined the network in 1964, and Sanders soon began appearing on the air for the daily five-minute segment *News with the Woman's Touch.* That same year, she became the first woman to anchor an evening news show. Jack Gould, TV critic of the *New York Times,* described the scene when Sanders filled in for the male anchor, who had lost his voice: "The courageous young woman with the Vassar smile was crisp and business-like, and obviously the sort who wouldn't put up with any nonsense from anyone." But, as Sanders has noted, "ABC broke the ice in 1964 and showed it could be done. No one else followed for many years."

In fact, it was not until 1971 that Sanders achieved another fill-in first when she substituted on ABC's late-Saturday-evening news show for regular anchor Sam Donaldson, who was on a three-month assignment in Vietnam. Sanders herself had been sent to Southeast Asia for three weeks in 1966—the first TV network newswoman to cover the Vietnam War. Throughout the late 1960s, Sanders was a visible presence on the hard-news beat covering the turbulent events of the 1968 presidential campaign: Eugene McCarthy's challenge

Sanders on location in Vietnam, 1966

to a sitting president, Robert Kennedy's assassination, the conventions, and the student antiwar protests.

The next decade was a time of growing critical acclaim for Sanders's work. In 1972, she went to work on ABC's documentary programs, exploring in depth such issues as the population explosion, child abuse, and the emergence of women in the political arena.

The success of her many award-winning documentaries paved the way for her appointment in 1976 as vice president and director of documentaries at ABC, making her the first woman to be named a vice president in any network news division. In that position, Sanders demonstrated that women could succeed both on the air and on the business side of broadcasting as she continued to produce documentaries focusing on serious issues such as the justice system, nuclear war, and the Equal Rights Amendment.

During this period Sanders not only continued to make her mark as a strong advocate on behalf of women in the broadcast industry, but she fought just as hard for the rights of women everywhere through her work. At a time when "women's issues" were not generally reported, she brought national attention to such issues as sexual abuse and women in leadership positions.

By the end of the decade, Sanders had joined CBS news as a correspondent and producer for the prestigious *CBS Reports.* She also covered major stories for *Sunday Morning* and the *Weekend News* and anchored hourly broadcasts for CBS Radio. Sanders later moved to WNET-TV,

Sanders in Vietnam, 1966

the PBS station in New York City, as host of *Currents,* a weekly public affairs program, and *Metro Week in Review* and *13 Live,* weekly programs that examined major local news stories. Sanders left the network in 1991 and became an educator, teaching at New York University and Columbia University.

The recipient of numerous awards throughout her long career, Sanders has continued her work on media-related gender issues, serving as program director of Women, Men, and the Media, a media watch group headed by legendary feminist Betty Friedan, and as professional in residence at the Freedom Forum. Sanders was married to Jerome Toobin, a director

At the desk at CBS News, 1987

of news and public affairs at WNEW-TV in New York, who is now deceased. To women who wonder whether they can balance career and a family, Sanders, having melded her trailblazing career and her role of wife and mother of two sons, answers with an enthusiastic "yes!"

While Sanders helped open the doors for many generations of women in broadcast news, she believes the fight for equality is not over. But if things aren't perfect yet, it isn't because Marlene Sanders hasn't tried. ∎

The Chinese are said to curse people by wishing them to live in interesting times. I have lived in interesting times, and finding myself in TV news in its early days was the defining feature of my career. My later designation as a role model for others was an unexpected bonus. In those early years, I was simply working to stay afloat, to advance, and to find my way in a relatively new business that was almost devoid of other women. I was aware of this early on, of course, but it was not until years later that I was able to do anything to change it.

My nearly forty years in television news coincided with some of the best stories of the twentieth century: the civil rights movement, the women's movement, the Vietnam War and its domestic turmoil, to name just a few of the stories that I have been privileged to cover. There were few women in TV news at the time, and by 1960, when my son was born, there were no other women whom I knew who were mothers and network correspondents. I had no one to talk to about how I would manage except my husband, who was confident that it could be done. And so it could.

Aside from managing a hectic family and professional life, my experience with covering the women's movement for ABC News, doing documentaries about it at the same time, and supporting feminist goals in the newsroom provided not only a challenge, but plenty of nervous moments. By 1970, the women in newspapers, magazines, and broadcast news discovered that, while women were fighting for better treatment, equal opportunity to move ahead, and salary equity in society at large, we had a way to go in our own places of business. Organizations were formed, and in some cases, lawsuits resulted.

Each network had a women's group, and at ABC we had regular meetings with management and made progress. Our core group consisted of low-level women employees and a few of us (there were only a few) in news. Those were exciting days. I look back with some amusement at our planning sessions before our meetings with management: how we divided up the responsibility, subject by subject; how we discussed tactics and, by the way, worried about how we should dress for these encounters! Were our jobs at stake? It didn't matter. This was the moment to seize the opportunity for progress.

The women at wire services, the newspapers, and the magazines made great gains, and some there paid a heavy price in lack of advancement as punishment for their activism. At CBS and ABC, management ultimately met many of our demands. At NBC, however, a long journey through the legal system was waged by a courageous group of sixteen, minus the support of the few highly visible women who could have joined them but did not. Feelings still run strong, and those of us who were there have long memories and remember who joined us and who waited for safer times.

I feel great personal pride today that women in TV news are making progress, rising to executive producer, anchoring major news broadcasts, and increasing their numbers in the ranks of correspondents, writers, and technicians. However, many years later, there remains more to be done. The glass ceiling still exists, even though a few women have broken through. I feel great pride in having contributed to that progress. It was based in large part on my feminist convictions and my indignation over obvious injustices. Entering the business so early and advancing to the point where I had some clout meant that I could at least assume a leadership role and try to make a difference.

As I look back, the progress we made is a source of pride. But mostly I remember the exciting and disturbing stories of the time and the issues that seemed to be never ending.

In the early days of the women's movement in the 1970s, we had high hopes that more women in the business would have a positive effect. We hoped that assignment editors, managers, and the reporters themselves would search out significant stories that affected women's lives, and also that women in management would not adopt the male model. This has come to pass in some cases, but not all. It is difficult to make a difference when there is not a critical mass, and mostly there is not.

I also note that many of the young women today do not know much about the history of the business and how we fought for the opportunities now available. This inspired my friend NYU professor Marcia Rock and me to write our book *Waiting for Prime Time: The Women of Television News,* so that the history would be out there.

We also hoped that there would be some sense of militancy after the initial goals had been reached. This has not taken place and probably will not happen until there is a more real sense of deprivation. Perhaps the publication of salary figures in each shop would do the trick! I know they would, if only those figures could be obtained without subterfuge.

I look back with satisfaction on my career. I miss covering the news, but not the news business and its increased focus on ratings, celebrity journalism, and short bursts, rather than long-form news. The consolidation of ownership has not been good for news gathering. But one thing is certain, and that is change. I look forward with hope that women will find a way to make the work more meaningful and find a way, as I have, to have full personal and professional lives.

—MARLENE SANDERS

Diane
Sawyer

■ LONG AGO, BEFORE THE ADVENT OF CABLE television, a seventeen-year-old Kentuckian named Diane Sawyer entered a Junior Miss pageant. For the talent competition, she didn't do the familiar tap dance or accordion solo. Instead, Sawyer read a poem she'd written about the Civil War, then sang a medley of tunes associated with northern and southern states. It was a gutsy performance, equal parts show business and substance. It was also an effective one. Sawyer wound up winning the Junior Miss crown and an $11,000 college scholarship.

Thirty-eight years later, she is still able to be both entertaining and informative under pressure. "Diane can do newsmagazines. She can do hard news," observed Roone Arledge, former president of ABC News. "She's intelligent. She's a personality. She is someone whose presence on a news program makes a difference. It's like putting Michael Jordan into the game." *People* magazine groped for a way to express her versatility, finally noting, "Sawyer herself is a combination of classical and commercial."

Political humorist Art Buchwald used to joke that President Nixon kept a bunch of cloned Henry Kissingers in the White House basement to send on shuttle diplomacy missions. The same theory can be applied to ABC News' deployment of

Diane Sawyer. Genetic engineering may be the only way to account for all that airtime: Sawyer coanchoring *Good Morning America,* Sawyer coanchoring *20/20,* Sawyer guest-hosting *Nightline,* Sawyer doing hitches on *Prime Time Live* and *Turning Point.*

"I can't pull back. I've never met the day that I could pull back," Sawyer once said, defending her workaholic metabolism to *TV Guide.* "I can't imagine doing anything else."

Why bother? It would be awfully tough to match her current level of success. Sawyer gets to do the exclusive interviews (from Michael Jackson to Hillary Clinton; from Saddam Hussein to Fidel Castro) and the juicy exposés (from Russia's biological warfare arsenal to life inside a maximum-security women's prison; from phony televangelists to neglect of patients at VA hospitals). She has bagged the big-game honors: three Emmys, a George Foster Peabody Award, a grand prize from the Investigative Reporters and Editors Association, entry into the Television Academy Hall of Fame and the Broadcasting and Cable Hall of Fame—"The sort of star news executives battle over," as *Time* called her.

Sawyer leads a dream life, with her celebrity status, her marriage to film director Mike Nichols, and high-profile gal pals such as Oprah Winfrey, designer Diane Von Furstenberg, and actor Emma Thompson. Sawyer was raised in Louisville—her father a county judge, her mother an elementary school teacher. Leisure time was a blur of ballet, tap, piano, fencing, and horseback riding lessons. She used that Junior Miss scholarship to attend Wellesley College, earning an English degree in 1967.

Afterward she ended up back in Louisville as a weather forecaster/reporter at WLKY-TV. Facing a cloudy future in TV meteorology ("I was forever reeling forward and backward, trying to focus my little astigmatic eyes on the temperatures out in San Francisco, and consequently reading them wrong"), Sawyer opted to make a change. Family friend Lamar Alexander, later the governor of Tennessee and a long-shot Republican presidential candidate, got her an interview with the Nixon administration. From 1970 to 1974, Sawyer served in the White House as an assistant deputy press secretary.

Sawyer prepares to go on-air on the *Good Morning America* set.

President Richard Nixon initially referred to her as "that smart girl." However, the two were destined to become much better acquainted during the Watergate crisis. After Nixon resigned, Sawyer stayed on for four more years as his personal assistant, primarily helping research his Watergate memoirs. The experience rendered Sawyer less cynical than most journalists about politics. "I think there are a lot of good people in Washington who work very long hours with fine motives," she says. "And I'm not sure that we don't, occasionally, simply relegate everyone to stereotypes."

Following the completion of Nixon's book, Sawyer was offered a job as a reporter with CBS News, much to the consternation of some staffers. But she quickly earned her stripes covering the near nuclear meltdown at Three Mile Island and the Iran hostage situation. That exposure led, in 1981, to a coanchor slot alongside Charles Kuralt on the *CBS Morning News*. Three years later, *60 Minutes* called, and she fit in perfectly on that all-star team as its first woman correspondent. As executive producer Don Hewitt said, "She is one of the girls who is one of the boys."

Before moving to ABC in 1989, Sawyer tried to corral Mike Nichols for a *60 Minutes* profile. The pretaping negotiations went well—so well that Sawyer ended up falling in love with Nichols before she got around to interviewing him. They married in April 1988, immediately becoming one of New York's glitziest power couples. Sawyer, apparently, isn't the straightlaced über-anchor viewers are accustomed to seeing. She's been known to groove to Motown music right up until the *Good Morning America* cameras roll, and Oprah swears that Sawyer can do a killer impression of a streetwalker with a bad cold. Who knew? "People think she's aloof," Winfrey told a *Ladies' Home Journal* reporter, "but Diane's funny as hell."

There's lots the world at large doesn't know about Sawyer. One day she'd like to take leave of television and write a "definitive" biography about some notable per-

Sawyer on the set at ABC News

son. And, truth be told, she's not crazy about her looks: "I hate my blond hair. I've always wanted to look like Cher."

That's the kind of personal tidbit she's known for coaxing out of other folks. But it doesn't mean she wants to *be* Cher. Sawyer insists she feels uncomfortable being placed high atop that celebrity-journalist pedestal. "I'm not sure we make a [proper] distinction between newspeople and celebrities. And I think there is a distinction," she says. "The distinction lies in what you do every day: what you do to get stories and how far you will go and how much you will dig for them. All the rest of the attention that comes to you because you're on the air seems to me an irrelevance." ■

It seems that almost every day of my life there is a defining moment. That's what it means to live in the turbulent wake of the news. I'm up, I'm down, I'm flattened on the ground, I'm soaring. And that's just one hour. I love the way new information, new insights, new people force me to rearrange my thinking about life. We are always on the lookout for stories that affect people's lives, always asking "Why aren't we questioning this?" For instance, when everybody was marching off to get mammograms without asking "What do I really know about the radiation in this machine? What do I really know about what it takes technically to get a good mammogram?" A good journalist has to stay absolutely curious, absolutely fresh, and indefatigably committed to answering those questions that help others live.

I am proudest of the investigative stories that have made a difference. Stories that have changed the life of someone walking in to get a mammogram, or someone dropping off their child at day care, or someone getting a Pap smear, or someone going in to apply for a job. Those stories are the ones that you get up in the morning and can't wait to come to work to do.

I think the biggest advantage of being a women in broadcasting, at least in the last fifteen years, has been when you go to some Third World countries. The men in charge are so disconcerted by a woman coming in that you usually have quite a long period in which to operate before they figure out that you are really a reporter. They can't believe it: a women is asking them questions; you can't be serious. I guess that allowed me to operate under the radar. It worked for me in the Soviet Union during the coup attempt against Boris Yeltsin. The tanks were supposed to fire on the building, but I wanted to get up to the floor where I could see him. The guards kept stopping me and saying, "No women are allowed in this building, no women allowed." Finally through an interpreter I said, "Tell him I'm not a woman, I'm a journalist. We're not women in that sense." He looked perplexed for a minute and then let me through. So it worked.

I know, and it has to be said over and over again, that there are still those extra obstacles that you can't see, that ultra-high-frequency resistance that takes place out in the business world if you're female. I know that there are major hurdles that a lot of women have to cross, just in terms of a level playing field. I think I'm so lucky that I never felt it, never knowingly experienced it. And short of being able to haul all my suitcases down the tarmac onto the plane, short of upper body strength, I've never personally experienced the inequality.

I do think that women have about six things to consider at all times where many men have only two. It can be more complicated because there are narrow margins between seeming too tough and not tough enough. I think we're held to a little higher standard on some of these fine gradations of tone or voice: "Did she wear the right thing for the interview?" "Is her hair looking good today?" "Oh, she looks a little tired." "Oh, that color of lipstick!"

So we do, I think, have about six report cards coming in at once, whereas men don't have quite that number. We've been trained over not just centuries but millennia to gauge a woman's age and to put her through more cosmetically than we do when we look at men. I think it's changing, but right now, a woman who looks tired is not given the same break as a man who looks tired. But I think it's going to change.

There is a giant sisterhood that exists. I think it confounds everyone who thought that women were notoriously cutthroat and competitive and who expected us to be like those old Hollywood movie scripts of women at one another's throats. In fact, we are one another's mirrors and shoulders and life rafts. The first call I get when I'm blue and anyone hears about it is from the women I know in the business. Also, the first celebratory calls usually come from my female friends. I think a lot of the men envy our sense of solidarity and our ability to get together and reinforce one another's confidence, to laugh with one another, to have a conversation that begins with campaign finance reform and ends with cellulite. There's something restorative about that.

There are additional tensions that we feel every single day. I think it's more difficult because we feel a sort of millennium-old responsibility for keeping the family cemented together. It is the torment not just of women in journalism, but also of women in the workplace, who are going to feel more responsible for children. Women are going to feel the burden of those thirty extra hours a week of work at home. Over time, we can only hope that several things will happen. First of all, that the community does more to ensure that women have day care they can trust and is in close proximity to their workplace. Over time, we can only hope that men who are concerned about the stresses on the family also start demanding some accommodation from the workplace in order to spend more time with children. Eventually I have to believe that will happen. But in the short term, a lot of women are operating at the breaking point.

I'd like to freeze-frame this moment: a husband I love, three glorious stepchildren, a grandchild, nephews I adore, my mother and my sister, and all the people I love healthy and whole. And the work I love. All I'd like to do is say, "Stop tape here," maybe forever.

—DIANE SAWYER

Dinah
Shore

■ DINAH SHORE'S VOCAL TALENT MAY HAVE made her a star, but her consistently warm personality made her an American broadcasting institution. After her years as a top recording artist, Shore hosted her own radio show and then five television series between 1951 to 1990 that won her eight Emmy Awards. In the early years of television, she became the first woman to host a successful variety show on television, thus helping to popularize the new broadcast medium. In her early series, she set the tone for the variety-show genre with her vivaciousness and ability to laugh off technical mishaps that live TV couldn't edit out. Later, in her talk shows, she proved that an interviewer can draw out guests without embarrassing them.

"Today most hosts are the anti-Dinah. They base their shows on making fun of people, whereas she was nice to them," says Robert Thompson, a TV historian at Syracuse University. "She was also important because she sat down and interviewed people in an era when most of the people who did that tended to be named Johnny or Jack."

For Shore, the tradition of graciousness and feminine strength started at home in Winchester, Tennessee, where, on February 29, 1916, she was born Frances Rose ("Fanny") to Russian Jewish immigrants Anna and Solomon Shore. Anna, an amateur opera singer, learned how to prepare traditional southern cuisine and delighted in entertaining guests at home. She taught her daughter how to make everyone feel comfortable. "A nervous hostess makes nervous guests," Shore wrote in one of the three cookbooks she published in the 1970s. "So enjoy your own party." Anna also impressed upon her daughter that a woman could be soft and sweet but also self-reliant and disciplined.

That spirit of determination proved crucial when little Fanny contracted polio at the age of eighteen months. Through physical therapy and athletics, she escaped paralysis and eventually even succeeded in losing her limp.

Shore appearing on a 1940s radio show

ern charm were an immediate hit with listeners. She also hosted *Mail Call,* a radio program for the armed forces. Risking her own safety, she entertained thousands of troops in German-occupied France. General George Patton presented Shore with a gun as a token of thanks, and a bridge in France was named for her.

In 1951, Dinah's own television musical variety series was launched, under the sponsorship of Chevrolet. *The Chevy Show* consisted of twice-weekly fifteen-minute broadcasts but quickly proved so popular that the company retitled it *The Dinah Shore Chevy Show* and expanded it to an hour on Sunday nights. At the end of each broadcast, Shore ebulliently urged audiences to "See the U.S.A. in your Chevrolet," then delivered the most enthusiastically thrown kiss in television history; it became her trademark.

The social skills Shore inherited from her mother—such as convincing the shyest person at a table to give an opinion—carried over to her shows. "She wasn't a persona created by some press agent; that was her real self," says Sheila Grattan, a publicist who worked with Shore. "I think that was part of her magnetism to other celebrities." On television, Shore genuinely had a good time, whether singing a duet with Ella Fitzgerald or landing on the floor when a bench accidentally overturned.

When the variety show ended its run in 1960, Shore headlined TV specials and played in nightclubs. In 1970, she debuted a half-hour daytime talk show, *Dinah's Place,* that featured household hints and cooking demonstrations. The

In Nashville, to which the family moved so Solomon could open a department store, the teenage Dinah frequented the Grand Ole Opry and got a job singing on a local radio station. In accordance with her father's wishes, Dinah enrolled at Vanderbilt University and graduated with a sociology degree in 1938. But with the big-band era calling her name, she moved to New York City and got gigs singing for WNEW radio and with Xavier Cugat's orchestra. At one audition, she performed the song "Dinah," the name she took to replace "Fanny." Soon after, she had her first hit, "Yes, My Darling Daughter."

Eddie Cantor, host of the popular radio show *Time to Smile,* found himself enchanted by Shore's voice and signed her as a regular. She became the most popular female radio singer; every jukebox in the country featured her records. In 1943, Shore was given her own radio show, *Call to Music,* and her spontaneity and south-

show ran for four years before NBC canceled it, but Shore soon returned to daytime TV with the ninety-minute *Dinah!*, which held its own against competitors *The Mike Douglas Show* and *Merv Griffin*.

One of Dinah's liveliest guests was actor Burt Reynolds, then in his thirties and at the peak of his reign as America's male sex symbol. When Reynolds fell in love with Shore, who was twenty years older, the resulting romance had Hollywood buzzing.

Shore also developed a passion for golf, and in 1972 she raised the profile of the game for women by lending her name to the first major competition for female golfers, the televised Colgate (later Nabisco) Dinah Shore Tournament. She played in the tournaments herself and spent time with those participating in, attending, and reporting on the events, using her personal presence to call attention to the women's sport.

In 1989, Shore returned to television and her Tennessee roots with *Conversations*

On the set with Bea Arthur

with Dinah, a one-on-one interview show on The Nashville Network. Her energetic lifestyle continued until 1993, when doctors found she had ovarian cancer. She died just months later, on February 24, 1994.

Shore left behind a son and daughter from her marriage to actor George Montgomery. (She had remained friends with Montgomery after their divorce, and in 2000 he completed a bronze statue of her that stands at the eighteenth hole of the Mission Hills Golf Course, the site of her tournament.) Hundreds of Hollywood friends, as well as fellow golfer and former President Gerald Ford, attended Shore's memorial service. The service featured film clips from throughout her career— and ended with a shot of her throwing out her famous kiss. ■

Performing with guest Nat King Cole on her show in the early 1960s

On singing and performing:

I can't remember a time when I wasn't singing. When I was four or five, my father had a general store in Winchester and I don't think the farmers could ever leave on Saturday afternoon until I had been placed on the counter to sing.

I stood backstage [at the Grand Ole Opry] every Saturday I could escape. I only got called five or six times, but I'd be there anyway, just hoping someone would sprain a tonsil and I'd get a chance to sing.

The first time I ever tried to sing in public—for money—was at a Nashville night club. I was all of 14 years old, but I had talked the manager into giving me a tryout, prudently neglecting to inform my parents of this interesting news. I practiced for days, borrowed an evening dress from my big sister, and went down to wow the customers with "Under a Blanket of Blue." That's just where I was, too—shrouded in indigo—when I marched out on the floor to discover, to my horror, that Mother and Daddy were sitting right in the front row of tables. Though they let me get through the number, I'll never know just how I did it. They marched me right back home before I had a chance to try my equally well-rehearsed encore, "I Can't Give You Anything But Love, Baby." But the manager still paid me my very first singing money—$10, to be exact.

My brother-in-law in Nashville . . . said if [singing] is what you really, really want to do, then I'll convince your father that it's the thing for you to do, and he did. My father put one proviso into the whole thing. He said, "You can go to New York and try, but you are never to sing with any of those musicians because I know what it is they want." I wish he'd been right.

Eddie Cantor . . . had me sing at that dreaded experience that most of us who have ever been in show business have had—the audition—and he had me sing on and on and on and on and on, and finally out of the darkened control room, this wonderful, neat gentleman walked out and he said, "You'll forgive me for keeping you singing so long, but I figure it's the last time I'm going to hear you for nothing." My mama didn't raise no dumb kid, so I knew I had the job.

On women's golf:

Though I never played it as a child, my roots in golf go back to my mother. Golf was one of the greatest joys of her life, and when I think about her playing golf in Tennessee, I marvel at her guts. After all, there weren't a lot of women golfers back home in those days. I wonder what she'd think if she saw how many women are playing the game today. I know she'd be just as thrilled as I am.

[Female golfers'] tenacity and belief in themselves and their right to recognition in spite of the most overwhelming odds are stunning when you realize how far they've come. Think about the days when great champions like Patty Berg and Louise Suggs played for twenty-five-dollar purses and tried to live a life of dignity and still have time to hone their golf skills, and you begin to realize the spirit and character of these women.

On accomplishments:

I'd like people to remember that I really tried everything within my range of reality. And that whatever I did, I did with all my heart.

— DINAH SHORE

Lesley Stahl

■ ALL REPORTERS ARE TRAINED TO FOLLOW A story. Lesley Stahl is one of the blessed few who will chase it right into the bathroom. Stahl made her mark at CBS News in the early 1970s, when the Watergate scandal was at full boil. One day after a congressional hearing, she tried to corner John Dean, then counsel to President Richard Nixon. He slyly made a beeline for the men's room. Undeterred, Stahl barged through the door fast on his heels, leaving Dean no avenue of escape.

"I know my reputation," Stahl once told a magazine writer who was profiling her. "I ask the hard questions. I'm tenacious, unrelenting."

Having spent thirty-one years in the CBS trenches, Stahl's tenacity has made her part of the heart and soul of that legendary news division. Beyond money, status, and her prized seat on the *60 Minutes* correspondents' bench, she is the first woman whose climb through the network's ranks is now approaching the rarefied heights previously reserved for such male CBS heavyweights as Edward R. Murrow and Walter Cronkite. Call it sweat equity. During the dizzy days of Watergate, "Lesley got a reputation as an incredibly hard worker," says one CBS bureau manager. "And she hasn't stopped working since."

Lesley R. Stahl was born in Swampscott, Massachusetts, on December 16, 1941. Her father, Lou, was an executive with a chemical company; her mother, Dorothy, a homemaker, continually reminded her daughter that she could "have it all": marriage, children, career— though she didn't mention someday covering the president of the United States. In 1963, Lesley graduated from Wheaton College, a women's college in Norton, Massachusetts, with dreams of becoming a doctor. She entered Columbia University to get a graduate degree in zoology before entering medical school. The only problem was that she found the whole business of vital organs and animals kind of, well, icky. "I couldn't touch anything in class," Stahl later confessed. "The smell disgusted me."

By 1966, Stahl had dropped out of

grad school, gotten married and divorced, and found a job as a speechwriter for New York Mayor John Lindsay. The exposure to the raucous City Hall pressroom quickly rubbed off on her. She decided she wanted to be a journalist and, in 1968, landed a job at NBC News as a researcher-writer for the presidential race. That led to a full-time job with NBC as a field producer in London for the Chet Huntley–David Brinkley evening news—despite the avuncular Brinkley trying to dissuade her by saying, "You're a pretty blonde. You should stay in New York and have fun." Two years later, Stahl went home to Boston to be a news producer for the local CBS affiliate, and in 1971 she wangled her way on camera. She was thirty years old but felt reborn. Indeed, Stahl half-jokingly refers to everything that happened to her in life before she became a TV reporter as a "prenatal" experience.

One of her biggest breaks was due in part to the Equal Opportunity Employment Act. In 1972, CBS News began actively recruiting women and minorities. Connie Chung, Bernard Shaw, and Stahl were all hired by the Washington bureau. The Watergate break-in occurred that summer and proved fateful for Stahl in two ways. First, her dogged reporting helped fast-track her career at CBS. Second, it brought her into contact with magazine writer Aaron Latham. The two fell in love, trading information about presidential shenanigans and unindicted coconspirators, and married in 1977.

Stahl is known for her aggressive style, a trait that serves her well in the competitive arena of investigative journal-ism. She pursues her stories with the vigor of a bounty hunter but has made progress, as she puts it, in "mastering my temper." And competitive? Stahl has been known to put her hand over the lens of a rival network's camera in order to keep the crew from horning in on one of her interviews. "I'm totally driven to get the story," she has said. "I can't stop. I'm compelled."

Stahl steadily climbed the broadcast ladder: from CBS national reporter to coanchor of the *CBS Morning News*, to White House correspondent, to *Face the Nation* moderator, to a second stint at the White House, and finally, in 1991, to the prime spot as coeditor/correspondent at *60 Minutes*. The latter promotion came after what she calls a "decade of rage" at being overlooked by CBS brass. Through the highs and lows, however, the work kept flowing. The stories piled high, accumulating like snowdrifts. She covered Jimmy Carter's Middle East peace accords,

Stahl with her colleagues on *60 Minutes*

Stahl at the 2000 AWRT Gracie Allen Awards Gala

and an Edward R. Murrow Award for Overall Excellence in Television for her exposé on Michigan militiamen.

For somebody who couldn't cut it as a doctor, Stahl wields a pretty good scalpel. She is regarded as one of the sharpest, most formidable interviewers in the business. Politicians who bob and weave their way around questions are a particular annoyance. "They are accountable to the public," Stahl griped on one occasion. "When they came on *Face the Nation*, their goal was to say nothing. And it infuriated me."

Stahl and Latham live in New York with their daughter, Taylor. It is, by her account, a normal life. On Sunday nights they like to sit around the house, eat Chinese take-out, and . . . watch *60 Minutes*. The show makes Stahl crazy happy. Best job on television, she insists; journalism heaven. What's more, it has let her spread her reporting wings by doing human interest stories in addition to those trademark make-'em-sweat investigative pieces. "Since I've been at *60 Minutes*, I'm not as two-dimensional to the public," Stahl has noted. "I can show another side of myself."

That other side is the kinder, gentler Stahl. But we're talking *relatively* kinder and gentler. She would still venture into any men's bathroom in the country in hot pursuit of a story. Nowadays, though, she might knock first. ■

U.S.-Soviet summits, and the attempted assassination of Ronald Reagan. She won an Emmy in 1992 for her "Lambs of Christ" report on radical prolife groups terrorizing doctors who perform legal abortions, another Emmy in 1996 for a look at former FDA commissioner David Kessler's assault on the tobacco industry,

Tenacity and perseverance are important in journalism, and they both came naturally to me. I had to plug away at all the other skills.

Once I realized what reporters did, I burned and yearned to become one. I finally got a job at NBC News when all the networks were gearing up for the 1968 presidential election. I was hired as a researcher/writer in the Election Unit, where I wrote handbooks for the correspondents, but also colored in maps—not exactly honing my skills. After the election, NBC sent me to London to work for *The Huntley-Brinkley Report,* but I quit after a year because I wasn't learning very much about reporting.

Dick Wald, the president of NBC News, told me at that time that I was never going to make it "from the top"—the top being the network level. He said that if I were "really serious" (something young women had to prove!), I was going to have to start "from the bottom" as a grunt at a wire service, a small newspaper, or a local television station. If I were ever going to be a reporter, he said wisely, I would have to go back, start all over again, and learn every step.

I was hired as a producer at WHDH-TV in Boston on a newsmagazine show patterned after *60 Minutes.* Unlike *60 Minutes,* though, the producers did everything. We reported and wrote the stories—did everything but appear on camera. I worked my tail off, but it didn't feel like work. I loved every phase, every step of the job, and every story. And if there was any sexism, I ignored it. I was just so grateful to be in the tent. Before I left Boston after two years there, I was finally on the air, a full-fledged reporter.

When WHDH lost its broadcast license, I went to work for CBS as a reporter in the Washington bureau. It was my dream job. I was hired in the affirmative action sweep of 1972, and so I shared "office space" (a corridor in the back) with Connie Chung and Bernie Shaw. We were often apprenticed to the senior male correspondents, yet even in that first year we occasionally made it onto the Cronkite show with our own stories. My first appearance was in a piece about a promising new cancer treatment. I was so proud. But when I called home my mother grabbed the phone and said, "Forty million Americans saw you tonight. One of them is my future son-in-law, but he's never going to call you for a date because you wore your glasses." Yo, Mom.

My next story for the evening news was one I'll never forget. I was ordered to reshoot my stand-up. Why? I asked. "Because you smiled." I smiled in the stand-up. I was told to never, ever smile again. Ever. As a woman I had to learn to be authoritative, which was code for More Like a Man. A woman smiling was seen then as soft.

My first long-running assignment was Watergate. Bob Woodward of the *Washington Post* told me, "You've got to make this your story. Stick to it like a barnacle." And so I did, working so hard that Watergate became all-consuming. It took over my life. But again, I loved it. It was my fun.

I've had three careers at CBS. My first was as a hard-news reporter. After Watergate, I covered politics (presidential campaigns, political conventions, and election nights) and then the White House (Jimmy Carter's, Ronald Reagan's, and George Bush's presidencies).

My second career was as anchor/moderator, first on the *CBS Morning News,* which I coanchored with Richard Threlkeld right after my daughter was born in 1977. Then, from 1983 to 1991, I moderated *Face the Nation,* the Sunday-morning interview show. Starting with the first show on the war in Lebanon, we covered the major news event of the week. Over the eight years I interviewed heads of state (Daniel Ortega, Margaret Thatcher, Boris Yeltsin, King Hussein) and virtually every major U.S. politician and officeholder.

I said good-bye to the White House and *Face the Nation* in early 1991 and started what I call my third career at CBS as coeditor of *60 Minutes.* The 1999–2000 season marks my tenth year at what I like to call "reporter's paradise." There is simply not a better job in all of television news, maybe all of journalism. As I say in my book, *Reporting Live,* I smiled all day the minute I started at *60 Minutes,* and I haven't stopped yet.

From the beginning of my life at the network there was always a sisterhood. At first it was a tiny little group, but ever since there's been a sense of family among the women reporters. Our circle was a refuge, a place where we didn't have to discuss sports, a place where we could be ourselves. This was far more true years ago, when there was a sense of hunkering down together. People tell me today that I work in a men's club, but that isn't true. Just about half the producers at *60 Minutes* are women.

Young women today (including my own daughter!) seem to have a disdain for feminism, a lack of appreciation for the women's rights movement, and for the trials and loneliness that some of us lived through in the beginning. I've been asked if that bothers me, and the answer is absolutely not. Why should they have to look back? They should do what I did: work hard, learn the steps from the bottom up, and have fun.

As for me, I want to stay in the game as long as Mike Wallace has.

—LESLEY STAHL

Susan Stamberg

■ THE HECK WITH DISCUSSING BRAHMS AND Beethoven. A few years ago, when Susan Stamberg, the founding mother of National Public Radio, interviewed a symphony conductor on air, one of the burning questions on her mind was whether his "arms didn't get tired" waving that itty-bitty baton so furiously. Matter of fact, the arms do wear out on occasion, the maestro said, though no reporter had ever before thought to ask.

Such small, unexpected revelations are what give Susan Stamberg's interviews their pleasurable kick. "I'm not afraid to ask silly questions or naive ones," she admits.

NPR's 250-odd member stations are regarded as something like safe havens from commercial radio on the FM dial; there, millions of news junkies can hear news and insightful editorials on such shows as *Morning Edition, All Things Considered,* and *Weekend Edition.* Stamberg, a twenty-nine-year NPR veteran, has played a prominent role in shaping the network's character and sensibility. When she helped lift *All Things Considered* off the ground back in the early 1970s, she became the first woman to coanchor a network news program. She has been honored with an Alfred I. Du Pont Award for educational broadcasting, a Distinguished Broadcaster Award from American Women in Radio and Television, and a seat on the board of the PEN/Faulkner Fiction Award and has been inducted into both the Broadcasting Hall of Fame and Radio Hall of Fame. Just like an orchestra conductor's arms, Stamberg's lips must sometimes get tired: she has, after all, racked up more than 35,000 NPR interviews.

Susan Stamberg practices the lost journalistic art of talking *with* people, rather than *at* them—whether her interviewee happens to be Nancy Reagan, jazz pianist Dave Brubeck, or a woman whose face has been disfigured by cancer surgery. Such go-with-the-flow encounters require a nimble, expansive mind, and Stamberg is "the closest thing to an enlightened humanist on the radio" in the opinion of novelist E. L. Doctorow. *Time* magazine credited her with being the key to *All Things Considered*'s charm.

One of her most prized pieces of work is a half-hour interview conducted with writer Joan Didion some twenty years ago: a long, discursive exchange between a dark-side-of-the-moon pessimist (Didion) and an eternally sunny-side-up optimist (Stamberg). It was one of those magical face-offs, Stamberg recalls, when both parties forget about the microphone and let their feelings fly. "I don't think I do interviews as much as conversations," Stamberg has said. "I mix up and scramble up with the people I'm talking to and get engaged in the ideas that they're discussing. I think that's appealing. The audience doesn't hear that elsewhere. Also, I don't mind laughing. And I do that a lot on the air."

On the air Stamberg exudes small-town congeniality, but she was born in Newark, New Jersey, and raised in New York City. She comes from practical stock. Her father, Robert Levitt, was a manufacturer's representative; her mother, Anne, a bookkeeper. Susan studied visual arts at New York's High School of Music and Art and graduated from Barnard College in 1959. However, she entered the working world in print. Her first job was as an editorial assistant with *Daedalus,* a scholarly journal in Cambridge, Massachusetts. In 1962, she married Louis Stamberg, a young State Department employee, and the couple moved to Washington, where Susan became an editor at *The New Republic* magazine. Unstimulated in that

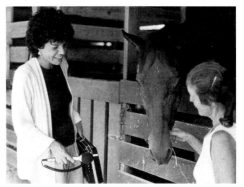

Stamberg on location in Austin, Texas, 1980

role, Stamberg put words into action when a girlfriend told her that WAMU-FM, American University's radio station, was looking for someone to produce a public affairs show.

"I said, 'I don't know anything about radio,'" Stamberg later recalled. "'What does a producer do?' And she said, 'A producer is someone who doesn't take no for an answer.' So I thought, 'Well, I can do that.'"

That was 1963, when it was possible to kick off a career in public radio with a high energy level and a low salary demand. Stamberg began at WAMU as a behind-the-scenes producer and program manager, but when the station was faced with a personnel shortage, she started anchoring. When like-minded stations across the country got together in 1971 to form the loose federation known as National Public Radio, she was asked to lend a hand in developing its signature afternoon news program, *All Things Considered.* A year later, she was elevated to coanchor.

Many of Stamberg's interviews and stories have coincided with events in her own life, such as motherhood, the pangs of

Sanford Ungar and Stamberg cohost NPR's daily show *All Things Considered*, 1983.

middle age, and life-threatening illness. In the fall of 1986, after undergoing a lumpectomy and radiation treatments for cancer, Stamberg took a break from the daily stresses of NPR. But when her strength returned so did she, hosting *Weekend Edition Sunday* from its debut broadcast in January 1987 until October 1989.

With son Joshua off pursuing an acting career and her husband retired, Stamberg has kicked back a bit with her work schedule. She pinch-hits as anchor when needed but serves primarily as a "special correspondent" on the culture beat—free to roam the landscape of art, music, dance, theater, film, and books.

Stamberg has long lobbied NPR editors to widen the parameters of their news coverage. She has spent most of her adult life in Washington but has never caught "Potomac fever."

"I've been a news hen all this time, but my true love is the arts," Stamberg once confessed to a reporter. "It was the thing that kept me going on the worst news day. You knew that at three in the afternoon, you'd talk to John Updike. That was the icing on the cupcake for me. I believe that politicians are not going to save us. It will be the artists who can show us new ways to tackle old problems." ■

I grew up with voices speaking to me from the magic box that sat on the kitchen table, telling me stories, making me laugh, informing me about war and peace and the death of President Roosevelt. Radio was the authoritative source and, when the chance came to work in it, I felt I was joining a world that had fascinated me since childhood.

The opportunity came in 1963, at a public radio station in Washington. The greenest member of a full-time staff of three, I learned to edit tape, lug around fifty-pound recorders, produce programs—and eventually I heard my voice through a headset, telling listeners the president had died in Dallas. National Public Radio hired me in 1971 to edit tapes for the new program it was about to put on the air. After a few weeks, I was reporting; and after ten months, I became host of *All Things Considered,* the first woman to anchor a nightly news program.

It was a revolutionary decision then, having a woman anchor reporting on the day's events as well as interviewing newsmakers about serious issues. Initially, some public radio station managers protested. They worried that a woman couldn't sound authoritative and wouldn't be taken seriously. NPR's then–program director, Bill Siemering, the man behind the creation of *All Things Considered* and the one who chose me as anchor, waited about eleven years before telling me about the opposition. Bill felt it might have affected my performance in some way. He had a good deal of confidence in me and felt that, if I kept at it, the reservations would fade. And they did. I must have had a good deal of confidence, too, because it never occurred to me that I couldn't do the job.

I'm so proud to have helped put public broadcasting on the map. Being a founding mother of National Public Radio, being present at its creation, and having that first-woman role as the anchor were real honors. In addition, in our very first years I served as managing editor of the program. Our staff was small; our resources were limited.

Public radio has a long and distinguished tradition, but it had never been national until National Public Radio. For decades there'd been individual small stations, usually on university campuses, broadcasting educational materials, language lessons, and classical music to very small, local audiences. In 1971, NPR linked all of those stations and audiences together and created a national audience. To have been there at the beginning, to have had an ongoing role in making all that happen, and to have helped create a program that would flourish are, I think, the main contributions I've made to broadcasting. That and establishing a permanent role for women, on the air and behind the scenes.

I've never felt there was such a thing as "women's issues." There are human issues. But as first woman, I lobbied for coverage of stories on the family, education, care for the elderly, health care—stories that touch all those caretaking roles that women have to play. At NPR, I made sure they became part of our daily broadcast agenda. The fact that I am a woman made that happen. Often people are more open with me because I am a woman. I think we're better listeners. We ask questions more than we give definitive answers, which helps us in our work because we *get* more answers. And if traditionally we've been a bit less confident, it means we'll check our facts more carefully and, perhaps, get more accurate information.

Age has often been a woman's greatest enemy, especially for women in television. But it's been an advantage for me. First of all, you can look older on radio, and who's to know? I could be 110 years old and stark raving naked at my microphone (not a pretty picture!), and keep on broadcasting. My reputation and my body of work have earned me a good deal of respect at National Public Radio. The fact that I am seasoned enough to usually know what I'm doing is also a tremendous advantage.

The growth of NPR has been fascinating in terms of working women. When we began, there were two working mothers on the staff. In those days it was difficult because women still hadn't quite made our mark, and we were hell bent to prove we could do the job just as well as men did. This meant total focus on work and little conversation about children or responsibilities at home.

A full eight or more years after I'd started, I came into a morning editorial meeting and my cohost then, a man named Sanford Ungar, had his baby daughter on his lap. Something had happened to the sitter's schedule that day, and Sandy brought his daughter to work. I looked at him and thought, "Good heavens, I could never do that!" I always felt I had to solve baby-sitting problems *before* I went to work. Later, several men at NPR had child care responsibilities. I loved hearing them standing around the coffee machine, talking about baby's first words or setting up after-school programs. It was the men who taught me how much more realistic a workplace could be for working parents.

I hope I can work forever. I love it. I love having a place to go every day, a group of people to see, be stimulated by, and swap ideas with. I love the world that opens up to me because I am a broadcaster. I love the places I get to visit, the people I meet, and the things I learn. I want to continue to make a contribution. For me that's crucial: making a contribution to society. That sounds so noble!

But this work is also such terrific fun. I hope I bring that sense of fun to my listeners. I like to laugh on the air, and that, apparently, was once unprecedented. There are marvelous ideas and events and people out there. I love trying to figure out ways to tap into them and then share them with others.

—SUSAN STAMBERG

Martha
Stewart

■ IN TODAY'S CULTURE, MARTHA STEWART IS practically omnipresent. Books (nearly 9 million sold), magazines (10 million a month), newspaper column (43 million readers a week), radio (1.5 million listeners a week), plus her daily television shows aired and rerun on multiple network and cable channels, regular visits to CBS's *This Morning*, merchandising through a national retail chain, and major ventures with catalogs and on the Internet—she uses each form of media and creates synergies among them to maximize her message. In financial terms, the results are also impressive: after Martha Stewart Living Omnimedia went public in October 1999, experts estimated her stake at $1.2 billion and put her additional personal net worth at $250 million, making her one of the richest self-made female entrepreneurs.

Television, however, has been a particularly effective means of reaching Stewart's audience since it allows her to "enter" their homes—the very place she is dedicated to helping them make a more attractive, gracious place.

In 1987, when Stewart's first television special, *Holiday Entertaining with Martha Stewart*, appeared on PBS, it was not her first TV appearance. In high school and college, she had made extra money as a model in commercials for products such as Lifebuoy soap and Clairol shampoo. *Holiday Entertaining*, however, was the first flicker of a revolution that would change not only Stewart's relationship with television but the role the medium could play in the lifestyle business.

By that time, cooking shows were appearing regularly on local and national television (Julia Child's PBS series, the first, had started in 1963). But Stewart was not only preparing a dish; she was creating a world. Meals were creative events served on exquisite table settings; holidays became showcases for handmade decorations; gift-giving times were opportunities to craft personalized expressions. All this came with a cheerful, positive attitude: somehow Stewart made viewers feel that putting effort into gracious living was possible, no matter what one's abilities, and infinitely worthwhile. What seemed a chore as taught by home ec teachers of the past became fascinating, desirable, and fulfilling in the hands of this friendly, talented neighbor.

The huge lifestyle advice industry Stewart is credited with creating had its origins not in television but in print. Stewart had built a successful gourmet food business and was doing a little writing, including a *House Beautiful* column, when she met the president of Crown Publishers at a party in New York. He encouraged her to write a book; she did. *Entertaining*, published in 1982, was the first full-color cookbook/entertainment guide because Stewart insisted that food looked better in color pictures. The first printing of 25,000 sold out quickly; it is still in print. Other books followed—now more than two dozen, on topics from hors d'oeuvres to pies, weddings to Christmas, gardening to wreath making. And in 1990, *Martha Stewart Living* magazine was launched by Time Warner, followed by another magazine, *Martha Stewart Weddings*.

The booming business of Martha in print paralleled her expanding television presence. She appeared twice a month on NBC-TV's *Today* show from 1991 until 1997, when she moved to CBS's *This Morning*. *Martha Stewart Living*, begun in 1993 as half-hour weekly syndicated shows, evolved over time to a daily show that was aired and rerun on CBS, PBS, and the Lifetime, Food, and Style cable networks. Her prime-time specials include

Martha Stewart's Home for the Holidays in 1995 and *Welcome Home for the Holidays* in 1996, both also popular in reruns.

In 1995, Time Warner created a new corporation, owned jointly with Stewart, called Martha Stewart Living Enterprises, which gave her control of both the business and creative sides of her activities. Two years later, she bought the company from Time Warner and formed her own, Martha Stewart Living Omnimedia. Time Warner continues to distribute the magazines and retains an interest in her ventures, but Stewart's company controls all existing products and activities and has created new ones, including an on-line service (marthastewart.com) and weekly ninety-second how-to segments that air on 270 radio stations. The company's successful initial public stock offering in October 1999 showed, in Stewart's words, that "people aren't just happy with our products but the company as well."

Stewart may have taken the lifestyle business to previously unimagined heights, but she acquired the building blocks of her success the same way most little girls of her generation did. Born August 3, 1941, she grew up in Nutley, New Jersey, one of six children of Edward and Martha Kostyra, both descendants of Polish immigrants. Her father was a pharmaceutical salesman and her mother a teacher before becoming a stay-at-home mom.

Young Martha learned to grow fruits, vegetables, and flowers from her avid gardener father; her mother taught her cooking, baking, and sewing. The traditional European recipes she learned at home were supplemented by lessons from a grandmother who loved to preserve fruits, one uncle who was a butcher and another who ran a delicatessen, and a family of German bakers next door. Even then, Martha was energetic and industrious, organizing birthday parties for neighborhood children because it paid better than baby-sitting.

While studying European and art history at Barnard College in New York, she worked for a time as live-in cook for two elderly sisters in their twelve-room apartment on upper Fifth Avenue. In 1961, after her sophomore year, she married Andrew Stewart, a law student at Yale (they divorced in 1987), then completed her degree and worked as a stockbroker on Wall Street. In 1973, the couple and their daughter moved to an abandoned Westport, Connecticut, farmhouse called "Turkey Hill," which they restored. Martha quit her job in the city, taught herself skills from Julia Child's classic cookbook, and over the next several years established a gourmet food shop and catering service. A few years later, her publishing career was launched, leading eventually to her multimedia empire.

For all Stewart's success, she retains a down-home appeal. Her TV look is casual chic: she wears slacks or jeans with tai-

Stewart with New York Stock Exchange President Bill Johnson outside the NYSE at ceremonies to mark the initial public offering of Martha Stewart Living Omnimedia Inc. shares

lored shirts and rolled-up sleeves; outdoor segments show her in gardening clogs or muddy boots.

Yet her competence can be a tad intimidating to the average homemaker, and perhaps therein lies the key to her television success. Having the real Martha visit one's home might inspire panicked visions of inadequacy; having the televised Martha sharing all that good advice feels just right. ■

I started my first book in 1982. And that book, *Entertaining,* became an instant success because it had wonderful color pictures and fabulous recipes. It was a big format book, the kind that was usually called a coffee table book; but people started to take this book into the kitchen. And I started to realize that we were filling a void.

So we kept writing books. We catered parties. The parties allowed me, financially, to write the books up until the publication of *Weddings.* After that book's success, I realized that, by myself, I couldn't possibly write as much as I want to write and get across as much information as I want to get across. So I went to my publisher and said that I had a series of how-to books I would like to publish with other authors working with me. But they didn't like the idea very much and passed on it.

So I decided the only other format that could contain all the information I wanted to gather and disseminate was a magazine. Now, this was in the early 1990s, and the magazine world was in disastrous economic shape. Not only was advertising at a nadir, but magazines were closing at a rate of several a day. Hundreds had closed by the time I started *Martha Stewart Living* with a very fine partner, Time Warner.

From day one, the magazine had a following. Other people might have been surprised, but I wasn't because it was right for the time. With all of us, and women especially, spending so much time on our work, I knew that we had sort of lost touch with the joys and satisfactions of caring for a home. I knew because I was one of them.

Well, it worked. It worked because I started to bring back the idea of tradition, the idea of teaching, the idea of allowing us to feel good about decorating, about home keeping, about collecting, about restoring. We started off with 250,000 readers the first issue. It was a sellout on the newsstands. Subscription cards were inserted into that first issue, and some of the charter subscribers those cards generated are still with us.

I then decided that to reach more people a television show would be the appropriate addendum to the magazine. Time Warner saw television as a secondary venture, so we started producing the show ourselves within the magazine company.

Martha Stewart Living Television started off in a very modest way, once a week—at 8:30 on Sunday morning, in fact, not an ideal time slot. But we produced it beautifully and soon it grew to being carried in over 200 markets. It became a five-day-a-week show in September 1996, and it's also rerun on cable networks.

Perhaps most challenging of all the television we've done are the Christmas prime time specials. For each of them, we've started working in June, beginning to develop creative ideas. Then we have to find guests. The first year, we had an amazing guest list with Hillary Clinton, Miss Piggy, and the icon of American cooking, Julia Child.

The second year, two weeks before shooting was to begin, we didn't have a guest! But I wasn't worried, and the guests turned out to be brilliant. Michael Jordan came, and when nobody else could put a star on top of the tree because they were too short, he did it.

And I had read in a gossip column that Dennis Franz loved me, though I'd never met the man. I had watched *NYPD Blue* a few times, with him playing the cute, fat Andy Sipowicz, but I didn't like him because his name is Andy—the same as my ex-husband. Nevertheless, it seemed he'd be perfect for the show, and when we called, he was thrilled to come on and he did a very funny scene with me.

Finally, Miss Piggy called and she wanted to be on again. So she came and she was a great surprise because she looked different. She'd had a makeover!

Aside from those television appearances, I always enjoy interacting with people individually when I give speeches around the country. In those settings, I find that people typically ask two main questions.

When young women who want to be entrepreneurs ask me for advice, I tell them to be sure to go into a business in which you have an idea that is unique, well thought-out, well planned. It does not, however, have to be heavily financed. I started with practically nothing and have built a sizable company by believing in what I was doing, treating it as serious subject matter, and projecting it as such.

Others have a more personal question: they want to know if I ever just put on my sweats and eat dinner from the pot. In response, I like to read a column I wrote about spending one Christmas alone when I was trying to write my first book. Here's what I said:

"I became a putterer. I shuffled around in heavy woolen socks and my nightgown, dusting the edges of tables with the hem of my flannel nightdress as I had done as a child. I turned on a TV and watched daytime programs I had never heard of before. . . .

"I invented chores that kept me from my desk. I washed every mirror and cleaned the intricate giltwork with cotton swabs. I set up my ironing board next to my four-poster bed. And after I had washed all my linen napkins, even the clean ones, I ironed them while watching old movies on TV all through the night.

"I ate liverwurst out of the tube, cottage cheese straight out of the container, and peanut butter and jelly right from the jar."

Surprised? Well, quite a while ago I figured out that Martha Stewart was both a person and something sort of removed from me, a brand. And if you take the brand part with a grain of salt and realize that it is something you can laugh about, you don't mind at all.

— M A R T H A   S T E W A R T

Marlo
Thomas

■ LOTS OF LITTLE GIRLS DREAM ABOUT ACTing, but few understand that performing is a job, not a fantasy.

Marlo Thomas, on the other hand, knew from the beginning that a career in show business meant due diligence. Born November 21, 1938, little Marlo would listen to her father, TV star and producer Danny Thomas, reviewing reel-to-reel tapes of his nightclub performances. "He'd say 'Hear this joke? It doesn't work.' Or 'This character is superfluous; he must come out.' I could see that to be a performer you must create something and work on it and make it fresh. You didn't just wing it."

Danny tried to discourage Marlo, his eldest child, from acting. "My godmother was Loretta Young," Marlo says. "Dad talked about how hard it was for her to balance kids and work. I think he just wanted me to be spared from rejection. He later told me he didn't want to relive those awful first years of his career with someone he loved."

So at her father's insistence, Marlo found something to fall back on. She attended the University of Southern California, earned certification as an English teacher, and, diploma in hand, headed to Manhattan to study acting. Her teachers included Uta Hagen, Lee Strasberg, and Sandra Seacat.

By the mid-1960s, Thomas was appearing as a guest star on such shows as *My Favorite Martian* and *Bonanza.* Based on her performance in a pilot called *Two's Company,* ABC executives felt she merited her own situation comedy. Thomas cocreated and helped pitch the idea for *That Girl,* featuring her as Ann Marie, an aspiring actress living on her own in New York City. The series, the first ever to revolve around a female character living on her own, debuted in 1966 and was produced by Daisy Productions, a company she formed.

"*That Girl* was an important step that TV needed to take," says Syracuse University TV historian Robert Thompson. "It went from decades of spinsters and housewives to a single woman who was concerned with career advancement and wasn't obsessed with getting married."

The series earned Thomas four Emmy Award nominations. After it ended its run in 1971, she concentrated on her interest in feminism, sparked in part by her maternal grandmother. Marie Cassannitti had cut back on her singing career because her husband felt it reflected badly on him to have a wife who worked. (Thomas's mother, Rose Marie, had also given up her career as a singer to raise her family.) But later, when she was in her seventies, Marie Cassannitti formed a band called Marie's Merry Music Makers in which she played the drums. "She was an independent woman who did what she wanted to," Thomas says.

In 1974, Thomas cofounded the Ms. Foundation with Gloria Steinem, editor of *Ms.* magazine, to support causes such as battered women's shelters and sexual abuse treatment programs. Thomas also took her message of equality to the masses by producing *Free to Be . . . You and Me,* a book, record album, and TV special that assured kids that it's okay for a woman to be a jackhammer operator and for a boy to play with dolls. Thomas convinced major singers such as Dionne Warwick to appear pro bono. The show also featured football star Rosey Grier singing about how it's okay for boys to cry. In a poem, Carol Channing explained that moms don't love to do housework and they would like some help from other members of the household. Thomas donated the *Free to Be . . . You and Me* proceeds to the Ms. Foundation.

Concerned about children's acceptance of not only themselves but their family members as well, Thomas created the book and CD *Free to Be . . . a Family* in 1988. "Some children feel ashamed of their families because their house is too small or their grandmother doesn't speak English," said Thomas. "They also might think family dynamics like arguments are their fault." The book and CD tell kids that whatever their family consists of, it is still a family and troubles such as arguments and divorces aren't their fault. The *Free to Be . . . a Family* TV special broadened the focus to include the whole family of humankind. The show featured the first satellite entertainment exchange between the United States and Soviet Union. In it, children from those two countries shared their mutual admiration of, among other things, Bon Jovi music.

Thomas has also taken on projects of a grave nature, such as the TV movie *Nobody's Child,* about a woman's battle with schizophrenia, for which she won an Emmy for best dramatic actress in a TV movie or miniseries. She subsequently starred in *Reunion,* the story of a mother who accidentally causes the death of her baby.

To prepare for *Nobody's Child,* Thomas spent a month with Marie Balter, the former mental patient depicted in the movie, and visited mental health institutions. "By the first day of shooting, Marlo *was* Marie," says actress Lee Grant, who directed the movie. "She didn't just depend on me to give her the character."

Despite her wealth of accomplishments, Thomas considers herself a lifetime

Thomas as *That Girl*

With characters from *Free to Be . . . You and Me,* which Thomas created, produced, and cowrote

learner of her craft. "Marlo goes to the bar every day, just like a ballet dancer," says Seacat, who has worked with Thomas for more than twenty years. "She has no ego. She comes to acting classes just like all my other students, and she's always willing to help out the newcomers by sharing her knowledge."

Thomas, who has won four Emmy Awards, continues to take on a wide variety of projects, including work as a television movie producer (of *The Lost Honor of Katherine Beck,* in which she also starred), a sitcom guest star (playing Jennifer Aniston's mother on *Friends*), a stage performer (in *Who's Afraid of Virginia Woolf?* and *Six Degrees of Separation*), and film actor (*In the Spirit* and *Thieves*). Residents of Manhattan, Thomas and her husband, talk-show pioneer Phil Donahue, are known in show business circles as loyal friends, fun-loving party guests, and proof that two celebrities can stay married. Taking place in 1980, the union has been all the happier because, like Ann Marie, Thomas didn't marry because she felt she had to; she waited until she wanted to. ∎

When I was a girl growing up, it was just about impossible for me to find a woman on television with whom I could identify. There were The Happy Homemaker, The Boss's Secretary, The Maid, The Old Maid. (Very often this last defined The Boss's Secretary and The Teacher and The Maid as well.) But I never saw a girl with a dream.

It may seem amazing now, but in 1960, a TV series about a young woman leaving home to live on her own seemed wildly avant-garde, even revolutionary. The network executives said it would never work, no way. They said if our heroine, Ann Marie, was going to New York to pursue her career, she'd have to take a chaperone, a little brother maybe or a maiden aunt.

"Face facts, Marlo," they said. "No one in the audience will identify with a girl who is not living in a family unit."

"Why does she need a family unit?" I protested. "The Fugitive doesn't even have a city, and people identify with him! This is a story about a girl with a dream!"

One executive earnestly asked, "A girl with a dream? Will anybody care about that?"

There were no women in the networks in those days. None. In fact, women in broadcasting were defined by what they did *not* do. They did not anchor the nightly news; they did not hang lights; only a very few directed and produced. So during that first year of production, I was the only woman at the creative table.

It was exhilarating and transforming, and, most important, it taught me how to negotiate. As the show's resident authority on the fine art of being a girl, I always seemed to be saying "But no girl would ever say that."

Once our writers came up with a very funny fight scene between Ann Marie and her father. "Great!" I said. "But now she has to go back and say something loving to him."

"But why?" came the response. "That'll blow the fun of the fight."

"She loves her father," I explained. "She wants to be independent, but she doesn't want to hurt his feelings."

They looked at me as if I were crazy, but since I was the "girl expert," they went along.

A woman engaged in creative discussions, possessing a certain amount of authority, was so unusual that nobody knew how to handle the situation. There were these nervous jokes about us. For example, Lucille Ball was the most powerful woman in television then—in fact, she was the only powerful woman. She was also our landlady. So the joke that went around was that if I was missing from the set, I must be in the men's room, having a meeting with Lucy.

I was so immersed in the common wisdom about women with power that, even though *That Girl* was my idea and the show was produced under my banner, Daisy Productions, it never occurred to me to take a producer credit. I think that, without even realizing it, having all that power embarrassed me. I was still trying to live up to the image of what was considered "feminine." I was so burdened by this stereotype, this common wisdom that any woman with executive power must be some kind of female impersonator, that I billed myself only as an actress.

By the second year of production, we finally had another woman on the creative team: Ruth Brooks Flippen, our story editor. She and I became close and supportive colleagues, and I no longer felt alone. But the first year's experience, the sensation of being out on a limb representing a whole gender, stayed with me and changed the way I thought.

I had learned that few things support a woman's career more effectively than the safety of freedom that comes with simple numbers. Being the exception doesn't teach you how exceptional you are. It just teaches you how vulnerable you are.

From that moment on in my career, I understood that it was not enough to be "the one" or "the other one," and I always made sure there were plenty of women working with me on every project.

Women today work in every job in broadcasting. Today young girls can turn on television and find women with whom they can identify. Women in our industry are finally enjoying a long-overdue confrontation with destiny, and the future looks very bright indeed. If I have any advice to give to those coming into the business, it's this: Remember that the greatest jokes are yet to be told, the greatest stories yet to be written, the greatest performances yet to be given, the best deals yet to be made.

When they tell you to "face facts," tell them to forget it. Never face facts. If you do, you'll never get up in the morning.

When they tell you "no way," hang in and find the way.

Stick to your dream.

—MARLO THOMAS

Dorothy
Thompson

■ IT TOOK MORE THAN FIVE YEARS OF PER-
sistent requests, but finally, in 1931,
Dorothy Thompson got the interview she
coveted: a meeting with Adolf Hitler at his
headquarters in Berlin. As a determined,
courageous journalist in pre–World War
II Europe, Thompson was only beginning
to understand the awful range of Hitler's
power, but she was ready when her desire
to tell her audience about him coincided
with his desire for international attention.
"He had a message for the world," she
said, "and so he was ready to see me." She
used the material from that interview in
her radio and print commentaries, as well
as in her 1932 book, *I Saw Hitler.*

As one of only a few female journalists in the early 1930s stationed abroad,
Thompson frequently risked her own
safety to report vigorously on the rise of
Nazism and the German arms buildup.
Eventually, Hitler saw that her reports
posed a threat to his plans, and he had
her removed from Germany in 1934.
Undeterred from her mission and true to
her nature, Thompson continued reporting from elsewhere in Europe, calling
attention to Hitler's actions and to other
injustices around the world from the
1920s until her retirement in 1958.

Described as a force of nature and hell
on wheels, Thompson reported on the
turbulent first half of the twentieth century,
both on radio and in print. As a pioneering radio journalist for NBC Radio and in
uniform as a war correspondent based in
London, she broke stories on the rise of
Nazism in Europe, World War II, and
political upheavals in the postwar years,
becoming a voice for freedom throughout
that time. Thompson's particular strength
was her ability to analyze the historical
moment, placing events within their
political context and describing their
impact for a vast audience.

Born July 9, 1894, in Lancaster, New
York, the oldest of the three children of
Peter Thompson, a Methodist minister,
and Margaret Grierson Thompson,
Dorothy endured a difficult childhood.
Her mother died in 1901, when Dorothy

was only eight. When her father remarried two years later, young Dorothy didn't find the understanding she needed in her emotionally distant stepmother, so she went to live with an aunt in Chicago. She went through school receiving mediocre grades but seemed to blossom at Syracuse University, from which she graduated with honors.

Thompson entered the workforce as a social advocate, first with the New York Woman Suffrage Party, where she lectured and wrote publicity papers for the movement to get women the right to vote. Later she worked with the Social Unit, a reform organization trying to improve political awareness of slum neighborhoods. However, Thompson longed to become a journalist who could call attention to social injustices throughout the world. She hoped to get published, but the stories she sent to New York magazines were seldom accepted.

Then, in 1921, Thompson made her break into journalism by traveling to Vienna, Austria, as a stringer for the *Philadelphia Public Ledger.* To supplement her income, she got work with the American Red Cross in the publicity department. By being in the right place at the right time, she was able to cover news-making events such as union riots and political demonstrations, and she pushed for interviews with newsmakers as well. She devoted extraordinary energy and self-discipline to cultivating sources and honing the news-gathering skills that would serve her throughout her career.

Thompson's efforts paid off. While in Vienna, she was hired as a regular corre-

Before the Senate Foreign Relations Committee speaking out in favor of the repeal of the policy of neutrality

spondent for the *Philadelphia Public Ledger,* and in 1924, she was appointed regional bureau chief for the *Ledger* and the *New York Evening Post,* becoming the first woman to be named a foreign bureau chief.

In 1936, Thompson started writing a thrice-weekly column, "On the Record," for the *New York Herald Tribune.* The column quickly became popular and continued for twenty-one years, reaching millions of readers. She explored subjects of every stripe, believing that she could influence public opinion and government policy through the power of her pen.

But while her articles caught readers' attention, it was radio that brought Thompson her greatest fame. Her job with NBC Radio kept her in front of a microphone with regular commentary from the 1930s until after the end of World War II. Fueled by the lessons she'd learned as a fiery speaker on the lecture circuit, Thompson's explosive style on radio goaded her audience to learn about and take action to stop the Nazi menace and other atrocities.

After World War II drew to a fiery close, Thompson took up the cause of refugees worldwide. She focused her sense of righteousness on the Middle East and was an active commentator in newspapers during the establishment of Israel. Starting in 1937, Thompson also wrote a regular column for *Ladies' Home Journal,* mostly focusing on domestic issues.

Thompson's personal life seemed just as tumultuous as her career. In 1922, she married Josef Bard, a Hungarian writer; they stayed together five years. Then, in 1928, fireworks sparked when she met novelist Sinclair Lewis, and they married within a week of first laying eyes on each other, or so the story goes. The couple's only child, Michael, was born in 1930, the same year Lewis won the Nobel Prize for literature. After Thompson and Lewis divorced, she married a Czech artist, Maxim Kopf, whom she described as "the man I should have married in the first place."

Even after she retired officially from writing her newspaper column in 1958, Thompson continued her efforts to inform the public by serving as an informal consultant to her many friends in broadcasting. While in Lisbon with her grandsons and daughter-in-law for the Christmas holidays in 1960, her health declined suddenly, and she died there on January 30, 1961—leaving a legacy of pioneering foreign reporting and paving the way for women to excel as serious journalists in broadcast and print. ■

Thompson on location in Czechoslovakia with Czech foreign minister Jan Masaryk (left) and General Miroslav, commander of the Czech forces (right), 1941

Because of our geography, our position between two oceans, the largeness of the nation, the necessary wideness of sympathy and imagination, this country is of all countries in the world the most susceptible to what happens outside its own boundaries. . . . Upon this country beat all the ideas and all the conflicts of the whole world for in this country are the peoples of the whole world, and in this country is a certain type of mind, which is impatient of boundaries, which is able to contemplate things near and very far.

This country is itself the synthesis of many cultures. Its founders were Anglo-Saxons—one of the most remarkable groups of men that history ever produced at the right moment. . . . But those Anglo-Saxons who framed the Constitution did not make America. . . . This nation was built by Germans, Swedes, Russians, Africans, by Italians, by Anglo-Saxons, and by Jews. It was built by people who came here with a dream.

For five generations people have been coming here with a dream. Sometimes the dream was grandiose. The men who built New England came here with a dream of religious freedom. They came here as refugees, persecuted because they wouldn't bend their consciences. Acadians trekked to Louisiana also to find a world in which they could be themselves. And some came here hoping to find gold in the streets. And some came because they were herded up in Hungarian and Slavic villages and brought over here like cattle under false pretenses, full of false hopes. But in all of their minds there was something in common. For all of them there was a magnet. And the magnet was that they thought that here, in their own way, they could stand up and look their neighbors in the face and call themselves men and not slaves. . . .

The attitude of Americans toward themselves and toward all other human beings, the fact that we are a race of races, and a nation of nations, the fact of our outlook upon two oceans—and the miracle of the creation of this country out of stock that for such a large part represents the frustrations of European dreams and the rejection of human material—all these combine to make us a messianic people, with a feeling of mission not only for ourselves but for the world. . . .

In all the great speeches of Lincoln, there is the same sense of the American mission. In his farewell speech at Springfield, he spoke of the United States as the last great hope of earth. And he closed the Gettysburg Address, that great apostrophe to popular government, with the words "shall not perish from the earth." He did not say "from this soil." He, like all great Americans and above all the poets, conceived that there was some cosmic significance about this country and about this great experiment.

And that feeling is still in the American heart. It is expressed in our reaction, our spontaneous reaction, to all assaults against human rights, to the degradation of personality, to all crimes against human freedom, to all persecutions and bigotries, and, above all, to all tyranny wherever it raises its head in the most remote quarters of the globe. And since we are a free people, and are not inhibited in our expression, all such crimes have been protested by the American people as individuals long in advance of the protests of their government. Time and again in our history we have broken off diplomatic relations with countries because they have persecuted Jews or Armenians, or any other branch of the human race. We have been told that it is none of our business; but in some undefined way, we know it is some of our business; that the sense and meaning of our life is that we should be sensitive to such things. . . .

This country in these days stands at the crossroads. It can seek to retire behind its two oceans, and wash its hands of the rest of the world. To wash its hands will mean to ignore the appalling sufferings that millions already endure. To wash its hands will mean to take a cynical view of the world scene as just another struggle in power politics, or a self-righteous view that all other peoples are more or less knaves, while we are not only rich but pious. The latter view is not in the least justified.

We are also to blame for the state of affairs in the world. We washed our hands in 1919. We inaugurated a policy the result of which had to be the bankrupting and impoverishment of Europe. We lent money in vast sums at enormous interest to countries that could not possibly repay it, at the same time that we closed our borders by the highest tariff barriers in our history. But, even were a cynical and self-righteous attitude justified, it would run against the grain of the whole American temper, and it will fail. Because we are intimately integrated with the world in which we live.

A war involving two oceans will surely involve us as every world war in our history has involved us. World anarchy will involve us as it has been involving us for the last 20 years. In the modern world, the world of paid communications, of universal exchange of commodities, and above all, universal exchange of ideas, the hope that we can divorce this continent from the planet on which it is is a forlorn hope. Sooner or later our power will be thrown into the balance. And the question is whether we should wait for the world to explode or whether we should make it clear right now that no one must count on the disinterestedness of the United States.

The attitude of a great democracy is greatness. The attitude of a great free country is to cheer up slaves and horrify despots. The attitude of the first great continental federation of free states, the first great nation with an unfortified frontier, a nation more cognizant, perhaps, than any of the grandeur and the possibilities of modern science and technology, is to call a halt to an attempt to throw the modern world back into an era of Caesarism.

From this country today should come comfort, and hope, and new strength to everyone, everywhere, who still loves freedom and still believes in a future for the common human being.

—DOROTHY THOMPSON

Lily
Tomlin

■ IN THE MID-1960S, A TELEVISION PRODUCER caught a stage show featuring a little-known comedian named Lily Tomlin. "I saw a woman tap-dancing barefooted. The taps were Scotch-taped to her feet," recalls George Schlatter. "I thought, 'This is the weirdest person I've ever seen.'"

Unusual, yes. Forgettable, no.

Not long after, Schlatter, who produced the hit show *Rowan & Martin's Laugh-in,* happened to see a clip of the same performer doing her "rubber freak" character—a woman whipped into a frenzy by bouncy polymer. He made the connection and knew he had to lasso this talent fast. "I had Lily come in to my office," says Schlatter, "and offered her a job on the spot."

His decision proved wise. On her first appearance, Tomlin debuted the character Ernestine, the phone operator given to petty power plays. Within days, "one ringy-dingy, two ringy-dingy" became a nationally known catchphrase and Tomlin a star. Over the years, her numerous other creations, such as the subversive five-and-a-half-year-old Edith Ann, captivated audiences and led to a career encompassing TV, stage, audio recordings, and films, earning her three Emmys, a Grammy, and an Academy Award nomination.

Even more significant than the gleaming trophies, however, are the dignity and complexity that Tomlin has brought to her female characters. In a world that too often classifies women as blondes or brunettes, nice girls or vamps, airheads or shrews, Tomlin has given us multifaceted, nonstereotypic female personae such as Crystal, the life-affirming quadriplegic, and Sister Boogie Woman, a seventy-seven-year-old evangelist. Her stand-up routines depart from standard comic fare about fat thighs and the differences between dogs and cats. Instead, Tomlin ponders life's seldom-considered puzzles: "Why is it when we talk to God, we're praying, but when God talks to us, we're schizophrenic?"

An overnight sensation on *Laugh-in,* Tomlin had been cultivating her material for two decades beforehand. Born to a housewife and a toolmaker, she grew up in a Detroit apartment building with occupants from many different walks of life. Young Mary Jean (she later adopted her mother's first name, Lily) liked to visit the residents, taking note of their idiosyncrasies and learning to appreciate the vast variety of human characters.

After high school, Tomlin enrolled at Wayne State University to study medicine. Elective classes in theater arts, however, convinced her that show business was her life's calling. She moved to New York City in 1965, performing at comedy clubs such as the Improvisation. Word about Tomlin's originality made it to the producers of *The Merv Griffin Show,* who invited her to make several appearances. The TV audience's favorable response was by no means a fluke. "Lily Tomlin was one of the first comedians who figured out that you have to try out material at clubs before taking it to TV," says Stephen Rosenfield, director of the American Comedy Institute.

Tomlin brings her special brand of humor to *Saturday Night Live* as host, June 24, 1976.

In 1969, Tomlin was delighted to win a cohosting job on *The Music Scene,* a new series featuring performers such as Janis Joplin and Jimi Hendrix. When the show proved a little too cutting edge for sponsors, prompting the network to cancel it, Tomlin remembered Schlatter's offer and signed with *Laugh-in.*

"I was scared to death," she says. "The show had been a top-five hit for years, and the other players were already famous." Again, preparation was the key to success. She worked with the wardrobe department to find an appropriate look for Ernestine, the telephone operator; they came up with a 1940s-style mididress and hairstyle. Schlatter, who shared Tomlin's iconoclastic spirit, suggested she have Ernestine dial with her middle finger, a subtle hint about the smug omnipotence of the telephone company, which at that time had a national monopoly. "We don't care. We don't have to. We're the phone company," Ernestine would say. But there was much more to the character. "I realized a kind of sexual repression within the heart of Ernestine's power," Tomlin says. "She tensed up so much that she snorted instead of laughed."

The overwhelming success of Ernestine notwithstanding, Tomlin had to talk *Laugh-in* producers into letting her try Edith Ann and building her oversized rocking chair. "A kid can do whatever she wants in Heaven," Edith Ann told adoring audiences. "And in Heaven your mother has to go to bed early—and that's the truth."

After the show ended its run in 1973, the comedian starred in her own specials, including 1975's Grammy Award–winning *Lily Tomlin,* and did an Oscar-nominated turn as a gospel singer in the Robert Altman film *Nashville.* Lorne Michaels, a writer on one of her specials, got a job producing *Saturday Night Live,* and invited her to guest-host four shows. Again, audiences loved her comic ingenuity.

In 1977, Tomlin made her Broadway debut in *Appearing Nightly,* a one-woman show written and directed by friend and artistic collaborator Jane Wagner. In addition to Ernestine, Edith Ann, and Crystal, the sold-out show featured Trudy the bag lady, Glenna the flower child, and former football player Rick, who cruised singles bars. Her visibility at a new high, Tomlin was featured on the cover of *Time* magazine, which called her "the new queen of comedy" and "the woman with the kaleidoscope face."

Throughout the next decade, Tomlin continued her TV and stage work and began starring in films, including the 1980 blockbuster *9 to 5,* in which she played an office manager who takes revenge upon her male-chauvinistic buffoon of a boss, and 1984's collaboration with another comic giant, Steve Martin, in *All of Me.* In 1986, she starred in another successful one-woman show on stage, *The Search for Signs of Intelligent Life in the Universe,* written by Wagner. They later adapted the show for HBO, winning a 1991 CableAce Award.

By the mid-1990s, Tomlin was playing a station boss on the sitcom *Murphy*

Tomlin and Candice Bergen on the set of *Murphy Brown*

Brown and doing movies every couple of years. She welcomed the millennium by starting a twenty-nine-city tour of *Lily Tomlin Live,* a stage showcase for Edith Ann, Ernestine, et al.

Throughout her career, Tomlin has stood out as a performer who communicates humor via in-depth characterizations. Her devotion to her craft still amazes even longtime associates. "When I watched Lily on *Murphy Brown.* I always wanted to see her do more, because I know what a rich motherlode of characters is inside her," says Schlatter. "Lily doesn't do characters; she becomes them." ∎

On an encounter with silent-screen legend Lillian Gish (best known for her roles in *The Birth of a Nation*, 1915, and *Broken Blossoms*, 1919):

When the movie *9 to 5* was opening in New York in 1980, I invited Lillian Gish to be my guest at the premiere. It was December and windy and cold, and I'd sent a car to drive the then-eighty-four-year-old Lillian to and from the event. When the screening ended, the streets outside the theater were jammed with cars, and my costars Jane Fonda, Dolly Parton, and I were ushered into a waiting car and the driver was ordered to take us to the party.

As we piled into the limo, I looked around and suddenly realized it was Lillian's car that had been commandeered, and I began to protest, "We can't take this car; it's meant for Lillian Gish." Suddenly I saw Lillian walking outside, half running up the street, holding her coat closed with one hand and her hat with the other, the wind whipping around her. I called out to her, "Lillian, Lillian," but with the traffic and the horns and the wind, there was no way she could hear me.

I couldn't believe my eyes: I saw Lillian approach someone in a Pontiac Firebird and hitch a ride.

When we got to the party, they started hustling us into the restaurant, and as I passed through the door, someone grabbed me and turned me around. There was Lillian with a big, rapturous smile on her face. She pulled me into the ladies' room, hugged me, and said, "Oh, Lily, this movie is going to be such a big hit. Tell me you have percentage [of the proceeds] and tell me it's not net."

On herself and her work:

When a reporter asked, "What do you feel when you see yourself on TV?" [I said], "What does a chameleon see when it looks into the mirror?"

Creating characters has great appeal for me. It is a process I invented to give me something to do. This is what captured me when I decided I wanted to become a performer. I can be in a store in the neighborhood where I live, suddenly picking up antics or body style of a man in a phone booth having an animated conversation.

I construct a compressed accuracy, a character essence that is as true and real as I can get it. I don't go for laughter. I never play for a joke per se. If the joke gets in the character's way, I take it out.

Commercial television specializes in escapist fantasy. I deal with culture reality.

Doing Ernestine is really a very sexual experience. I just squeeze myself very tight from the face down. The line with Ernestine is that she's a very sensual person. She's a woman who knows she has a very appealing body and likes to show it off.

As Trudy, the bag lady:
It is my belief that we all secretly ask ourselves at one time or another, "Am I crazy?" In my case the answer came back a resounding "Yes."

My space chums think that my unique hookup with humanity could be evolution's awkward attempt to jump-start itself again. Just maybe, going crazy could be the evolutionary process trying to hurry up mind expansion.

I forget more important things, too. Like the meaning of life. It'll come to me. Let's just hope when it does I'll be in.

Reality is the leading cause of stress amongst those in touch with it.

It's my belief we developed language because of our deep inner need to complain.

If evolution was worth its salt, it should've evolved something better than "survival of the fittest." I think a better idea would be "survival of the wittiest." At least that way, creatures that didn't survive could've died laughing.

As Tina Trip:
I'm coasting on my own chemistry, and I am volatile, baby. When I woke up today, I felt like I had brain surgery done over my entire body. I'm thinkin' half the damn day, "What chemicals did I take to make me feel so wrecked?" And then I remembered, I hadn't taken anything. Here I was trying to blame a drug for what it feels like to be straight.

As Sister Boogie Woman, a southern evangelist:
Boogie's not a meanin', boogie's a feelin'. Boogie takes the question marks outta yer eyes, puts little exclamation marks in their place. Are ya on my beam? Boogie's when the rest of the world is lookin' you straight in the eye sayin' you'll never be able ta make it and ya got your teeth in a jar and those teeth say, "Yes I can, yes I can. Yes I can. Yes I can." I say, "Think of yourself as a potato chip and life as a dip." I say, "Think of yourself as a chicken leg and life as Shake 'n Bake."

—LILY TOMLIN

Barbara
Walters

■ BARBARA WALTERS IS THE KIND OF PERSON Barbara Walters would interview—a pioneer, legend, and industry leader, with a high-profile career that spans four decades. When it comes to television news, it seems as if she has always been there; but she got there and stayed there because of the quality of her work. A generation of women beginning careers in broadcasting have patterned themselves after her, thinking they want to be "like Barbara Walters."

She entered the television news business at a time when women were included more for their attractiveness than their skills as newswomen. However, from day one, Walters was known for her professionalism. She has conducted interviews with an amazing range of the famous and infamous; but not only is she renowned for getting the interview, she has a flair for getting her subjects to answer revealing and thought-provoking questions as the cameras roll. She was the first woman cohost on a network morning show and the first woman coanchor in network evening news. After those jobs ended, she refashioned herself as a television news-magazine host, a celebrity interviewer nonpareil, and, most recently, as an entrepreneur producer of an all-woman talk show.

For a professional as successful as Walters has been, respect comes with the territory. But what is sometimes forgotten is that Walters's early success and respect had to be earned, and it was a long road.

Born September 25, 1931, in Boston, Massachusetts, Barbara first encountered the entertainment world through her father, Lou Walters, a talent promoter. In her earliest years, while Lou was struggling, the family lived in somewhat genteel poverty. Then Lou had a big hit with the Latin Quarter nightclub in New York City, a popular hot spot that did so well he opened other clubs in Boston and Miami. Suddenly the family was rich, and mingling with stars became second nature to Barbara.

But the alternating experiences of bad and good fortune, as well as the frequent moves for the family, instilled in Barbara a powerful longing for the family to be financially secure. This gave her a sense, very early on, that she was the family member responsible for taking care of her parents and older sister, Jackie, who was mentally retarded and lived at home. Her lingering fears were realized when Lou's businesses later failed and he found himself broke and forced to move with his wife and Jackie to Florida. Barbara supported them all.

Walters's drive to succeed, however, was also motivated by her ingrained dedication to hard work and professionalism. She had briefly considered acting as a career but settled on teaching instead, earned a B.A. in English from Sarah Lawrence College in 1954, and began work toward a master's in education. Her career took a significant turn when she took a job in television, first as a writer and producer at WNBC-TV in New York City, then at WPIX-TV for a job producing women's programming and a short

Walters and guest Christopher Reeves

stint at CBS's morning show writing for Dick Van Dyke and Jack Paar.

Still working behind the camera, Walters was hired in 1961 for NBC's *Today* show to write stories with a woman's focus. At the time, *Today* featured a well-known woman, usually an actress, as "the *Today* girl," responsible for making small talk, smiling at the camera, and reading commercials. When the slot opened up in 1964, Walters was given a chance, on a trial basis, to fill in. But no one made the mistake of referring to her as "the *Today* girl." She was an interviewer. Viewers' response to her well-informed, professional presence was overwhelmingly positive.

Soon Walters was a mainstay of *Today*, though she was not given the title of cohost until 1974, ten years later.

After fifteen years with NBC, Walters moved to ABC News to coanchor the

Walters and guest Queen Noor of Jordan

On the set of *20/20*

evening news and host specials. Her widely reported million-dollar salary made her the highest-paid newscaster in the industry. But being the first woman in one of the most prestigious jobs in television journalism was stressful, especially since coanchor Harry Reasoner was publicly and privately uncomfortable with the arrangement.

But from the beginning, Walters's interview program, *The Barbara Walters Special,* won rave reviews. The shows quickly became the industry standard and have consistently been among the top-rated specials year after year. She continues them to this day, along with cohosting the weekly newsmagazine *20/20.*

"She just keeps getting better and better," says Roone Arledge, ABC News president. "She has a way that has matured over the years of getting people to say things on the air that they never thought they were going to say."

Over the years, those people have included world leaders ranging from Fidel Castro to the shah of Iran, Indira Gandhi to Moammar Qaddafi, Margaret Thatcher to every U.S. president since Richard Nixon. She conducted the first joint interview with Egyptian president Anwar Sadat and Israeli prime minister Menachem Begin and reported on President Nixon's historic trip to China in 1972. She has also interviewed celebrities across generations, from Sir Laurence Olivier to Ricky Martin, Bette Davis to Elizabeth Taylor, Audrey Hepburn to Tom Hanks, John Wayne to Tom Cruise.

In 1997, Walters decided to try something new and launched (along with her longtime producer) *The View.* This ABC daytime program is hosted by five women, including Walters, of different generations, experiences, and backgrounds, who share their opinions on topics of the moment.

Throughout her career, Walters has received a multitude of honors, including seven Emmy Awards. However, just as important is the credit those who followed in her footsteps give to her for paving the way.

Today she's still serving as a role model. Says Katie Couric, current coanchor of *Today,* "What a lot of women in the business admire is that she is still hungry and so competitive. She will never rest on her laurels. She's in her sixties and still on the air. It gives all women a real boost." ■

When I began my career in television, I never thought that I would be in front of the camera. I had graduated from college and expected to teach. My father was in show business and had a very famous nightclub in New York at that time—and in other places as well, such as Miami and Boston—called the Latin Quarter. One of my early jobs was as the assistant to the director of publicity at NBC's local station, WNBC, because I knew all the columnists. I was Lou Walters's daughter. That's how I began in television. I wrote the releases for all the talk shows. I was then made a producer, the youngest producer at the time. I think I was twenty-four.

I next worked at CBS, and then at a public relations firm, until I finally went back to the *Today* show as a writer, still not thinking I would be in front of the camera because, before me, they had used only actresses and models. I was hired to write only the feminine things: fashion shows, celebrity guests. My big breakthrough came when the producer, who knew me from CBS, said, "She can write the same things the men can write." So they began sending me out to cover all kinds of stories.

The very first time I was on the air as a reporter was to cover the funeral of President John Kennedy. After that, I did everything from a day in the life of a nun to interviews with murderers to being a Playboy bunny. During the Democratic National Convention in Atlantic City in 1964 that nominated Lyndon Johnson, the woman who was the "*Today* girl," Maureen O'Sullivan, did not work out, so they put me on the air for nineteen weeks. I stayed for thirteen years.

In those years, I was not allowed to do the so-called hard-news interview. The host, a man named Frank McGee, insisted I could not ask a question until he had already asked three. The only way I could do the more substantial interviews was if I got them myself. So I began to do as many as possible outside the studio. That's when I started interviewing major international figures, and that's when I got the reputation of being very pushy, because it took phone calls, it took energy, it took perseverance.

Those were very happy and productive years on *Today*. I had a small child, and I used to say I could be up for the five o'clock feeding. In those days, you didn't bring your children into the studio; there was nowhere you could keep them. I used to say it would be like bringing in a dog that wasn't housebroken because nobody wanted it around.

When Frank McGee died, NBC said, "We're going to find the next host." I said, "No, cohost." It was in my contract that, if Frank McGee ever left the show, I would be cohost. They never expected him to leave. He was relatively young when he died of cancer. Only then was I named cohost. Since that time, every woman has been called cohost on all the morning programs.

I came to ABC after a lot of thought. I had a seven-year-old daughter—it was twenty-six years ago. I was always exhausted, and I thought the change would give me a better chance at having a normal life with her. I wanted to be able to see her at night and not always be tired. If there was a turning point, that was it.

It was a turning point of failure, though, because I arrived with the much-trumpeted assignment of being the first female coanchor of a leading network news program. I think it was much overrated. We have women doing the news on the weekends and on all the morning programs, which I think is harder to do. But it was considered to be a big deal.

I coanchored the program with a newsman named Harry Reasoner. He was a man who didn't want a partner. It wasn't that he didn't want me in particular; he didn't want a partner, period. And I was forced on him. I hadn't realized this was going to be the case.

I also got terrible publicity as the "million-dollar baby." Actually, I made the same salary as Harry Reasoner for doing the news, $500,000, but I was also doing four one-hour prime-time specials a year for another $500,000. ABC had a huge bargain in me. The specials alone made a tremendous amount of money then and have continued to do so for twenty-six years.

But there was enormous resentment. I was a woman. I was a new generation. I had been raised with television and as a television writer. The publicity was horrendous. Harry Reasoner was openly hostile. It was the low point in my career, and what saved me was my private life: my daughter, my friends, my family.

A year later, Roone Arledge became the new president of ABC News. Everything turned around because he was a creative genius. He decided I was the future, and Harry went back to CBS and *60 Minutes.*

Years later, when Harry wrote a book, I did the first interview with him on *20/20.* I always knew it was nothing personal.

And by then my career was back on solid ground. I had survived.

— BARBARA WALTERS

Oprah Winfrey

■ OPRAH WINFREY IS NOT JUST A BROADcaster, she's a phenomenon:

• *Time* magazine named her one of the most influential people of the twentieth century.

• Her talk show reaches over 22 million U.S. viewers and is seen in 113 countries.

• At the 1998 Emmy Awards, Winfrey received a Lifetime Achievement Award at the relatively young age of forty-four; by then, her show had already won thirty-one Daytime Emmys.

• Her on-air book club has dramatically expanded the readership of quality fiction, making her selected books instant bestsellers; and

• Her name itself represents the phenomenon, as in the *Wall Street Journal's* "This upending of tradition—from keeping one's heart under control to wearing it always loudly and tearfully on one's sleeve—has come to be known as Oprahfication" and *Jet's* "I wasn't going to tell her, but after a few drinks, she Oprah'd it out of me."

The scope of Winfrey's potential influence became clear by the mid-1980s, when her talk show went national and the ratings soon surpassed the previous number one, *The Phil Donahue Show.* Winfrey soon made sure her audience-drawing power was matched by her power over her show and her share of its revenues. When she created her production company, Harpo Productions, in 1988, she became only the third woman in movie and television history (after Mary Pickford and Lucille Ball) to own a major studio. Her percentage of King World, her show's distributor, grew until she became one of that company's largest shareholders; when CBS bought King World, she became one of the largest shareholders in CBS.

Yet for all her success and influence, what lies at the heart of the phenomenon is that Winfrey seems like your best, down-to-earth girlfriend—someone who cries when the world treats you badly, bucks you up when you're down, celebrates when things go right, and always, always helps you become a better, truer person than you could be on your own.

Oprah's compassionate TV persona succeeds largely because she openly shares her own problems with viewers. Born on January 29, 1954, to an unwed mother on a tiny farm in Mississippi, followed by years with a bullying though loving grandmother in a house with outdoor plumbing and chickens in the yard. Reunited with her mother in Milwaukee from the age of six until fourteen—tough years in crowded rooms, feeling like an intruder and running around with older boys to escape the pressure. Giving birth to a premature baby who died soon thereafter. Suffering sexual abuse by a male relative. Moving to her father and step-

mother's home in Nashville, where strict discipline refocused her energy to become a star student, determined to succeed.

People had always seen something shine in Oprah when she was before an audience. At church recitations as a little girl in Mississippi, neighbors told her grandmother she was gifted. In Nashville, the teenage Oprah became a popular speaker on the church circuit, and speech and drama were her favorite subjects in high school.

Then, in her senior year, came the opportunity she'd been waiting for without knowing it. After winning a contest sponsored by radio station WVOL, she was named Miss Fire Prevention, which gave her the opportunity to go on the air and

Hosting *Oprah*, 1996

Oprah Winfrey touts her acclaimed segment Oprah's Book Club.

read copy. A disk jockey she spoke with was so impressed with her voice and presence that she was offered a weekend job at the station. She became an instant hit.

The next year, when she enrolled at Tennessee State University, she applied for a reporter job with WTV-TV, Nashville's CBS affiliate. At nineteen, Winfrey lacked television experience, but she knew where to look for inspiration. "I had no idea what to do or say," she recalls. "And I thought in my head that maybe I'll just pretend I'm Barbara Walters. I will sit like Barbara. I will hold my head like Barbara. So I crossed my legs at the ankles, and I put my little finger under my chin, and I leaned across the desk, and I pretended to be Barbara Walters."

It worked, and Winfrey got the job. Soon she was promoted to the nightly news, and three years later she was recruited to anchor the evening news at WJZ-TV in Baltimore, a larger and more prominent market.

But after enormous anticipation, Winfrey's first appearances in her new job fell short. She felt uncomfortable with hard-news interviews, especially when told to pressure people in a crisis to talk into a microphone. Her discomfort with the setting and her sympathy for her subjects were evident on camera.

A new station manager insisted, however, that the problem wasn't Winfrey; rather, she was in the wrong job for her talents. Following the success of Phil

Donahue's nationally syndicated talk show, the station had decided to try out a local version. Winfrey began appearing as cohost of *People Are Talking* in 1977; and suddenly everything came together for her.

"I came off the air," she says of that first show, "and I knew that was what I was supposed to be doing. It felt just like breathing. It was the most natural process for me."

The program flourished, outperforming Donahue in the Baltimore market.

Soon even bigger markets came calling, and Winfrey accepted a hosting job on *A.M. Chicago* on WLS-TV. Within months, the show's ratings were so high it was expanded from a half hour to an hour. Then, in 1986, the retitled *The Oprah Winfrey Show* entered into a national syndication deal with King World Productions and quickly became its hottest-selling show. As the ratings and advertising dollars climbed, Winfrey took greater artistic and business control of the show, forming Harpo Productions and becoming a significant shareholder in King World.

Winfrey has now branched out into other media as well. Harpo has produced miniseries and movies for television and a feature film. In May 2000, she launched *O: The Oprah Magazine,* to promote empowerment and self-awareness. She is also one of the key players, along with Marcy Carsey, Tom Werner, and Caryn Mandabach, involved with Geraldine Laybourne's Oxygen Media, an interactive cable network for women.

Yet to speak of her influence is to go beyond a list of her projects. Winfrey has transformed the talk show into a community in which sharing emotions, admitting mistakes, and seeking growth are welcomed and supported. Deborah Tannen, a Georgetown University professor who specializes in communication styles, describes Winfrey's style as "rapport talk"—the give-and-take that characterizes women's conversation and often includes self-revealing intimacies.

Bringing this style of discourse to television has expanded the definition of what the medium can do. In other words, it's been Oprafied. ∎

I've been an orator really, basically, all of my life. Since I was three and a half, I've been coming up in the church speaking. I did all of James Weldon Johnson's sermons. He has a series of seven sermons, beginning with "The Creation" and ending with "Judgment." I used to do them for churches all over the city of Nashville. I've spoken at every church in Nashville at some point in my life. You sort of get known for that. Other people were known for singing. I was known for talking.

■　■　■

I started this [the Angel Network, which encourages others to volunteer and donate to good causes] because I believe people are ultimately good. I think television is a good way of opening people's hearts.

■　■　■

A good talk show will stimulate thought, present new ideas, and maybe give you a sense of hope where there wasn't any—a feeling of encouragement, enlightenment; inspire you.

■　■　■

I want to use television not only to entertain, but to help people lead better lives. I realize now, more than ever, that the show is the best way to accomplish these goals.

■　■　■

I'm a woman in the process of creating and striving for new dreams, new goals, new ideas. It never ends and that's what's so exciting; the journey itself.

■　■　■

I want to be a catalyst for transformation in people's lives—to help them see themselves more clearly and to make choices that lead to a fulfilled and happy life.

—OPRAH WINFREY

About AWRT

AWRT

American Women in Radio and Television, Inc. (AWRT) is the premiere organization to serve and promote women in the electronic media industry. Founded in 1951, AWRT is a national, nonprofit organization dedicated to advancing the impact of women in electronic media and allied fields by educating, advocating, and acting as a resource to AWRT members and the communications industry.

AWRT works to improve the quality of the electronic media; to promote the entry, development, and advancement of women in the electronic media and allied fields; to serve as a medium of communication and idea exchange; and to become involved in community concerns.

As a national organization, AWRT takes positions on policy issues of importance to women. Over the past several years, AWRT has worked to promote ownership opportunities for women in broadcasting and to create effective and efficient equal employment opportunity rules. AWRT is also an advocate on behalf of women for pay equity and training initiatives to help launch women into senior executive ranks.

The Foundation of AWRT

Through the broadcasting industry's oldest foundation, AWRT raises the awareness of appreciation for the pivotal role of women in electronic media to create positive change. Founded in 1960, the foundation supports and promotes educational, literary, and charitable programs related to the electronic communications industry. The Foundation of AWRT supports scholarships and holds quality educational programs related to the electronic communications industry.

AWRT's Gracie Allen Awards™

The Gracies™ recognize programs that are created by women, for women, and about women, as well as outstanding individual achievements in electronic media. Produced by the Foundation of AWRT, the Gracies encourage the positive and realistic portrayal of women by honoring excellence in television, cable, radio, and new media programming. Held in New York City each spring, the Gracies Gala brings together industry luminaries, broadcasting professionals, and students, who gather to celebrate the outstanding achievements of their colleagues. The Gracies are named in honor of the radio and television pioneer Gracie Allen, a trailblazing woman who helped to underscore the growing importance of women in electronic media.

How to Become a Member of AWRT

Membership in AWRT is open to individuals who work in the electronic media or allied field, students, and retirees. Members receive *News and Views*, a bimonthly newsletter; CareerLine, a national listing of job openings; the *AWRT Resource Directory*; networking opportunities; career resources; and member discounts. Through a network of more than thirty local chapters, members have access to mentor programs, regional career banks, and industry education programs. To obtain membership information, visit the AWRT Web site at www.awrt.org or contact the national headquarters at (703) 506-3290.

Left to right: Agnes Law, Edythe Meserand, and the other founding members of AWRT at the 1951 organizing convention, Astor Hotel, New York City

Honor table at the 1965 convention. Standing left to right: Edythe Meserand, Elizabeth Bain, Jane Dalton, Doris Corwith, and Nina Badenoch; seated left to right: Agnes Law, Margaret Mary Kearney, Montez Tjaden, and Esther Van Wagoner Tufty.

Marlo Thomas (left) celebrates AWRT's twenty-fifth anniversary at the 1976 AWRT convention in Philadelphia.

Silver Satellite Award winner Barbara Walters addresses members of AWRT at the 1985 convention.

(Right) AWRT members on the steps of the U.S. Capitol, 1990.

Deborah Roberts, ABC News, and Jane Pauley, *Dateline NBC,* celebrate at the 1998 Gracie Allen Awards.

Hannah Storm, NBC Sports, poses with Donna de Varona of *Donna de Varona on Sports,* a radio program, after each received a 2000 Gracie Allen Award.

Leeza Gibbons accepts the 2001 AWRT Silver Satellite Award.

Acknowledgments

AWRT wishes to thank the many people who generously gave their time and effort to make this book possible. A heartfelt thank-you, first of all, to the membership of AWRT in chapters across the country for the selection of the fifty women honored here. Sincere gratitude to the Library of American Broadcasting, an amazing resource at the University of Maryland, for partnering with AWRT to develop a list of outstanding women in broadcasting for possible selection of the fifty greatest, as well as for helping with research and providing photographs of those chosen. In particular, we would like to recognize the gracious efforts of Chuck Howell, curator, and Karen Fishman, assistant curator.

Key to the success of this book are the talented writers who profiled the fifty women and helped acquire their essays and photographs. For this we sincerely thank Louisa Peat O'Neil, Rebecca Reisner, Judith Marlane, Jane Lawrence, Lynn Page Whittaker, and Tom Dunkel. A grateful thanks as well to Jeannine Dugan for her diligence in acquiring photographs.

Others whose efforts were instrumental in the collection of information and photographs are Dr. Allida Black, Alice Cahn, John Cannon of the National Academy of Television Arts and Sciences, Cynthia Clements, Don West of Broadcasting and Cable, Kay Daly, Phyllis Diller, Elizabeth Edwards of Desilu, Dee Emmerson in Phyllis George's office, Jim Golden, Sheila Gratten, Marge Gregory at Radio One, Ann Hodges of the *Houston Chronicle*, Jeannie Kedas at MTV, George King, Eric Lindquist of the University of Maryland, Dick Moore of Dick Moore & Associates, Lee Moorer of the New York Public Library/Dorot Jewish Division, Erica Nasser at Shukovsky/English Productions, Audrey Pass at Harpo Productions, Coral Petretti at ABC Photos, Shannon Rhodes at NPR, Shelby Scott of AFTRA, Richard Seymour, Cheryl Smith at Oxygen Media, Jeremy Tarcher, Mallory Tarcher, Robert Thompson of Syracuse University, and the *Washington Post*.

We thank Jean Zevnik Lucas and the rest of the team at Andrews McMeel for their belief in this book and all their efforts on its behalf; we especially thank Jean for her patience and cheerful support during its development.

We thank Lynn Whittaker of Graybill & English, our literary agent, for her guidance and vision from the very beginning of this project; her dedication to this book is best exemplified by her willingness to step in to write some of the profiles in a moment of dire need.

AWRT also thanks the team at Association Management Bureau for their support in the development of the book.

Finally, AWRT wishes to acknowledge all the organizations and individuals who share with us a commitment to the advancement of women in radio and television. It is only through our collective efforts that we can truly make a difference.

ACKNOWLEDGMENTS

Essay Credits

Lucille Ball—Excerpted from Lucille Ball, *Love, Lucy*. New York: G. P. Putnam, 1996. Used with permission of Desilu.

Candice Bergen—Excerpted from Candice Bergen, *Knock Wood*. New York: Linden Press, 1984. Used with permission of Candice Bergen.

Dr. Joyce Brothers—Excerpted from Dr. Joyce Brothers, *The Successful Woman: How You Can Have a Career, a Husband, and a Family—and Not Feel Guilty About It*. New York: Simon & Schuster, 1988. Used with permission of Dr. Joyce Brothers.

Dorothy Stimson Bullitt—Quotes © 1995 by Delphine Haley. Reprinted from *Dorothy Stimson Bullitt* by permission of the publisher, Sasquatch Books, Seattle.

Carol Burnett—Excerpted from Carol Burnett, *One More Time*. New York: Random House, 1986. Used with permission of Carol Burnett.

Diahann Carroll—Excerpted from Diahann Carroll, *Diahann!* New York: Little Brown & Company, 1986. Used with permission of Diahann Carroll.

Marcy Carsey—Excerpted from speech by Marcy Carsey to the Los Angeles Business Women, 1995.

Sylvia Chase—Excerpted from Press Foundation Interview conducted by Donita Morrhus at Columbia University, New York, July 31, 1992.

Nancy Dickerson—Excerpted from Nancy Dickerson, *Among Those Present*. New York: Random House, 1976; and interview for AWRT Broadcast Pioneers Library Oral History Project.

Pauline Frederick—Excerpted from a personal interview with Judith Marlane, February 20, 1973, New York.

Dorothy Fuldheim—Excerpted from Dorothy Fuldheim, *I Laughed, I Cried, I Loved*. New York: Random House, 1966.

Anne Hummert—Reprinted with permission from the University of Wyoming American Heritage Center.

Shari Lewis—Excerpted with permission from the Dorot Jewish Division of the New York Public Library's oral history collection.

Ida Lupino—Excerpted from Debra Weiner, "Interview with Ida Lupino," in *Women and the Cinema: A Critical Anthology*, ed. Karyn Kay and Gerald Peary. New York: Dutton, 1977.

Penny Marshall—Foreword to Garry Marshall, *Wake Me When It's Funny: How to Break into Show Business and Stay There*. New York: Newmarket Press, 1997. Used with permission of Penny Marshall.

Mary Margaret McBride—Excerpted from Mary Margaret McBride, *Out of the Air.* Garden City, New York: Doubleday & Company, 1960.

Edythe Meserand—Excerpted from address by Edythe Meserand when being honored by AWRT on her fiftieth anniversary in broadcasting, Northeast Area AWRT Conference, October 1976.

Mary Tyler Moore—Excerpted from Mary Tyler Moore, *After All.* New York: G. P. Putnam, 1995. Used with permission of Mary Tyler Moore.

Irna Phillips—Quotes from interviews with Irna Phillips that appeared in *Fortune,* June 1938; *Time,* June 10, 1940; *Newsweek,* July 13, 1942; *Chicago American,* May 12, 1964; *New York Times* magazine, Sept. 8, 1968; *Chicago Tribune,* March 17, 1970; *Broadcasting* Nov. 6, 1972.

Eleanor Roosevelt—Excerpted from "On Reaching Her 75th Birthday, Eleanor Roosevelt Praises Television's Contributions to the Senior Citizen," *TV Guide,* October 17, 1959. Used with permission from *TV Guide,* © 2000 TV Guide Magazine Group, Inc.

Martha Stewart—Excerpted from address by Martha Stewart to the National Press Club, Washington, D.C., November 12, 1996.

Dorothy Thompson—Excerpted from Dorothy Thompson, *Let the Record Speak.* New York: Houghton Mifflin Co., 1939.

Oprah Winfrey—Quotes provided by Harpo Productions.

Photo Credits

Gracie Allen p. 1: Courtesy of San Francisco Performing Arts Library

Christiane Amanpour p. 7: Photo by Nigel Parry, TM & © 2000 CNN, a Time Warner Co.; pp. 8, 9, 10: Photos TM & © 2000 CNN, a Time Warner Co.

Lucille Ball pp. 13, 14, 15: Photos courtesy of Library of American Broadcasting, University of Maryland

Candice Bergen p. 20: Photo courtesy of Candice Bergen; p. 22: Photo by Geraldine Overton, © 1992 CBS Inc.; p. 23: Photo © 1992 CBS Inc.

Dr. Joyce Brothers p. 26: Photo courtesy of Dr. Joyce Brothers; p. 28: Photo © Bettmann/CORBIS; p. 27: Photo © Ed Kashi/CORBIS

Dorothy Stimson Bullitt pp. 32, 33, 35: Photos courtesy of Priscilla Bullitt Collins; p. 34: Photo by Forde Photographers, courtesy of Priscilla Bullitt Collins

Carol Burnett p. 38: Photo courtesy of AWRT; p. 39: Photo courtesy of Photo Division, CBS Television Network Press Information; p. 40: Photo © 1990 Touchstone Pictures & Television

Diahann Carroll pp. 43, 45: Photos by Harry Langdon, courtesy of Diahann Carroll; p. 44: Photo courtesy of ABC Photography

Marcy Carsey p. 49: Photo courtesy of Carsey-Werner; pp. 50, 51: Photos courtesy of Marcy Carsey

Peggy Charren p. 55: Photo by Ed MacKinnon Photography; p. 56: Photo by Standard Studios; p. 57: Photo by David Gould

Sylvia Chase p. 60: Photo © 2000 ABC, Inc., courtesy of ABC Photography; p. 61: Photo © 1995 Capital Cities/ABC, Inc.; p. 62 Photo © 1983 American Broadcasting Companies, Inc.; p. 63: © 1995 ABC, Inc, courtesty of ABC Photography

Julia Child p. 66: Photo by Michael McLaughlin; p. 67: Photo by Paul Child; p. 68: Photo © Jack Lueders-Booth

Connie Chung pp. 71, 72, 73: Photos courtesy of Connie Chung

Joan Ganz Cooney pp. 78, 79, 80, 81: Photos courtesy of Sesame Workshop

Katie Couric pp. 84, 85: Photos courtesy of NBC

Nancy Dickerson pp. 89, 90: Photos courtesy of Library of American Broadcasting, University of Maryland; p. 91: Photo © Bettmann/CORBIS

Phyllis Diller pp. 94, 95, 96: Photos courtesy of Phyllis Diller

Linda Ellerbee p. 100: Photo by Gordon Munro; pp. 101, 102, 103: Photos courtesy of Linda Ellerbee

Diane English pp. 106, 107, 108, 109: Photos courtesy of Diane English

Pauline Frederick p. 113: Photo by Hally Erskine, © 1948 The Conde Nast Publications, Inc.; pp. 114, 115: Photos courtesy of NAB/ABC, Inc.

Dorothy Fuldheim p. 119: Photo courtesy of Library of American Broadcasting, University of Maryland; p. 120: Photo courtesy of John Carroll University Media Archives/WEWS; pp. 120, 121: Photos courtesy of WEWS

Phyllis George pp. 125, 128: Photos by Jonathan Exley, courtesy of Phyllis George; p. 126: Photo courtesy of Phyllis George

Cathy Hughes pp. 132, 133, 134: Photos courtesy of Cathy Hughes

Anne Hummert pp. 138, 140: Photos © CBS Photo Archive

Charlayne Hunter-Gault p. 142: Photo by Christopher Little for MacNeil/Lehrer Productions; pp. 143, 144, 145: Photos courtesy of *The News Hour*

Kay Koplovitz pp. 148, 150: Photos courtesy of Kay Koplovitz

Geraldine Laybourne pp. 153, 155, 156: Photos courtesy of Geraldine Laybourne and Nickelodeon

Shari Lewis pp. 160, 161, 162, 163: Photos courtesy of Richard Seymour, Lewis & Lamb

Ida Lupino pp. 166, 167, 168: Photos © Bettmann/CORBIS

Penny Marshall pp. 171, 172, 173: Photos courtesy of ABC Press Relations

Mary Margaret McBride pp. 177, 178, 179: Photos courtesy of the A/P Wide World Photos

Judy McGrath p. 182: Photo courtesy of MTV; pp. 183, 184: Photos courtesy of Judy McGrath

Edythe Meserand p. 187: Photo by Frumkin Stuaw, courtesy of AWRT; pp. 188, 190: Photos courtesy of Library of American Broadcasting, University of Maryland; p. 189: Photo by Essque Studio, courtesy of AWRT

Mary Tyler Moore p. 193: Photo courtesy of AWRT; p. 194: Photo courtesy of Library of American Broadcasting, University of Maryland; pp. 195, 196: Photos © CBS, Inc.

Jane Pauley pp. 199, 200: Photos courtesy of NBC; p. 201: Photo by Alan Perlman, courtesy of AWRT

Jane Cahill Pfeiffer pp. 204, 205, 206: Photos courtesy of Jane Cahill Pfeiffer

Irna Phillips p. 209: Photo © CBS Worldwide, Inc.; p. 210: Photo courtesy of NBC/Globe Photos

Cokie Roberts pp. 214, 215, 216: Photos by Steve Fenn/ABC, © 2000 ABC, Inc.; p. 215: Photo by Craig Sjodin/ABC, © 2000 ABC, Inc.

Eleanor Roosevelt pp. 220, 221: Photos courtesy of the National Press Club; p. 222: Photo © Underwood & Underwood Studios, courtesy of the National Press Club

Marlene Sanders pp. 225, 226, 228: Photos courtesy of Marlene Sanders; p. 227: Photo by Curtis Brown, Ltd., courtesy of Marlene Sanders

Diane Sawyer pp. 231, 232, 233: Photos by Ida Mae Astute/ABC, © 2000 ABC, Inc.

Dinah Shore pp. 236, 237, 238: Photos courtesy of the Dinah Shore Fan Club

Lesley Stahl p. 241: Photo ©1999 Ingrid Estrada; p. 242: Photo © 1998 CBS World Wide Inc.; p. 243: Photo by Alan Perlman, courtesy of AWRT

Susan Stamberg pp. 246, 247, 248: Photos courtesy of National Public Radio®

Martha Stewart p. 251: Photo © S.I.N./CORBIS; p. 253: Photo by Peter Morgan/ Reuters, © Reuters NewMedia Inc./CORBIS

Marlo Thomas pp. 256, 258, 259: Photos courtesy of Marlo Thomas

Dorothy Thompson p. 262: Photo courtesy of Library of American Broadcasting, University of Maryland; p. 263: Photo courtesy of the A/P Wide World Photos; p. 264: Photo © Hulton-Deutsch Collection/CORBIS

Lily Tomlin p. 268: Photo courtesy of NBC Photo; p. 269: Photo by S. Nannarello, © 1996 CBS Inc.

Barbara Walters pp. 272, 273, 274: Photos © ABC Photography Archives

Oprah Winfrey p. 277: Photo by Timothy White, © 1998 Harpo Productions, Inc.; p. 278: Photo © 1996 Harpo, Inc.; p. 279: Photo by George Burns, © 1999 Harpo Productions, Inc.

AWRT pp. 284, 285, 286: Photos courtesy of AWRT